An important and valuable di:
countries that used to run the

— Jo

How does one of the world's
and influence when internatiₒₙₐₗ conditions are unfavourable
and its resources do not match its commitments? This was Britain's
burden in the 1970s and 1980s when the international order was
transformed. Much became unsettled and Britain had to adapt
policy to suit new needs and opportunities.

Michael J. Turner elucidates the efforts that were made to maximize Britain's role on those matters and in those parts of the world
that were of special importance to British strategy, prosperity and
security. He examines key decisions and their consequences and
places British policy-making in an international context, suggesting that British leaders were more successful in preserving
power and prestige on the world stage than has sometimes been
appreciated.

Michael J. Turner is Roy Carroll Distinguished Professor of British
History at Appalachian State University, North Carolina. He has
published widely in the fields of British political history and foreign policy.

British Studies Series

General Editor JEREMY BLACK

Alan Booth **The British Economy in the Twentieth Century**
Glenn Burgess **British Political Thought, 1500–1660: The Politics of the Post-Reformation**
John Charmley **A History of Conservative Politics since 1830 (2nd edn)**
David Childs **Britain since 1939 (2nd edn)**
John Davis **A History of Britain, 1885–1939**
David Eastwood **Government and Community in the English Provinces, 1700–1870**
Philip Edwards **The Making of the Modern English State, 1460–1660**
W. H. Fraser **A History of British Trade Unionism, 1700–1998**
John Garrard **Democratisation in Britain Elites, Civil Society and Reform since 1800**
Brian Hill **The Early Parties and Politics in Britain, 1688–1832**
Katrina Honeyman **Women, Gender and Industrialisation in England, 1700–1870**
Kevin Jefferys **Retreat from New Jerusalem: British Politics, 1951–1964**
T. A. Jenkins **The Liberal Ascendancy, 1830–1886**
David Loades **Power in Tudor England**
Ian Machin **The Rise of Democracy in Britain, 1830–1918**
Allan I. Macinnes **The British Revolution, 1629–1660**
Alexander Murdoch **British History, 1660–1832: National Identity and Local Culture**
Anthony Musson and W. M. Ormrod **The Evolution of English Justice: Law, Politics and Society in the Fourteenth Century**
Murray G. H. Pittock **Inventing and Resisting Britain: Cultural Identities in Britain and Ireland, 1685–1789**
Nick Smart **The National Government, 1931–40**
Howard Temperley **Britain and America since Independence**
Andrew Thorpe **A History of the British Labour Party (3rd edn)**
Michael J. Turner **Britain's International Role, 1970–1991**

British Studies Series
Series Standing Order
ISBN 0–333–71691–4 hardcover
ISBN 0–333–69332–9 paperback
(*outside North America only*)

You can receive future titles in this series as they are published by placing a standing order. Please contact your bookseller or, in case of difficulty, write to us at the address below with your name and address, the title of the series and the ISBN quoted above.

Customer Services Department, Macmillan Distribution Ltd
Houndmills, Basingstoke, Hampshire RG21 6XS, England

Britain's International Role, 1970–1991

Michael J. Turner

palgrave
macmillan

First published 2010 by
PALGRAVE MACMILLAN

Palgrave Macmillan in the UK is an imprint of Macmillan Publishers Limited, registered in England, company number 785998, of Houndmills, Basingstoke, Hampshire RG21 6XS.

Palgrave Macmillan in the US is a division of St Martin's Press LLC, 175 Fifth Avenue, New York, NY 10010.

Palgrave Macmillan is the global academic imprint of the above companies and has companies and representatives throughout the world.

Palgrave® and Macmillan® are registered trademarks in the United States, the United Kingdom, Europe and other countries.

ISBN: 978–0–230–57771–8 hardback
ISBN: 978–0–230–57772–5 paperback

This book is printed on paper suitable for recycling and made from fully managed and sustained forest sources. Logging, pulping and manufacturing processes are expected to conform to the environmental regulations of the country of origin.

A catalogue record for this book is available from the British Library.

A catalog record for this book is available from the Library of Congress.

10 9 8 7 6 5 4 3 2 1
19 18 17 16 15 14 13 12 11 10

Printed in China

Contents

Acknowledgements

I would like to thank Jeremy Black, the series editor, and Sonya Barker and everyone at Palgrave Macmillan who oversaw the production of this book. I am very grateful to Courtney Steed, who read through my original typescript and made many helpful suggestions, and to the two anonymous referees who commented on a later version of the typescript. I have also benefited from conversations with History Department colleagues at Appalachian State University. For regularly luring me away from my computer, sustaining my morale and making me smile – a lot – I want to thank friends at FPC Boone, teammates in Boone 40 United and High Country Beer Fest FC, and above all my wife Catherine and our children Grace, Jill and Ethan. Few academics could enjoy what they do without the backing of an understanding and supportive family: I am truly blessed.

Some of the discussion in this book is based on material that first appeared in chapters 9 and 10 of my *Britain and the World in the Twentieth Century: Ever Decreasing Circles* (Continuum, 2010).

Any errors or shortcomings in this book are entirely my own responsibility.

MJT

Introduction: 'Doomed steadily to diminish'?

> British foreign policy had been one long retreat. The tacit assumption made by British and foreign governments alike was that our world role was doomed steadily to diminish. We had come to be seen by both friends and enemies as a nation which lacked the will and the capability to defend its interests in peace, let alone in war. Victory in the Falklands changed that. Everywhere I went after the war, Britain's name meant something more than it had.
>
> (Margaret Thatcher, *The Downing Street Years*, 1993)

To Margaret Thatcher, who served as Britain's prime minister from May 1979 to November 1990, and to her colleagues and supporters, the Falklands War of 1982 marked a resurgence of British power and prestige after thirty or more years of decline. 'The significance of the Falklands War was enormous', Thatcher insisted, 'both for Britain's self-confidence and for our standing in the world'.[1] In offering this version of events during her premiership, Thatcher had necessarily to contrast the recovery of the 1980s with what had gone before. Yet the political and economic problems of the 1970s and the limits they imposed on Britain's international role and influence were not as debilitating as was claimed, and similarly the increase in power and prestige of the 1980s was less dramatic and far-reaching than many contemporaries thought. These years present no simple trajectory of weakness and difficulty displaced by strength and success. What they present is a mixed record, but this is not to deny that there was something behind the idea that Britain's standing in the world was much higher than it might have been, and higher than it should have been in view of Britain's economic situation and military capabilities relative to the other great powers of the late twentieth century. Historians who focus on the reasons for Britain's decline perhaps lose sight of an equally interesting and important phenomenon: how and

1

why decline was minimized. Britain *did* decline, but despite the lack of resources and despite events that did not go its way, Britain remained one of the world's great powers.

In 1970 it was confirmed that most of Britain's commitments in the Middle East and Far East would be given up and that Britain's security, economic and political relationships with Western Europe would be extended. At the end of 1991 the scene was set for a transformation in Britain's dealings with Europe, as details were finalized for the Treaty of Maastricht, which created the European Union and led to the establishment of a common currency, the euro. Each of these developments, in 1970 and 1991, represents a fundamental reorientation of British policy and activity, although in both cases the full implications were not realized at the time. In between, in 1982, Britain won the Falklands War. Though there is a sense in which this war looks like a small and anachronistic colonial conflict, its significance was magnified because of the wider international context and because the British knew that the world was watching to see how they would respond. The long-term impact of victory in the Falklands continues to be debated. So does the impact of the collapse of the Soviet Union. Its official dissolution was announced in 1991. This was uncharted territory for the British, as they found themselves in a post-Cold War as well as a post-imperial age.

Britain's role in the world, which had changed greatly since the end of the Second World War, was shaped by several prominent relationships and organizations. Along with the United States, France, the Soviet Union and China, Britain was a permanent member of the United Nations Security Council. The UN was set up in 1945 to foster peace, cooperation, respect for international law, and economic and social improvement. Post-war optimism faded, but there were other structures from this period, along with the UN, that survived to provide a framework for international relations. Trade and financial stability were promoted by plans made in 1944 and 1945. Under the Bretton Woods system currency values were fixed to the value of the US dollar. The International Monetary Fund (IMF) provided for the regulation of exchange rates and the balance of payments and borrowing, and the World Bank made loans to facilitate reconstruction and combat poverty. The British participated in all these initiatives and also entered into military alliances. The Brussels Pact of 1948, for example, was a mutual defence treaty signed by Britain, France, Belgium, Luxembourg and the Netherlands. National security was subsequently enhanced by NATO, the North Atlantic Treaty Organization. Formed in 1949, NATO consisted of the United States, Britain, Canada, France, Belgium, Luxembourg, the Netherlands, Portugal, Italy, Norway, Denmark and Iceland. Greece and Turkey were admitted in 1952 and the Federal Republic of Germany (FRG) in 1955.

Suspicion and rivalry, especially between Britain and America on one side and the Soviet Union on the other, meant that the post-1945 order in Europe and beyond was fraught with instability and discord. The Soviets set up satellite states in Eastern Europe while Western Europe began to develop into an economic unit protected by US security guarantees. Occupied at the end of the Second World War, Berlin remained a divided city, a situation that was given added physical expression in 1961 with the erection of the Berlin Wall. Germany was split into two states in 1949: the FRG in the west and the communist German Democratic Republic (GDR) in the east. The Cold War was intensified by the establishment of competing military blocs. NATO was consolidated in the early 1950s, and in 1955 Moscow formed the Warsaw Pact, which consisted of the Soviet Union, Rumania, Poland, Hungary, Czechoslovakia, the GDR, Bulgaria and Albania. In 1956 the Soviets quashed an uprising in Hungary, demonstrating that no satellite would be allowed to depart from an approved path in domestic and foreign affairs. In 1968 a reform movement in Czechoslovakia was suppressed and the 'Brezhnev Doctrine' enunciated. Named after the Soviet leader, the 'Brezhnev Doctrine' held that it was the duty of all states in the eastern bloc to safeguard one another's institutions and that military action should be taken to deal with agitation for political democracy and economic liberalism. The purpose was to reinforce Soviet control over the bloc. No satellite was permitted to leave the Warsaw Pact or to undermine the unity of the bloc. Non-communists were barred from entering government. There was an economic as well as a political-military divergence in Europe: Moscow had established the Council for Mutual Economic Assistance (Comecon) in 1949 to bind bloc countries together and channel their trade away from the West and more towards each other.

The Cold War spread into other parts of the world. There were armed struggles in Korea and Indochina in the early 1950s, and affairs in Asia became increasingly complex as the Americans, Soviets, British and others intervened. The USSR's initially close relationship with communist China deteriorated in these years, and there was a serious rift between the two by the end of the 1950s. Asia was further destabilized by the Vietnam War, which escalated during the mid-1960s and complicated America's dealings with its allies, including Britain, and with the Soviets and Chinese. The Cold War affected Britain's activities in Asia and in Africa. On both continents, crises were exacerbated by interference from outside. Washington DC typically reacted more strongly than London to extra-European developments. Containment of communism was a constant American preoccupation, and US foreign policy was greatly affected by the loss of China to communism in 1949 and the loss of Cuba in 1959. Mao Tse-tung led China until his death in 1976. Cuban leader Fidel Castro ruled his country for nearly fifty years, despite US attempts to remove him.

One of the most important developments in twentieth-century British history was decolonization. India, for so long a strategic and economic asset, was granted its independence in 1947. Withdrawals from Asia, Africa and the Middle East continued for several decades, quickening noticeably during the late 1950s and early 1960s. Britain no longer had the means or the will to retain most of its colonies, world opinion had turned against colonialism generally, and nationalist groups had arisen in the colonies to demand self-government. The British preferred peaceful, negotiated withdrawal that would make possible the establishment of new and advantageous relationships with former colonies, and many of the latter joined the Commonwealth, an intergovernmental organization of equal and independent nations likened by its enthusiasts to a family. Decolonization was hardly an unqualified success, however, for there were violent disorders in some places and a number of former colonies did not wish to retain links with Britain. There was huge controversy over Rhodesia and South Africa. The white minority in Rhodesia blocked Britain's efforts to implement a power-sharing arrangement with the black majority and issued a unilateral declaration of independence in 1965. South Africa's system of apartheid also incensed many in the Commonwealth, especially its African members. South Africa had left the Commonwealth in 1961. Britain was pressed to do more, through sanctions, diplomatic action and other methods, to topple the illegal regime in Rhodesia and to promote change in South Africa. As the Commonwealth expanded and became multi-racial in character, British leaders had to find a way of combining influence with sensitivity.

Outside Europe, efforts to protect British interests and shore up influence were hampered by the gap between resources and commitments and by the emergence of new challenges. The world role could not be sustained. This was coming to be accepted by the late 1950s, although it was not until the mid-1960s that economic problems and political circumstances resulted in clear decisions about reducing Britain's activities abroad. Successive statements on defence policy pointed to the need for reorganization and retrenchment, and the withdrawal from East of Suez was announced in January 1968, though Britain still had residual interests in the Far East and Middle East in the 1970s and 1980s. The ongoing tension, economic importance (mainly because of its oil) and strategic location of the Middle East meant that Britain's involvement there did not end, even if its role was much smaller than in former times. The enmities enflamed by the creation of the state of Israel in 1948, the plight of Palestinians forced out of their homes, the Arab-Israeli wars of 1948–49, 1956 and 1967 and the support provided to the belligerents by the United States and USSR placed obstacles in the way of Britain's goals in the region. After 1967 there was an uneasy lull in hostilities and to many observers it seemed that yet another war was coming.

In Western Europe, meanwhile, integration was boosted by the formation of the European Coal and Steel Community in 1952. Its members were France, the FRG, Italy, Belgium, Luxembourg and the Netherlands ('the Six'). In 1957 they signed the Treaty of Rome, which established the European Economic Community and the European Atomic Energy Community. From 1967 these bodies were known collectively as the European Communities (EC). By this time, integrated Europe was dominated by the Franco-German axis and it proved very difficult for London to counter the influence enjoyed on the continent by Paris and Bonn. The British, with their 'special relationship' with America and ties with the empire-Commonwealth, had not initially cared enough about cooperation in Europe to involve themselves in integrationist schemes. They were loath to give up sovereignty and disliked supra-nationalism. Euro-scepticism remained strong, but as 'the

Six' prospered the notion arose that membership of European bodies might bring economic benefits and offer a means of sustaining international influence. This affected British policy even if there was no conversion to the idealism and principles of integrationists in Europe. Britain applied to join the European Economic Community in 1963 and 1967. Both attempts failed, primarily because of French objections.

In the mid-1940s, Britain's wartime prime minister Winston Churchill spoke repeatedly about the three 'circles' of world power: the English-speaking alliance between Britain and the United States; the British empire-Commonwealth; and Europe. The assumption was that Britain, which, uniquely, was involved in each of these 'circles' *and* could unite them, was well positioned to remain one of the world's leading powers. Fifty years later, Britain's status did not accord with what had previously been hoped for and expected. Difficulties had surfaced in all three 'circles'.

By the 1990s there were elements in the US government that were dismissive towards Britain. They no longer attached much importance to the 'special relationship' and were amused by the manner in which the British kept referring to it, as if expecting favours. There are numerous illustrations. For instance, in February 1993, soon after Bill Clinton became US president, British prime minister John Major arrived in Washington DC for talks. As the president waited for his visitor to arrive, one of his aides observed: 'Don't forget to say "special relationship" when the press comes in'. 'Oh yes, the special relationship', Clinton said. 'How could I forget?' Then he threw back his head and laughed.[2]

If the relationship with America was no longer delivering the benefits it once had, the same was true of the Commonwealth. During the 1970s there was still an impression that the Commonwealth was useful to Britain, but in the 1980s this was much less evident. Serious quarrels had developed between the British government and Commonwealth countries, and Britain had moved towards a closer association with Europe.[3] As one commentator noted in 1984, British leaders no longer saw much point in cultivating the Commonwealth. There was 'a feeling amongst the major sections of the politically relevant elites in Britain that the Commonwealth is becoming less capable of providing tangible rewards' and 'a decline in identity with the Commonwealth'. Two years earlier the cardinal point was made by a Commonwealth historian in a clear and direct fashion: 'how far were British interests still served by membership of a scattered community of states, in which Britain's pre-eminence was no longer tacitly acknowledged? With leadership to be earned, not conceded, what attitude was to be taken?'[4]

As for Europe, it became one of the most contentious issues in British politics during the 1980s, with Thatcher and those of her mindset standing against further and quicker integration and their opponents maintaining that Britain would do better to participate wholeheartedly in the formation of new rules and goals for a common future. By obstructing the proposals emanating from leaders in Western Europe, said the prime minister's detractors, she was making them less likely to listen to her advice and forfeiting a role for Britain in the van of policy-shaping efforts in the EC. Thatcher was unrepentant. She wanted the EC to be 'a force for freedom' and detested 'a contrary tendency in the Community – interventionist, protectionist, and ultimately federalist. The sharpness of the contrast between the two views of Europe would only become fully apparent as the years went by. But it was never far beneath the surface of events and I was always aware of it'.[5]

Opportunities to exercise influence in the world, through the 'special relationship', the Commonwealth and the EC, were now decreasing. Yet Britain did not cease to act and to be regarded as one of the world's great powers. Notwithstanding the relative decline that could not be reversed after the Second World War, British interests and opinions still mattered. This book offers a detailed examination of Britain's role in a time of rapid and perplexing change. The international order, comparatively stable in the 1950s and 1960s, became more unsettled and Britain had to adapt. Britain could not expect to be treated as the equal of the United States or Soviet Union, and ongoing adjustments were required in British priorities and methods in view of developments at home and abroad, but the continuing desire was to maximize Britain's influence on those issues and in those parts of the world that were of special importance to British strategy, prosperity and security. This book elucidates the motives behind pivotal decisions, discusses their consequences, explains why some options were taken and others rejected, and places British policy-making in the appropriate international context. British leaders were not uninformed, or unreflective, or unsuccessful in managing decline and sustaining influence. By explaining the circumstances in which they were placed, the options that were available to them, the goals they had in mind and the international environment that conditioned all, this book demonstrates that British leaders deserve more credit than some historians have appreciated. British power and prestige were not 'doomed steadily to diminish'.

A prominent theme in the relevant historiography is indicated by phrases such as 'the collapse of British power', 'the wasting of the British economy', 'the eclipse of a great power', 'Britannia overruled', 'descent from power' and 'Britain in decline'.[6] This is the conceptual framework that has been used by many historians. Their comments about Britain's international influence and capabilities tend to be downbeat and negative. This book is offered as a contribution to debates about 'decline' and 'power' and as a reminder that Britain continued to play a significant international role during the 1970s and 1980s even as the opportunities to do so were decreasing.

The structure of the book is partly chronological and partly thematic. There is some overlap between chapters, so that arguments can be properly developed and the interconnectedness of events and problems clearly demonstrated. Chapter 1 explores the international difficulties that challenged Britain in the early 1970s, including the Rhodesian and South African questions, Commonwealth relations, European integration and war in the Middle East. National defence and nuclear weapons are also discussed, along with the results of US and Soviet policies and China's new openness. Chapter 2 carries forward the examination of defence debates in the light of détente. The thaw in Europe and a more constructive dialogue between America and the USSR were important influences, but military and diplomatic competition continued as well, meaning that international tension was not greatly mitigated, for all the talk of flexibility. The British had reservations about détente and about its corollary – the idea of a 'new world order' – which is investigated in Chapter 3. There were negotiations for arms control and an ongoing arms race, predictions about and efforts to promote peace and stability in a time of wars, coups and unrest. All this put pressure on Britain and its allies. Unity was difficult to preserve on vital contemporary issues and Chapter 4 deals with some of the quarrels that arose between Britain, the United States and Western Europe. Disagreements about how to respond to Soviet actions are the focus of Chapter 5.

NATO strategy, the pros and cons of détente, the measures pursued by Moscow at home and abroad and the determinants of the policies of Britain and other great powers are also analysed. Chapter 6 explores the concept of multipolarity, new defence planning, nuclear proliferation, the search for effective disarmament mechanisms and the links between these phenomena. Chapter 7 discusses the reasons behind the break-up of the Soviet Union and eastern bloc in the late 1980s. Britain's interaction with the Soviets and their satellites is also examined. Chapter 8 casts light on developments outside Europe, especially in Africa, where Britain had abiding interests, and discusses the causes and consequences of the Soviet invasion of Afghanistan in 1979. Middle East affairs in the 1970s and 1980s and Britain's involvement in the region are investigated in Chapter 9. Chapter 10 deals with the outbreak of the Falklands War and with the impact of crisis and victory on Britain's self-image, prestige and influence.

1 Accommodating Change

At the time and afterwards, some commentators regarded the 1960s as years of retreat for Britain, and this pattern appeared to carry on into the 1970s. The British had to contend with a growing number of challenges in Europe, Africa, the Middle East and the Far East and in the organizations and relationships that had become so important to Britain's international role and status, not least NATO, the Commonwealth and the 'special relationship' with America. At home and abroad, debates about Britain's place in the world centred not only on specific regions and institutions but also on the foundations of power, especially economic performance and military capability.

Tests of influence: Europe, Rhodesia, South Africa and Commonwealth relations

The 1970s were not a very rewarding time for Britain in terms of exercising or maintaining influence. Edward Heath's Conservative government, in office from 1970 to 1974, finally managed to negotiate Britain's entry into the EC, which took effect on 1 January 1973, but there was controversy over the terms of membership and the issue remained divisive. The hope in London was that membership of European bodies would help Britain economically and politically and serve as a vehicle for the effective promotion of wider interests, but on this and on other matters there was frustration. Outside Europe, there was the embarrassing situation in Rhodesia. Heath's foreign secretary, Alec Douglas-Home, did work out a settlement, but an inquiry in 1972 showed that the Africans were not satisfied. Sanctions against the white Rhodesian regime remained in place and the Conservative Party headed towards an open split on this policy.[1]

Home's proposals were always likely to be inadequate from the African perspective, and there was no escaping the fact that black leaders found it impossible to trust the illegal white regime led by Ian Smith. The Rhodesian imbroglio continued to sour Britain's relations with the Commonwealth, strengthening the prime minister's notion that Britain's future lay in Europe. Matters were not helped by the ease with which sanctions were evaded. The bigger picture was one of relative economic decline. The use of economic means to support diplomatic pressure had offered British leaders options and opportunities in former times, but the Heath government did not have this advantage, and though Washington DC shared London's view of the white Rhodesian regime, the Americans were not committed to sanctions and rarely intervened to shield British policy from international criticism.[2]

Rhodesia's blacks thought that Home's proposals, if implemented, would delay majority rule. Their protests continued, and the Smith regime responded with detentions and tear gas. In January 1972 the *Economist* doubted that sanctions would make much difference. It was not clear that the British parliament wanted to persist with them, and it *was* clear that other nations were not observing them. The government's claim that its policy rested on a 'cool calculation' of what was best for Rhodesia was crumbling.[3]

Newspapers in America opposed the United Nations economic boycott of Rhodesia (introduced in 1968), regretted the failure of Home's proposals, complained that African states and 'their communist allies' would push for stiffer action at the UN and ultimately military intervention to oust the Smith regime, and emphasized that Rhodesia's blacks could gain nothing from the rejection of Home's settlement, the polarization of races and the shedding of blood. The UN explicitly censured the United States, Portugal and South Africa for trading with Rhodesia, while in Britain the sanctions debate rapidly widened. There were popular demonstrations and many public figures took sides. Some insisted that the Rhodesian people, black and white, should be left to solve their problems in their own way, while others maintained that black Rhodesians were subjects of Queen Elizabeth II and that the British government had a duty to help them. The *Guardian* and the *Observer* pointed out that matters were being complicated by the trickery of the Smith regime, which oscillated between promises to negotiate and declarations of intransigence, and by its links with right-wing Conservatives in Britain.[4]

Writer and journalist Roy Lewis argued that after years of fruit-less effort the House of Commons, the foreign office and the British public no longer cared about Rhodesia. They just wanted an end to all the fuss. Therefore a new approach was needed. The main reason why Britain could not change direction, according to Lewis, was the attitude of the UN. A majority of UN members favoured sanctions and expected Britain to act accordingly, but it was absurd to go on pretending that Britain still exercised colo-nial authority in Rhodesia and that sanctions would end the rebel-lion against this authority. How could Britain find a solution when Rhodesia's white leaders would not accept what the blacks wanted, and any formula approved by the blacks would go too far for the whites? The UN and black African states kept up the pressure, and it was Britain that took the blame for the fact that sanctions were not working. Lewis concluded that the best course would be for parliament to pass legislation that removed Rhodesia from the queen's dominions and continued sanctions in line with Britain's membership of the UN. This would not make Rhodesia independ-ent or transfer power to Smith. The effect, rather, would be to pass authority to the UN. Then it would be up to the UN to pursue its policy on Rhodesia, with Britain cooperating in the same manner as other members of the organization.[5]

As tempting as this might have seemed, Home and Heath con-sidered it too radical. In any case, an abdication of responsibility on Britain's part was bound to affect the country's international standing and embroil the government in even greater controversy at home. Addressing the Commons in July 1973, Home said he would go on trying to arrange talks between the Smith regime and Rhodesia's black leaders. Sanctions, he added, would have to con-tinue in line with UN recommendations. Some MPs objected that Britain had been bearing the burden of sanctions almost alone. Home replied that the government was doing all it could to make other trading nations assist, but that this was really a matter for the UN.[6]

If the Commonwealth disliked what was happening in Rhodesia, it was also in uproar over Britain's arms sales to South Africa. Heath's government reversed the ban of the previous Labour cabinet. The main reasons were economic (the wish to prevent other countries from gaining contracts that should have been Britain's) and strategic (Britain's concerns about the growth of the

Soviet navy). The loudest protests were from African members of the Commonwealth. Immigration policy was a related problem. Claims were made that Britain was discriminating against non-whites. Immigration was a major issue for right-wing Conservative MPs, who were often at odds with the prime minister, although on South Africa there was common ground. Heath's government announced that Britain was obliged to fulfil the weapons contracts because refusal to do so would breach the Simonstown Agreement of 1955 on defence cooperation with South Africa. The prime minister rejected complaints from the Commonwealth and emphasized his personal opposition to apartheid. He found Commonwealth leaders to be 'largely indifferent to our wider strategic considerations'. Heath also suspected that the commotion over Rhodesia and South Africa was part of 'an attempt to bully Britain' into stepping back from a closer association with Europe.[7] He and his colleagues knew that Britain's trade with Western Europe had long since overtaken trade with the Commonwealth. Rhodesia, South Africa and related issues were difficult for the British to manage, and developing nations were quick to criticize Britain, once the foremost imperial power in the world, no less for its history than for its present policies.[8]

Signs of weakness?

On taking over as prime minister in June 1970 Heath had promised to restore Britain's world position, but lack of resources made him even more determined to make Britain a part of Europe, where he expected a collective diplomacy to be forged. Britain could work with the Europeans, Heath decided, rather than pursue narrow national interests. In opposition Heath had attacked Labour for weakness. When he was prime minister the same charge was made against him. Many Conservative MPs and voters believed that the government was wrong on Rhodesia, South Africa and withdrawal from East of Suez. Assailed from the political right, Heath also angered moderate opponents and those on the political left, as when he refused to condemn French nuclear tests in the Pacific and when he welcomed Portugal's right-wing prime minister Marcello Caetano to Britain in July 1973 at a time of lurid press reports about 'massacres' in the Portuguese colony of Mozambique.[9]

Some forms of tyranny appeared to be acceptable to some people, reflected the *Guardian*, while others did not, and it was unlikely that the Labour Party would apply the same standards to a foreign socialist leader that it wanted to apply to Caetano. *The Times* called for an international inquiry into the situation in Mozambique. In the Commons, Labour leader Harold Wilson stressed his party's opposition to the visit of 'the Portuguese dictator', while Home condemned Wilson's 'political opportunism' and said that respect for Portugal as a member of NATO and an old ally of Britain did not entail approval for Portuguese actions in Africa. Home recalled that Wilson had refused to denounce the United States when allegations were made about atrocities in Vietnam. Wilson had maintained then that it would be wrong to cast blame on a friendly government until the full facts were known.[10]

As for the French nuclear tests, Heath denied on 19 June 1973 that there was any need for international talks on the matter, but on 10 July he told MPs that there had been some discussion. On 23 July the prime minister was urged openly to oppose the tests, just as the leaders of Australia, New Zealand, Canada, Chile and Japan were doing. News came through of a French attack on a vessel manned by anti-nuclear activists, but the government denied that this had anything to do with 'British interests', and on 25 July it was declared that there was no evidence of nuclear fall-out 'in any form' as a result of French testing. This was beside the point, wrote one anti-nuclear campaigner. Lord Chalfont had been an army officer, defence correspondent for *The Times*, and more recently a minister at the foreign office (1964–70). In July 1973 he argued that French nuclear tests were going on 'in pursuit of a policy which has no military significance, which is based on a false sense of national pride, and which puts existing and future arms control agreements at risk', all of which was also true of Britain's nuclear forces. To the *Guardian*, the tests were polluting air and water that did not belong to France and rested on 'the illusion that a country the size of France can still defend itself by its own efforts against all comers'.[11]

Heath had first made proposals for nuclear coalition with France in 1967. Once he became prime minister, however, he ran into opposition from the foreign office and was advised by the defence secretary, Lord Carrington, that the practical difficulties would be insurmountable. The idea was for Britain and France to develop their nuclear weaponry together and to maintain it 'in trust' for integrated Europe, the other members of which would be regularly consulted. Britain's most important external attachment would be with France, not the United States. Heath saw all this in relation to Britain's bid to join the EC. In the 1960s, the Americans had refused to allow Britain to share information and technology with third parties. Now, in the early 1970s, US president Richard Nixon was willing for Heath to explore the possibilities with French leader Georges Pompidou, yet the French were sensitive about their nuclear independence and Pompidou never took the talks seriously.[12]

In opposition the Conservatives had vowed to reverse some of Labour's cuts East of Suez. This was partly for electoral purposes. Heath also had to sound patriotic for internal party reasons, in order to win over those Conservative MPs, activists and voters who had doubts about the move towards Europe. Therefore he stressed that Britain would still have a global role. It was hoped that a party schism on foreign policy could be avoided (Wilson had a similar problem inside the Labour Party, which is why he promised to hold a referendum on British membership of the EC).

In office, Heath and his colleagues decided that little could be done about the withdrawal from East of Suez. Britain could not afford to remain. There was concern about leaving a vacuum in the Persian Gulf and the Far East, into which the Soviets could move, and it was agreed that a residual British presence should continue. Nevertheless, most of the cuts announced by the Labour government in the late 1960s had to be accepted. The Americans began to regard Iran, not Britain, as their main ally in the Gulf region. In the Far East, London arranged for the formation of a joint defence force involving Britain, Australia, New Zealand, Malaysia and Singapore. Primarily consultative in nature, this pact of April 1971 was not a firm or effective security alliance of the type that Britain had subscribed to in earlier times. In 1954 Britain had been a founder-member of the South East Asia Treaty Organization (SEATO). By 1971 the British commitment to the region was fast declining. Britain would still have troops in Singapore, a small garrison in Hong Kong and five surface ships stationed permanently in the Far East, but politically, economically and militarily Britain was focusing more on Europe. Elsewhere, the wish was to share responsibilities with others.[13]

Thaw with China

A thaw in relations with China was a welcome distraction at a time when British prestige appeared to be shrinking. Home wanted to find out what was behind the quarrel between China and the USSR, since this had huge importance for the West. Britain and the People's Republic of China agreed to exchange ambassadors in March 1972, and in October 1972 Home made an official visit to China. The Chinese foreign minister Chi Peng-fei visited Britain in June 1973. The British had not had normal diplomatic relations with China since the communist takeover there in 1949, mainly because of Washington DC's animosity towards the regime in Peking, and the Anglo-Chinese thaw was partly a by-product of President Nixon's effort to foster a new friendship between the United States and China. In fact, American policy undercut Britain's position and London had to settle for less favourable terms than it had originally envisaged. This helps to explain why Britain finally broke with the United States' position on Taiwan, which had survived as a nationalist stronghold since the Chinese civil war of 1946–50. Washington DC was still maintaining that Taiwan should retain China's seat on the UN Security Council, but Britain and most other members of the UN were unwilling any longer to put up with this anomaly.[14]

The British had been thinking for some time about how to improve links with China, in order to safeguard Hong Kong and contribute to global détente. Heath was struck by the 'increasing fluidity' in relations between the United States, Western Europe, Japan, the USSR and China in this period, and the British government decided that China needed closer ties with the West, both politically (in view of the enmity between Peking and Moscow) and economically (China was commercially underdeveloped). For Britain, the prospect of trade was a big incentive. The path to agreement was smoothed by Britain's statement of respect for Peking's claim that Taiwan was part of China, and soon Heath arranged to visit China himself. The 'normalization' of Anglo-Chinese relations in the 1970s had diplomatic, political, economic and cultural sides to it. The process was made easier by Nixon's policy but was not dependent upon it. Some advances had been made before Heath became prime minister and before Nixon made overtures to the Chinese.[15]

Britain's thaw with China was facilitated, and probably necessitated, by other events in the early 1970s. Several countries officially recognized the People's Republic of China and the question of China's representation at the UN was resolved. As China came out of its former isolation, and the Nixon administration and governments in Western Europe responded, Britain had to do the same. The context was also shaped by instability in South East Asia. In 1970 the Vietnam conflict had spread into Cambodia. Washington DC had claimed that this was unavoidable, and Britain's prime minister at the time, Wilson, sided with the Americans on this, agreeing that intervention in Cambodia was necessary to protect the sovereignty of South Vietnam. All this had implications for British interests in Singapore and Malaysia. At the same time, Wilson and his successor Heath expected the Americans to negotiate an end to the war, and it was clear that progress in this direction would largely depend on China. In January 1973, in Paris, a tentative agreement was reached for peace in Vietnam. Britain was subsequently involved in talks on the implementation of the accords reached at Paris, but optimism faded. The Khmer Rouge overthrew a pro-US regime in Cambodia. The Pathet Lao took control of Laos. North Vietnamese forces eventually overran the whole of Vietnam and reunified the country in June 1975.[16]

Anglo-Chinese relations steadily improved. In 1972 there were agreements on trade and industry, science, technology, sporting links and air services. Chinese students were invited to study in Britain. In 1972 Britain's exports to China were worth £12.2 million. In the first half of 1973 they were worth £36.3 million. Between 1971 and 1974 the value of exports to and imports from China more than doubled. In the spring of 1975 over sixty British companies participated in a large industrial exhibition in Shanghai.[17]

The new understanding with China was affected by Anglo-European and Anglo-Soviet relations. In 1971 the Heath government demonstrated that it was not unwilling to stand up to Moscow when it expelled Soviet diplomats who were suspected of spying. This move had something to do with the French belief that Britain was too close to the United States: in Paris it was thought that if Britain joined the EC, Europe would be even more exposed to US influence. Heath wanted to prove that Britain was not dependent upon the Americans, and at a time when US-Soviet relations were improving London deemed it appropriate to take a harder line with Moscow. Détente was relevant too, and Heath and Home wanted to establish a common negotiating position, which is why they favoured European Political Cooperation (EPC) and asserted that a joint policy was needed with respect to the Conference on Security and Cooperation in Europe (CSCE). The British fell in behind their European allies on the question of détente in Europe, but moved ahead of them with regard to China, and this was facilitated by Britain's robust attitude towards the USSR. Chinese leaders were impressed. In the longer term, the Anglo-Chinese thaw led to an agreement on the future of Hong Kong, British withdrawal from the territory in 1997 and its incorporation (with special status) into the People's Republic of China.[18]

In late 1972 Home expressed the government's 'real satisfaction' that China had 'voluntarily ended her self-imposed exile in favour of international contact and co-operation'. Home expected commercial benefits but advised that 'we must not be too ambitious' and admitted that trade agreements would have to be compatible with British membership of the EC. *The Times* argued that Britain was highly regarded by Chinese leaders, having been the first western state to recognize the communist regime in China (1950) and having restrained the Americans during the Korean War and sponsored the Geneva Accords on Korea (1954). China's suspicion of the USSR was helpful, as was the fact that the Americans were looking for a way out of Vietnam. History made the British more important to China than France or the FRG could be, and Britain's membership of the EC would reinforce this: 'the image of a politically mature and stable power playing a part in the new Europe engages China's interest'. The *Guardian* and the *Economist* pursued this theme, as did American newspapers, which also noted British frustration with the policy of the United States. Indeed, Washington DC often told the British to stand aside so that US-Chinese negotiations could proceed, and the British had little choice because America and China gave precedence to their own bilateral relationship.[19]

Oil shock and economic concerns

More damaging to Britain's international position was the Arab-Israeli War of October 1973, which disrupted oil supplies from a region that met half of Britain's energy needs. Arab governments imposed restrictions as part of their war effort. Prices rose and Britain's oil imports were cut by about 15 per cent, an unexpected shock that seriously affected Britain politically and economically.[20]

In 1971 OPEC, the Organization of Petroleum Exporting Countries, had agreed to guarantee existing prices for five years, but awareness of Britain's vulnerability prompted Heath's government to look at other energy sources, including nuclear, the coal industry, Alaskan deposits and North Sea oil. When the Yom Kippur War broke out on 2 October 1973, Heath was hosting the FRG's chancellor Willy Brandt. Both leaders saw the dangers for Western Europe. Heath's immediate concern was that the conflict should be contained. He did not think that the USSR would intervene. If there was a danger of escalation, he complained, it came from the Americans, who placed their forces on alert. They also wished to use their bases in Europe to supply Israel during the war. Britain refused to permit this, as did other countries in Western Europe. The only exception was the Netherlands. The Heath government made much of its even-handed approach and on 16 October 1973 announced that Britain would not provide any of the combatants with armaments. Arab leaders, meanwhile, decided to step up their use of oil as a political tool and declared that supplies would be cut each month until Israel withdrew from lands occupied in the war of 1967 and the Palestinians were granted self-government. There was a complete embargo on the sale of oil to the Americans and the Dutch.[21]

In these emergency conditions, Heath later wrote, the British priority was clear: 'We had to ensure our own economic survival without, if possible, alienating any of our friends in the world'. A ceasefire was agreed on 24 October but the end of the fighting did not mean that the problems behind it, or the wider effects, had been properly tackled. On 6 November the nine members of the European Community (Britain, France, the FRG, Italy, Belgium, the Netherlands, Luxembourg, Ireland and Denmark) issued a declaration based on the UN resolution that had been passed after the 1967 war, which called upon Israel to leave the occupied territories and respect Palestinian rights. Britain's view was that Europe had to remain strictly neutral. This would earn Arab trust and enable London and Paris to take the lead in an effort to get the oil flowing again. Heath intended to use 'quiet diplomacy' to obtain oil for Britain's European partners, but quarrels broke out as the British and French were accused of putting their own interests first. Moscow was a keen observer of these developments. The Soviets had not encouraged the oil embargo. According to Victor Israelyan, a senior figure in the Soviet foreign ministry, the USSR's prime minister, Aleksei Kosygin, and foreign minister, Andrei Gromyko, were worried that if oil was used as a weapon against the West, NATO forces would be sent into the Middle East. When NATO did not intervene, Soviet leaders began to change tack. After the war of 1973 they came to see the oil weapon in a more positive light.[22]

The oil shock damaged the British economy and caused further trouble for Britain in Europe, as when West Germany insisted that in view of the financial pressures of the time, the planned European Regional Development Fund (ERDF) could not be as large as Britain wanted. A serious dispute arose between the British government and the oil companies. Britain's balance of payments problem was exacerbated, and the wage demands of the clamorous miners' union made a collision between the miners and the government inevitable. At the end of 1973 Heath and his colleagues decided to limit the working week to three days and ration electricity in order to conserve fuel. There were substantial reductions in public expenditure, restrictions on credit and an increase in taxes. Disputes continued in Western Europe as each government tried to safeguard its own oil supplies. The Arabs exploited this, treating nations differently according to how sympathetic they had been to Israel. Heath, who had called for unity in the face of common danger, was disappointed, though not to the extent that he offered to share North Sea oil. He had envisaged a time when European initiatives would matter more to Britain than the 'special relationship' with the United States, but the quarrel over oil showed that there was some way to go before integrated Europe would have an agreed position on international problems. If the British saw EPC as a supplement to national policy and a way of gaining support for a wider, extra-European role, others did not. Moreover, London never wanted EPC to develop into a set of formal obligations. What British leaders really required was effective cooperation in times of crisis. As with other aspects of European integration, they did not wish EPC to go too far.[23]

Home maintained that Britain's conduct during the Arab-Israeli War of 1973 was appropriate. The arms embargo meant that both sides would be treated the same, though he was prepared to review the situation should the existence of Israel be placed in jeopardy. Any future settlement, he thought, would have to combine security for Israel with the return of occupied land. Home approved of Heath's determination to stand up to Britain's allies on the oil question, and agreed with Heath that North Sea oil should not be included in a collective energy agreement and that the FRG was wrong to press Britain on this by holding up arrangements for the ERDF. He also argued with the West Germans about the US military alert, for Bonn suspected collusion between London and Washington DC. In private discussions with Henry Kissinger, Nixon's national security adviser from 1969 to 1973 and subsequently US secretary of state, Home argued that Britain should be free to object to certain aspects of American policy in order to make British support on other aspects more useful.[24]

Oil was a main topic of discussion in the US press in October 1973. The *New York Times* did not expect America to be seriously affected, since only 6 per cent of its oil came from the Middle East, but the *Wall Street Journal* warned that the longer the crisis continued, the more dangerous it would become: 'Most oil-consuming countries can ride with the shortages for a while. They have about two or three months of oil in storage. But what will happen in mid-winter, especially in Europe or Japan, is anyone's guess'.[25] British publications, such as the *Economist*, could not tell how long Western Europe's reserves would last and expected rationing in Britain and on the continent. Though the Americans were less dependent on Arab oil, they were headed in the same direction as Britain and Western Europe and this had implications for the future, but for the present the Arabs had to accept that their embargo would not (yet) weaken the US commitment to Israel. Perhaps the real purpose was to persuade America's allies to turn against its policy in the Middle East. The *Guardian* pointed to the contradictory actions of Washington DC and Moscow: they were working for peace in the Middle East and yet they supplied the weapons used in the war there. As for the claim made by Britain's chancellor of the exchequer, Anthony Barber, that the oil shock would double the country's balance of payments deficit, but that the increase would be matched by a rise in exports to the Arab world, a growth in Arab holdings of sterling and higher prices for British exports generally, the *Guardian* regarded all this as 'utterly unpredictable'. 'Accustomed as we seem to have become to the acceptance of economic problems and defeats', stated *The Times*, the war in the Middle East underlined the fact that Britain needed urgently to develop its own energy supplies. North Sea oil could restore the balance of payments and insulate the economy from the 'virtual anarchy' of the international oil market. This would help to remove constraints on foreign policy.[26]

The oil crisis raised concerns about economic security. The British began to exploit North Sea reserves in the 1970s. France and the FRG expanded their use of nuclear power. Events had demonstrated the increasing sensitivity of economies to events outside the national boundary. This also contributed to the breaking down of distinctions between domestic and foreign affairs.[27] Britain's activity abroad was heavily influenced by successes and failures in economic management at home.

Nuclear deterrence, strategic planning and NATO affairs

Lack of resources bedevilled Britain's attempts to preserve influence and status. In the 1970s attention often focused on the nuclear deterrent. Doubts were expressed about its usefulness, many commentators denied that it was worth the money, and as disenchantment spread it was suggested not only that the deterrent did not restrain the Soviets, but also that it had failed to convince the world that Britain was still a great power. Following an agreement of 1962, Britain had purchased the Polaris system from the Americans. In 1979 Britain agreed to buy Trident from the United States, but even when the new system became operational, it was revealed, British missiles would be able to take out only 9 per cent of the USSR's land-based missile force. By this time, moreover, Britain and the West seemed to be threatened less by the nuclear capabilities of the Soviet Union than by rogue regimes that were thought to possess nuclear weapons. The Trident deal was important to Britain, nonetheless, and the Americans offered the kind of generous terms that they were unlikely to offer anyone else, which confirmed the survival of the 'special relationship', especially on defence matters. British leaders never showed much enthusiasm for arms control of the type that might affect the development of

Trident, which laid them open to the charge that they were breaking the spirit of non-proliferation.[28]

In the early 1980s there were signs that the strategic balance was shifting to the advantage of the Americans and their allies. Some contemporaries suggested that the Soviets were essentially cautious and that the West attributed to the USSR a war-making capacity it did not have.[29] If this is true, however, it can only have become apparent with the passing of time, and for Britain in the 1970s and 1980s, as for other western powers, vigilance and resistance were still seen to be necessary in dealing with Moscow.

Britain was not involved in the major East-West summits held between 1972 and 1974 and attended by Nixon and Soviet leader Leonid Brezhnev. Britain could do nothing about the loss of control over old imperial lines of communication through the Mediterranean and Red Sea. Somalia had become a Soviet ally in 1969, Malta's government requested the departure of British forces in 1971 and the Libyans (led from 1969 by a military dictator, Colonel Muammar Gaddafi) ended their defence treaty with Britain in 1972. Reducing commitments saved money, and in the event British forces did not leave Malta completely, but the sense of resignation and compromise was growing stronger. The Nixon administration's more constructive relationship with the USSR did not have much to do with Britain. It was shaped more by the situation in Vietnam, by US domestic politics and by changes in international affairs. As Washington DC and Moscow dealt directly with each other, Britain's opportunities to influence the course of events were fewer. This made it easier for Heath and Home to think about distancing Britain from the United States and using the superpower thaw further to reduce Britain's obligations around the world. On the other hand, there was a limit to what could be done in terms of shifting policy onto a new basis. Britain's need for American help could not be ignored. Membership of European institutions was part of an effort to cope with change, but by itself it could not provide all the answers.[30]

Heath took a neutral line during the Arab-Israeli War of 1973, but it was impolitic to defy the United States in other respects and there was dismay as pressure grew within the United States for a scaling down of its military commitments in Europe. American leaders and public opinion were seeking to draw back from activism around the globe in the early 1970s, as economic problems at home, the oil shock and Vietnam eroded ambition and self-belief. Washington DC was frustrated by the efforts of America's allies to take a more independent path. The Europeans were thinking in terms of greater cooperation among themselves, and Washington DC was worried that they would no longer care about reconciling their interests with those of the United States. There was to be an ongoing problem for the Americans: they wanted a stronger 'European pillar' and expected the money and manpower to come from the Europeans, not the United States, but they feared that if Western Europe did do more to defend itself, it would become less amenable and American influence would be lost. Paris became notably agitated whenever the Americans tried to get what they wanted by threatening to reassess their security role in Western Europe. The French thought they could enhance their own leadership credentials by challenging America and asserting that the future course of European integration should not be determined by US preferences.[31]

Although NATO would survive these pressures, in the 1970s there were doubts that it would be able to carry on functioning to good effect. The crucial US guarantee that underpinned the safety of Western Europe could no longer be taken for granted. Nixon's authority was undermined by the Watergate scandal and Vietnam, and Congress moved to restrict executive powers, especially those relating to international affairs. One proposal was to withdraw US troops from any country that did not pay to keep them there. In the 1960s the FRG had overtaken the United States in the provision of troops for Western Europe, and from then on the FRG made the largest military contribution to NATO strength in the European theatre. The FRG kept up its force levels to compensate for the declining deployments of America and most other members of NATO. This reassured Washington DC, as did the opinion of US defence analysts in the 1970s that the strength of the Warsaw Pact had been overestimated.[32]

Heath wanted Britain to go its own way more often, instead of routinely falling in behind American policy, but his attitude towards the United States was not entirely negative. Though he doubted America's reliability he knew that Britain needed its friendship, and the tendency to distinguish Britain's interests from those of the United States eventually petered out. Heath supported the US plan (in the aftermath of the 1973 oil shock) for the establishment of the International Energy Agency, despite French opposition, and began the process of modernizing Britain's Polaris force. He accepted that British policy had to take account of American wishes, and his reservations about the 'special relationship' were balanced by Home's enthusiasm for it. The foreign secretary got on well with Nixon and other American leaders, notably Kissinger's predecessor as US secretary of state, William P. Rogers, and the American ambassador to the UN, George Bush. In Washington DC Home was respected for his robust anti-communism.[33]

Britain's troubles with Europe continued after Heath. Wilson's Labour government of 1974 to 1976 renegotiated some of the terms of Britain's membership of the EC, adding to the acrimony of the European debate in Britain and offending some of Britain's European partners. The economic situation also had to be dealt with. The rise in oil prices had knock-on effects for several years. Negligible growth, combined with relentless inflation, brought 'stagflation'. This, and the possibility of 'mutually assured destruction' (MAD) created by the nuclear strike capabilities of the two superpowers, made for a pessimistic mood. It was extremely difficult to marry together political preferences, security objectives and economic goals. Although Britain's average rate of economic growth between 1970 and 1974 was comparatively good, at 3 per cent per year, this masked deeper problems. Most of the increase happened in 1973 and was related to a brief world boom. The benefits were seen in consumption rather than investment. The 1970s were difficult for all the advanced economies, but Britain probably suffered most. Economic adviser Alec Cairncross later suggested that more than anything else, the Heath government was unlucky. The sharp rise in oil prices exacerbated the deficit; Britain already had a record of balance of payments problems; and the struggle with the miners complicated the attempt to deal with wage inflation.[34]

Heath's successors were unable to improve Britain's economic position. A sterling crisis in 1976 forced the Labour government to seek international relief. Washington DC offered credit but imposed conditions. The credit agreement did not help and the government then applied to the International Monetary Fund. Again, the Americans made sure that strict terms were attached to the aid Britain received. In particular, they wanted more rigorous deflationary measures. The Americans had less reason to give

assistance now that the Bretton Woods system had been disman-
tled and the British military presence East of Suez virtually ended.
The British government claimed that it had intended to set defla-
tion targets anyway, but the affair damaged its prestige abroad and
its reputation at home.[35]

MAD continued to shape military thinking into the mid-1980s,
meanwhile, and one of the reasons why America's Strategic Defence
Initiative (SDI), or 'star wars' programme, would be so controversial was because it was a departure that seemed to make nuclear
war more likely. The arms race intensified in the late 1970s and
early 1980s because of the old Cold War assumption that it was
unwise to seek bargains with an adversary without first gaining a
position of superiority.[36]

British sensitivity about the loss of status was palpable in the
1970s. To many people the turn to Europe was a sign that Britain
counted for less in the world. Yet the British still valued their 'special relationship' with the United States and still had extra-European interests. They did not wish to be confined only to a European
role. The continentals were annoyed by this, and blamed Britain
for blocking closer union in Europe for the sake of an unequal relationship with the Americans. In the late 1970s the British refused
to join in the European Monetary System (EMS) and argued in
favour of a wider and more inclusive approach to economic and
financial reorganization, involving the United States. Here was
another example of the tension between Britain's global perspective and what London took to be a narrow European viewpoint.
Nevertheless, there were opportunities for British and European
governments to work together, especially on security matters, and
one of the most important developments in this respect was the
rise of the Eurogroup. Established in 1969, the Eurogroup set up
regular informal talks between Western Europe's defence ministers. The main purpose was to arrive at a coordinated position
before full meetings of the NATO council.[37]

Summary

For all the disappointments experienced by Britain in the 1970s,
there was an expectation that problems would pass, or be dealt
with, and that British influence could be shored up. Britain was
in trouble, but Britain was not alone in this, and power, prestige

and status were always contingent rather than fixed and absolute. Most situations were managed as well as they might have been in the circumstances: the British had developed expertise in minimizing and delaying relative military and economic decline. Britain was quite successful in accommodating change. In fact, Britain's flexibility and pragmatism were great attributes. Britain's record speaks for itself. Decolonization, the decision to withdraw from East of Suez, the reallocation of resources and shift in economic and political relationships indicate that timely adjustment had become the normal practice for British governments before the 1970s. Thereafter, the need was to focus on the most vital issues and regions so that British interests were served and Britain's power and position did not deteriorate to the point that they were in danger of possible collapse.

2 Questions of Defence and Détente

The needs and opportunities associated with defence and détente became increasingly important to British policy-makers. As the international order changed, security concerns remained constant, although they had to be addressed in new and sometimes unexpected ways. Despite moments of pessimism of the 1970s, the Helsinki Accords of August 1975 inspired hopes that détente was really working and that the world was a safer place as a result. The West recognized Soviet interests in Eastern Europe and the Soviets agreed to open up the eastern bloc for trade and to respect human rights. This appeared to represent a significant breakthrough. Yet there was no end to ongoing controversies within Britain. The most immediate and pressing issues included the modernization of the nuclear deterrent, the wish to preserve the 'special relationship' with the United States, and the difficult and connected tasks of improving Britain's economic position and sustaining high levels of defence spending.

Defence policy

Though nuclear disarmament was a favourite cause of the Labour left, Wilson's government of 1974–76 decided that an attempt should be made to update Polaris. This had been under discussion since 1967. The resulting Chevaline project entailed a huge expenditure and was ultimately of limited benefit, since the Polaris system became irrelevant before the improvements were completed. In 1974, the cabinet had been informed that the cost would be about £250 million. Within two years the cost had soared to four times this amount. Wilson's successor as prime minister, James Callaghan, decided that so much had been spent on Chevaline, and it had progressed so far, that it should not be discontinued. National security therefore rested on the long-established commitment to an expensive deterrent, with governments consistently understating the costs in public. Meanwhile, Wilson and Callaghan managed to maintain good relations with the United States, and Callaghan worked well with President Jimmy Carter, who occupied the White House from January 1977 to January 1981. Britain's economy could not be quickly repaired, however, and as Callaghan had said in April 1974 when he was foreign secretary, Britain's role in the world was shrinking because long-term political influence depended on economic strength, and that was running out. In May 1977 the members of NATO agreed to augment their defence spending, which had implications for Britain and proved that détente had not ended military competition with the Soviets after all.[1]

The Carter administration agreed to a 3 per cent annual increase in the US defence budget, in line with the rest of NATO, because the envisaged spending would be less than what had been proposed by Carter's predecessor, Gerald Ford, who was president from August 1974 to January 1977. Carter later announced a bigger increase, 5 per cent, in 1979, following the Soviet invasion of Afghanistan. In fact, the new Soviet weaponry that came into service in the mid-1970s had already given a spur to US modernization efforts. This arms race led British leaders to regard Polaris as insufficient, but at least Chevaline meant that Britain would not lose the ability to strike targets in the USSR while postponing a decision on the new generation of submarine-launched missiles. The nuclear relationship with the United States remained close. Still, the Labour government appointed in 1974 could not easily balance the need to finance Chevaline with the need to control public expenditure. This government had inherited a huge balance of payments deficit, and predictions about the overall economic outlook were not encouraging. The Heath government had intended to reduce the defence budget by £178 million. Labour's new chancellor of the exchequer, Denis Healey, a former defence secretary (1964–70), had to make a further reduction of £50 million. Although Wilson decided that Chevaline was necessary, the fact that the extent and cost of the programme were kept from the cabinet suggests that he expected it to be blocked unless he hid the truth. The British had also to give attention to conventional forces, as did their allies. NATO's 'flexible response' strategy involved keeping open a range of options, both conventional and nuclear, to deal with various threats: hence the decision of May 1977 for a 3 per cent annual increase in defence spending for five years from 1979.[2]

Britain's circumstances were such that higher defence spending would not be easy to sustain. The Callaghan government, in office from 1976 to 1979, agreed that NATO's conventional forces should be strengthened, but where were Britain and other members of NATO to find the money? It is likely that the agreed targets would have been forgotten had it not been for the fall of Nicaragua to the left-wing Sandinistas in June 1979; the Kremlin's threat to retaliate when NATO deployed Cruise and Pershing missiles to counter the USSR's SS20 mobile, multiple warhead, intermediate range ballistic missiles; and the Soviet invasion of Afghanistan in December 1979. Britain worked hard to meet the NATO spending targets. Callaghan was confident that Britain could fund its contribution from North Sea oil revenues. The rising cost of Chevaline was a worry, however, and more money was needed in due course for Trident, which Britain had to have, it was decided, if the deterrent was to remain credible and if Britain was to influence Washington DC, uphold prestige and status, and restrain the Soviets, who would have to take account of a second nuclear decision-making centre in NATO.[3]

Officially, Britain remained committed to détente. The agreements reached at Helsinki in 1975 were among the most important of this era, and Wilson and Callaghan helped to bring them about. In conversations with Kissinger, Callaghan suggested that the Soviets not only wanted détente but also needed it, for they were spending more than the Americans on defence and had only half of the United States' gross national product (GNP).[4] In 1975 Callaghan and Wilson assured their cabinet colleagues, and the Americans, that even if the Soviets continued to use the rhetoric of international struggle, in practice Moscow would be reasonable.[5]

European thaw, the Helsinki process and its contexts

The Conference on Security and Cooperation in Europe had been launched with preparatory talks in November 1973. The British were initially sceptical. The main point for the foreign office was that CSCE should not interfere with Bonn's 'Ostpolitik' (the FRG's dealings with the eastern bloc) or with British activity in the EC.

It was assumed that the Soviets intended to use CSCE to reinforce their position in Eastern Europe, retard economic and political cooperation in Western Europe and weaken NATO, yet it was impossible for Britain peremptorily to reject Soviet calls for negotiation. Governments and peoples across Western Europe wanted a thaw; Brezhnev had been pushing for a security conference since the mid-1960s; and the Nixon administration, under pressure domestically to withdraw US troops from Europe, was interested in 'mutual and balanced force reductions' (MBFR). In May 1971 Brezhnev agreed that there should be two sets of negotiations, CSCE and MBFR. The Soviets wanted to confine CSCE to security matters but the West insisted that humanitarian issues should be included.[6]

The British foreign office saw that 'Ostpolitik', the Strategic Arms Limitation Talks (SALT), MBFR and CSCE were all pointing in the same direction. It was not thought that Britain could stem the tide, but there was a determination not to accept a CSCE framework shaped by Moscow or by wavering allies. The goal was to frustrate Soviet designs without appearing to disrupt détente. Britain could not endorse the 'Brezhnev Doctrine', which provided for Soviet intervention whenever one of the USSR's satellites departed from an approved socialist path. Nor could Britain approve of the break-up of NATO and the Warsaw Pact in favour of pan-European arrangements. Britain would have to make some compromises, though, or risk isolation; and working with European partners would help to promote EPC, in which there might be benefits.[7]

European détente coincided with adjustments in Britain's international role, and it is not surprising that the attitude remained equivocal. Overseas commitments were being reduced, the focus was more on exercising influence in Europe, and there was an acceptance that Britain ranked below the United States and USSR. Although Britain still had some remnants of empire and the global reach and was respected as one of the founders of the post-1945 world order, power and potential were limited. Among Britain's key tasks was the resolution of disputes within NATO, especially between the Americans and Europeans. The British wanted to contribute to détente while ensuring that it did not endanger NATO unity. The FRG had more to offer the USSR and its allies in Eastern Europe, especially economically, while Britain lacked common interests with the USSR and eastern bloc. There was some trade, but it never represented a significant portion of Britain's overall trade, and London's bilateral relationship with Moscow normally depended on the general state of East-West relations. Britain had little incentive and few opportunities to take a lead in European détente.[8]

London approved of 'Ostpolitik' and encouraged Nixon to pursue détente with the Soviets while stipulating that US-Soviet bargains should not cut across the interests of America's allies. The British hoped that MBFR talks would nullify the pressure that was growing in Congress for an unconditional downsizing of the American military presence in Europe. The Americans were reluctant to get involved in CSCE. The British pressed for full US participation, though they had some of the same reservations as the Americans. In particular, it was thought that the USSR should not be forgiven for the invasion of Czechoslovakia in 1968, or allowed to gain legitimacy for their control over Eastern Europe, or given a chance to separate Western Europe from the United States. Meanwhile, the Kremlin's willingness to negotiate increased as a result of 'Ostpolitik'. Bonn's decision to recognize the East German state, conclude agreements about the status of Berlin and accept Poland's western frontiers was seen by Soviet leaders as an acknowledgement of the USSR's ascendancy in Eastern Europe. Moscow wanted a further improvement in East-West relations. The British were pleased that CSCE could get under way, but did not expect it to bring significant results. They cautioned against excessive optimism and, like the Americans, argued that agreements should not be legally binding (the Helsinki Final Act would not be a formal treaty registered with the United Nations). London assumed that economic and cultural links could be improved quite easily. Security issues and human rights would be more contentious.[9]

Quarrels developed in the West over aims and tactics. Some governments wanted to focus on humanitarian issues from the outset. Others were anxious about alienating Moscow. Some wanted to keep everything vague, in order to introduce specific proposals at a time of their own choosing. There was disagreement on the question of setting up a permanent body as part of CSCE. Britain backed the idea, the Americans did not, and Western Europe was divided on the matter. The preference for temporary bodies that were limited in scope gained ground because it was supposed that a permanent body might be used by Moscow to slow up the process of integration in Western Europe. Another problem that had to be addressed was security. Washington DC wanted to press ahead with MBFR and sought to prevent CSCE from getting in the way. London and Paris opposed any linkage between the two sets of negotiations and warned that MBFR might disadvantage the West militarily, but other NATO members wanted a linkage in order to have a say in the outcome of MBFR. Finally it was agreed that arrangements for CSCE would only be made after or in parallel with discussions on MBFR.[10]

Once the MBFR negotiations began, it was clear that progress would be slow. An agreement was not signed until 1986. Moscow was determined to preserve the Warsaw Pact's superiority in conventional forces, but was willing to talk about force reductions in order to gain leverage on other matters, notably CSCE. In NATO the prevailing opinion was that large reductions would be dangerous, since they would give the Warsaw Pact an even greater advantage in the European theatre, but leaders in the West had to negotiate in order to maintain domestic support for their defence policies. More divisions emerged. For a time the FRG pushed for radical force reductions across the board. Later the French advocated limits on both nuclear and conventional weapons and stringent monitoring of the arms trade. None of this appealed to Washington DC or Moscow.[11]

By the time the CSCE preparatory talks opened in November 1973, the British had been making plans for over a year. It was known that the Kremlin had little interest in economic or technological cooperation and opposed any serious negotiation on freedom of movement and other human rights issues. Members of the Warsaw Pact wanted their frontiers to be formally recognized. British experts decided that some were less willing than others to have CSCE confirm Soviet hegemony in Eastern Europe, but that it would be difficult to exploit this. On human rights the USSR's allies were expected to be cautious, not wishing to provoke Soviet intervention. It was assumed that ruling elites in the eastern bloc were reluctant to allow more contact with the West in case this weakened their authority. A foreign office paper of February 1972 had stressed that CSCE was really Moscow's idea, and 'western countries have had to accept it largely because of domestic political pressure: they have had, in effect, to accept the

Soviet thesis that support for a conference is the only acceptable evidence of willingness to work for détente'. Above all, Moscow wished to create 'an atmosphere in Europe in which the presence of American troops appears increasingly unnecessary and in which all-European co-operation seems more attractive than West European integration'.[12]

Addressing the Commons in December 1972, Home declared that while there were grounds for optimism, it would be wrong to expect too much from the different negotiations that had begun or were soon to commence. Misgivings about CSCE persisted. Britain's chief negotiator, Sir David Hildyard, informed London in October 1973 that certain western representatives were siding with the Soviets, making it difficult to bring up issues that Moscow was reluctant to discuss. Home insisted that CSCE had to be treated as a complete package. Committee I was to deal with security in Europe, Committee II with economic, scientific, technological and environmental cooperation, and Committee III with humanitarian and other matters. Britain's position was that the humanitarian strand and the security strand should 'proceed as far as possible in parallel'.[13]

Labour took office in the spring of 1974. Thinking that CSCE had made insufficient progress, Wilson and Callaghan sought to inject new impetus into the negotiations. They had both visited the USSR previously and had contacts in the Soviet leadership. Callaghan had a fairly good working relationship with Gromyko, who had been Soviet foreign minister since 1957. The Labour government decided that the time was right to take the initiative. Callaghan hoped that the Americans would respect the wishes of 'neutral' nations and urged that a distinction had to be maintained between what the West wanted and what the West would be willing to settle for. In February 1975 he and Wilson arrived in Moscow for talks. Wilson focused on trade, Callaghan on security and stability in Europe. Human rights, left-wing subversion in Portugal and the need for a CSCE accord were among the matters discussed. The visit helped to make agreement at the CSCE summit in Helsinki in August 1975 more likely. The Americans still had reservations, but a deal was made under which the Soviets made pledges about human rights and East-West contact in return for the recognition of post-1945 frontiers and the Soviet sphere of influence in Eastern Europe. Privately, the Soviets also agreed to end their involvement in Portugal (where a long period of right-wing dictatorship had been ended and a socialist government installed under Mario Soares). Wilson was concerned that Soviet interference there might destroy détente.[14]

Before the signing of the Helsinki Final Act Callaghan had reason to complain about last-minute difficulties created by the Soviets, who claimed that Britain had gone back on certain undertakings. Callaghan told Nikolai M. Lunkov, the Soviet ambassador to Britain, that this was 'complete rubbish'. Britain's representatives were not 'plenipotentiaries', after all, and as the foreign secretary wrote to the negotiator Hildyard in June 1975: 'We had to carry our friends and allies along with us and could not order the Germans or the Dutch to do what we wanted. The Soviet Government could perhaps treat its friends in this way but we could not ... we could not impose a solution'. In the following month Hildyard reported that the Final Act was ready to be approved and that the British team had played a 'major role' in putting it together, especially the sections on confidence-building measures, economic cooperation and above all humanitarian issues.[15]

Callaghan believed that Helsinki represented a momentous step forward. Washington DC was not so sure, but at least seemed willing to give the process a chance. Anglo-Soviet relations improved, with more trade and cultural links, and talks with Gromyko in the spring of 1976 led to the relaxation of restrictions on dissidents. Callaghan continued to press the Soviets on human rights, but he did not ask for official or public undertakings. As he extended Britain's bilateral dealings with the USSR, he thought he could detect a loosening of Moscow's position. None of this represented an entirely independent course on Britain's part, because the British government was committed to NATO and, even more, to the 'special relationship' with America.[16]

While the British remained ambivalent about the thaw in Europe, the FRG forged a new relationship with the East German regime, the USSR and other states in the eastern bloc. London and Washington DC feared that the FRG was becoming less open to its allies' advice. As superpower détente continued, moreover, British leaders worried, as others did, that the Americans and Soviets would bargain above their heads. Kissinger noted that in periods of tension Western Europe feared US rigidity, and in periods of thaw it feared US-Soviet 'condominium'. In London there was also a concern that the Helsinki process might prove troublesome. If it raised expectations and more concessions had to be made to keep it going, the West could end up giving way on fundamentals. The British argued repeatedly that the strength and cohesion of NATO mattered more than the conclusion of a comprehensive settlement with the USSR and its satellites. Although the Helsinki Accords were welcomed in London, in February 1976 parliament was reminded by Roy Hattersley, minister of state at the foreign office, that détente had to be approached prudently. British ambivalence reflected a sense of marginalization, perhaps, for Britain did not often play the principal role in the East-West bargaining of the period, and in CSCE the British contribution was much clearer on human rights than on other issues.[17]

Even on human rights, though, it has been claimed that Britain did not abide by the spirit of the Helsinki Accords and that, across Africa, Latin America and the Pacific, Britain did nothing to prevent atrocities and profited from the conditions in which they took place.[18] It is clear that abuses continued in Europe and elsewhere, but to blame Britain alone and to ignore the efforts made by British leaders and campaigners on human rights, especially in relation to the Helsinki process, is to hold an unbalanced view of history.

Shortly after the signing of the Helsinki Final Act, Britain's ambassador in Moscow, Sir Terence Garvey, offered an analysis of Soviet perceptions. Soviet leaders believed they had made important gains. Without abandoning the 'right' to intervene in Eastern Europe, as encapsulated in the 'Brezhnev Doctrine', they obtained a multilateral endorsement of the political situation there. They had brought about the conference that they had long been seeking and added weight to their claim that the USSR was for peace, and in the Helsinki Accords were statements that the Kremlin could use to attack its critics in the West as enemies of détente and to demand more binding agreements. In addition, although the Soviets had promised to participate in MBFR talks in Vienna, CSCE left them free to resist anything that would diminish their superiority in conventional forces. On the other hand, Garvey continued, there were aspects of the Helsinki process that made the Soviet leadership uncomfortable. The Kremlin had been reluctant to accept the obligation to notify the West about Warsaw Pact military manoeuvres, for instance, fearing that this would lead to western observers actually being present. But it was the human rights part of CSCE that represented 'the main debit' for the Kremlin, which did not want information and ideas spreading from the West into the USSR and eastern bloc. On every matter on which Soviet practice was not in line with the Final Act, Garvey argued, the West should make determined protests. If the West was united, moved gradually, kept up its defences and settled for 'nothing less than a fair balance of concrete advantage', Garvey was confident that the results would be favourable. Détente did not have to be what Moscow wanted it to be, and in the long run it was possible that détente would alter the USSR and render its rulers less intractable.[19]

The change of governments in Britain in 1970 and 1974 had made little difference to British policy on European détente, for a consensus had developed, and the attitude towards CSCE remained mixed. The wish for agreements coexisted with a concern to prevent disunity, excessive optimism and unnecessary compromises. British leaders were pleasantly surprised because, to their way of thinking, the Helsinki process turned out to be better than expected, and they were pleased to have the machinery in place to review the implementation of the Final Act so that the process could continue. One useful by-product was the development of EPC. This closer cooperation gave Britain new ways of exercising influence, which was important because it had not been possible to draw the Americans more into CSCE by using NATO links. Britain saw that certain goals could be pursued through EPC that could not be achieved by acting as a mediator between the United States and its European allies. Britain's caution with regard to CSCE was reinforced as détente lost its impetus. Little progress was made with MBFR or the next stage of SALT, and the Americans and Soviets went on competing with each other in Africa and Asia, often through proxies. While supposing that the underlying East-West rivalry could probably not be removed, most British leaders rarely said so openly. The government's defence statement of March 1976 brought together a range of activities and pointed to the need for progress in each one: nuclear deterrence, détente, CSCE, MBFR and SALT.[20]

Although many leaders in the West and in the East wanted the European thaw to continue, the Helsinki process highlighted the limits of détente and the difficulties that were caused by events outside Europe. After 1975 the Soviets regretted the concessions they had made and complained that the Helsinki Final Act was being used improperly against them, but they did not pull out of CSCE. Indeed, neither side wanted CSCE to collapse: or rather, neither side wanted to be blamed if it did collapse. The process was worthwhile because it provided bargaining tools, and there was still a lot of ambiguity in CSCE. East and West could both claim that they had made advances. The follow-up conferences at Belgrade (1977–78), Madrid (1980–83) and Stockholm (1984) were marked by disagreements that reflected the course of international events. Britain's position was made clear by Callaghan in July 1976, when he told the Soviets that the Helsinki Final Act should not be treated as a definitive, static document, and by foreign secretary David Owen, who declared in March 1977 that Helsinki had created a long-term framework and a code of behaviour.[21]

In the mid-1970s the Labour government stressed its commitment to détente alongside sound defence. The deterrent factor became more important because of Soviet military activity outside Europe, especially in Africa. The leader of the opposition, Margaret Thatcher, was sure that the Soviets had used détente to gain strength. She called upon the government to do more to counter them. Thatcher was unhappy about Helsinki and opposed the trade and credit deals that were being made with Moscow, because she thought that these would enable the USSR to divert more of its resources into armaments. Nevertheless, there were influential figures in the West who believed in the Helsinki process, including corporate tycoons like Donald M. Kendall of PepsiCo, who chaired the US-USSR Trade and Economic Council. It took time for the US government to commit itself to CSCE, but when MBFR delivered no quick benefits the human rights aspects of the Helsinki process took on greater importance. Congress involved itself more energetically, and the White House could not ignore the openings that materialized, especially when Moscow intimated that compliance with human rights agreements would be facilitated by economic assistance. Aid and trade did increase. Then the Soviet invasion of Afghanistan and the US military build-up and strengthening of NATO pushed East and West farther apart.[22]

Helsinki meant different things to different people. What Brezhnev had in mind was a transitional period, during which tension could be lowered despite the increase in armaments. The end in view was a global shift in favour of the USSR. The Kremlin believed that CSCE could be used to persuade the West to accept this shift, and in the meantime détente would enable the USSR to obtain western technology and consumer goods at no political cost. For the Americans, the main point of détente and trade was to bring the USSR into interdependence. The desired outcomes were the ending of the arms race and the stabilization of super-power relations. CSCE was not important in this scenario. For the Europeans, though, it was vital. They were seeking to overcome the division of Europe and moderate the military competition between East and West. Perhaps the actual terms of the Helsinki Final Act were immaterial, and its main importance was that it fostered relationships without which European détente could not have developed. Helsinki was less helpful in terms of superpower détente.[23]

There were informed commentators in the West, especially in the United States, who urged their governments to rethink détente. Some insisted that the only way forward was through trade, which should not be dependent on anything else, and that to continue challenging Moscow on human rights would be dangerous. Samuel Pisar, a former adviser at the US state department, wanted the Americans and Soviets to give up moral and ideological arguments and return to the pragmatism of the early 1970s. Robert Legvold, a political science professor at Tufts University, Massachusetts, wrote that the USSR would not fit into an expected pattern of behaviour. The West assumed that the USSR had problems associated with economic and technological deficiencies, bureaucratic sclerosis and reform agitation, and that it needed help from the West to deal with these, but this was not necessarily how the Soviets saw themselves.[24]

The invasion of Afghanistan in 1979 suspended détente, sur-prised many in the West, and coincided with a shift to the right in British and American politics. A Conservative government took office in Britain in May 1979 with Thatcher as prime minister. In November 1980 the Republican candidate, Ronald Reagan, gained a landslide victory over Carter in the US presidential election. Thatcher and Reagan went on to forge the closest working rela-tionship between Britain and America since the early 1960s. They were determined to take a tough line against the Soviets, although the situation began to change after Mikhail Gorbachev became Soviet leader in 1985. In the meantime, for all the revived Cold War rhetoric and the new closeness with the United States, Britain was still losing influence and status. The West German economy had been more successful than Britain's for some time, and the FRG was making a larger contribution to European defence, and at a relatively lower cost, than were the British, who had to impose further limits on their spending even while trying to *act* as if they remained militarily strong. By 1979 Britain's defence expenditure had fallen to 5 per cent of GDP[25] but this was more than the expenditure of the FRG and France. During the 1980s there had to be a reassessment of Britain's defence posture. While the government remained firmly committed to NATO, Britain's armed forces were reshaped to perform narrower tasks within the alliance. In Europe and beyond, Britain still faced the old predicament: how to match responsibilities with resources.[26]

The resource gap and multipolarity

Britain's post-1945 defence spending had been consistently high. It peaked at 11 per cent of GDP in the early 1950s (during the Korean War), falling to about 6 per cent in 1970. Continuing reductions brought spending down to 4.7 per cent of GDP in 1978, but then new NATO spending targets took effect. Financial worries mounted in the early 1980s because of an economic downturn. Defence accounted for 5.4 per cent of GDP in 1983–84, and in 1985–86 Britain was one of the few members of NATO to spend at the agreed level. In 1986–87 defence spending was down to about 4.7 per cent of GDP. In absolute terms Britain's expenditure was about the same as that of the FRG and France, but as a proportion of GDP it was higher. For the FRG the figure was 3.3 per cent, and for France 4 per cent. Britain's smaller economy was subjected to greater pressure. Within NATO, Britain remained one of the highest proportionate spenders. The complexity of Britain's defence requirements meant that savings were not easily made. There was the continental commitment, necessitating a presence in West Germany. There was a need for ships and aircraft in the Atlantic and the waters around the British Isles. There was Britain's own security to attend to, which was based primarily on air defence. There was the nuclear deterrent. There were also 'out of area' responsibilities, notably in Hong Kong, Belize, the Persian Gulf and the Falklands.[27]

Most members of NATO fell short of the spending targets set in 1977. There was disputation about this lack of uniformity. Another problem was disagreement about how the money should be spent. Burden sharing remained a sensitive issue: Washington DC wanted the Europeans to do more. In 1984 the US Congress was still insisting on this, and America's secretary of defence Caspar Weinberger was obliged to commission a report on the matter. The report revealed that most European members of NATO had been paying a reasonable share of the alliance's costs for some time. During the 1970s US defence spending had fallen by 7 per cent, while the Europeans' spending had risen by about 23 per cent. Nevertheless, controversy continued. Leaders in Western Europe knew that they could not do without US security guarantees, but they disliked the restraints that this imposed upon them and worried that Washington DC, in projecting American power throughout the world, might involve them in a war against their wishes or otherwise put off for years a big reduction in defence spending.[28]

Quarrels about defence spending marked the early days of the Thatcher government. The prime minister was determined to bring public expenditure under control, and the chancellor of the exchequer between 1979 and 1983, Geoffrey Howe, tried to impose sweeping cuts. Thatcher regarded defence as a special case, however, and defence secretary Francis Pym insisted that the 3 per cent NATO commitment was one that Britain was bound to honour. When Howe pointed to projects that were already over budget, Pym threatened to resign. Thatcher agreed to minimize the cuts in defence, though she accepted Howe's analysis of the situation and backed him on the need to scale down the Trident programme. Pym was subsequently moved from the ministry of defence.[29]

As well as spending more on defence than most other advanced industrial nations, both in absolute terms and as a proportion of GDP, Britain maintained larger professional military forces. France and the FRG relied on conscripts, while Britain had no compulsory military service. In 1985–86, Britain's armed forces numbered 323,800 personnel in total. France had 557,493, but 253,000 of these were conscripts. West Germany had 485,800, but 228,850 were conscripts. At this time Britain was still the world's third largest spender on defence, and its military capabilities placed it among the top military powers. Only the British, Americans, Soviets and French had the whole range of military force, covering land, sea and air, nuclear and conventional, and covering the spectrum from strategic to battlefield weaponry. The commitment to European security, through NATO, had emerged as Britain's main responsibility in the late 1960s. It was the one that could not be reduced in the way that other commitments could. As a result, high expenditure carried on alongside the survival of multiple responsibilities. Influence was lost less because of military weakness than because of an inability to mobilize other sources of power, especially economic and technological.[30]

In the 1980s, as the FRG's political, economic and military importance increased, Britain was still trying to perform more defence roles than the FRG and other European members of NATO, but with a comparatively weaker economic base. In 1984 the Thatcher government announced that it would abandon the 3 per cent annual increase in defence spending from 1986. Extra burdens had been taken on, notably the cost of Trident and the cost of maintaining substantial forces in the South Atlantic after the Falklands War of 1982. Defence choices continued to be hotly debated.[31]

American thinking on national security and foreign policy had been changed forever, meanwhile, by the Vietnam War and its aftermath. Nixon and Kissinger had managed to arrange a US withdrawal, but only after an escalation of the conflict and at the cost of serious domestic and international repercussions.[32] America's allies and enemies waited to see if the United States would act differently in the world after Vietnam. Both as leader of the opposition from 1965 to 1970 and as British prime minister from 1970 to 1974, Edward Heath maintained that Britain should not get drawn into Vietnam. His initial opinion was that the United States would win the war, but he came to see involvement in Vietnam as a source of humiliation for America. He considered this dangerous, suspecting that the Americans would review their commitments around the world and probably pull some of their forces out of Western Europe. When the Americans began to withdraw from Vietnam, Heath approved, but he hoped for a gradual process: the Americans had to leave in such a way as to dispel any idea that their power was fading, otherwise the Soviets might grow bolder. The Americans were conscious that the USSR's nuclear arsenal had grown and that the Soviets intended to match the United States. By the early 1970s the Soviets had more intercontinental ballistic missiles (ICBMs) than the Americans, although the United States had superiority in other types of nuclear weapons, as well as a strategic bomber force, and Britain and France also had nuclear weaponry. Still, Nixon could not fail to respond to the Soviet arms build-up and the spread of Soviet influence in sensitive areas, notably the Middle East. He had to show firmness, but he also wanted a more positive engagement with the Soviets, in order to ease tension, and his diplomatic approach to China was part of this. He expected it to facilitate détente and to promote a shared US-Soviet understanding that the old bipolar Cold War world no longer existed. Nixon also presumed that Moscow and Peking wanted a thaw as much as he did, in which case his overtures to them would not be rebuffed, and he was fortunate in that an opening already existed: SALT. He was sure that SALT could be linked with other initiatives, and he was hoping in particular to secure Soviet help with the Vietnam peace plan.[33]

The movement away from a bipolar perspective had an impact on international relations and on what politicians, expert advisers and historians said and wrote about the Cold War. By the 1990s, indeed, the bipolar paradigm had fallen into disrepute. According to one commentator, it was 'inadequate as an analytical tool in studying the forces of change that have reshaped the international order'. Even before the Nixon years, it was argued, there had been more to the Cold War than the two superpowers and their military competition, and over the whole of the period from the 1940s to the 1980s the international order had been influenced most not by US-Soviet interaction but by the 'essential interrelatedness' of many different types of influence. Moreover, the changes in world affairs during the 1970s and 1980s served to demonstrate that the Americans and Soviets did not have everything their own way.[34]

How did the Nixon thaw and the talk of multipolarity go down in Britain? Late in 1969 the Labour foreign secretary Michael Stewart remarked that new departures in US foreign policy would not necessarily bring a dramatic shift in international relations. Indeed, though many observers in Britain agreed that détente promised much, they doubted that Nixon was the man to lead it. They did not believe that he would do what was needed to make peace in Vietnam, or make the concessions Moscow desired in return for its full commitment to détente. At the time of the US presidential election in November 1972, *The Times* called upon Nixon to respect the interests of the United States' allies, consolidate the thaw with the USSR and China, make progress in SALT, assist with CSCE, be more even-handed in the Middle East, and conclude long overdue agreements with the leaders of Britain and Western Europe on trade and on America's contribution to collective security. The *Economist* suggested that although he was not personally popular, Nixon had convinced American voters that his foreign policy was worthwhile, but in the *Guardian* the Europhile and left-of-centre commentator Peter Jenkins declared that it would be disastrous if Nixon remained president, for he 'succeeds by bringing out the worst in people'. His diplomatic manoeuvres were 'external diversions' that could not make up for the manipulation of fear and greed in America, and he was relying mainly on force and threat to deal with the USSR, China and North Vietnam. After Nixon's electoral victory, the *Observer* expected his priorities to be economic. American politicians and businessmen were in a hurry to make trade agreements with the Soviet Union and China. The idea seemed to be that by selling to its enemies, America could prompt them to sue for peace.[35]

Some British leaders were not sure what to make of American overtures to Moscow and Peking or Nixon's talk of a multi-polar world. In his time as foreign secretary, Home concluded that the West was right to seek an accommodation with the USSR, but in London there was plenty of criticism of Nixon's agenda. This was partly because Nixon's policy represented an attempt to transform his country's international position with an 'imaginative leap', as John Young calls it, and the British tended not to go in for such things. Lack of imagination was not necessarily a flaw. Pragmatism and even cynicism served Britain well on particular issues, and a 'realist world-view' was a consistent theme in British policy-making. It gained added purchase when the thaw slowed down, when the disadvantages of multipolarity became clearer, and when Cold War tensions rose again. To the 'realist', international relations were shaped primarily by power struggles and the world was anarchic, with no overarching authority to settle disputes and each state relying on its own efforts and resources. Conflict was inevitable. It was assumed that détente would probably not last and that potential aggressors were impressed less by negotiation than by threats backed up with credible military force. This 'realist world-view' featured prominently in Britain's foreign policy debates of the 1970s and 1980s. So did other ideas and models, however, and there were times when cooperation in international affairs was more obvious than conflict. No single formula could determine policy, though British leaders did continue to ask questions about détente and multipolarity. There was a similarly consistent body of opinion in Washington DC. Indeed, Nixon's apparently more flexible approach might not have represented much of a depart-ure at all, because multipolarity came to be regarded as a source of instability.[36]

Summary

On defence and détente, there was a pattern to British goals and activities. The maintenance of adequate defences was a cardinal requirement, and this included attempts to enhance Britain's cap-acity to deter. The British were also committed to thaw, though their approach remained cautious. They wanted to protect themselves and their allies. There was also an ongoing need to rearrange Britain's obligations in line with the available financial and manpower resources. Some of the changes that took place in the world during the 1970s and 1980s engendered pessimism and uncertainty, but Britain also evinced real resilience. There was no relaxation of efforts to influence the course of events and to fur-ther British interests. Increasingly, this was done in collaboration with allies. The British could still occasionally act alone, however, depending on the issue, the timing and the opportunity.

3 The Beginning of a New World Order?

In the early and mid-1970s, many observers thought they were witnessing the construction of a new world order based on bargaining, tolerance and mutual respect. The Americans and Soviets were serious about negotiating with each other, and SALT produced important agreements. Superpower détente affected and was affected by the thaw in Europe, where the status of Berlin, links between the two Germanys, and diplomatic, economic and other contacts between Western Europe and the USSR and eastern bloc were all being addressed. Britain's international role and relationships began to change in line with these developments, but the change should not be exaggerated. The Cold War in Europe and beyond was certainly not ended, and hostility and suspicion were never eradicated. Western governments quarrelled with each other on a range of issues. In Asia there was a war between India and Pakistan. There was a coup in Chile. The Middle East saw war and an intensification of long-existing rivalries. The United States and Soviet Union went on competing with each other even while pursuing détente.

Strategic arms limitation: the background

Although the Soviets did not trust Nixon, who had been an outspoken anti-communist in his younger days, they were willing to give détente a chance in order to see what they could achieve. Initially the focus was on SALT, which officially opened in April 1970. There was an immediate problem because the USSR wanted to cover only those weapons that could hit Soviet and US territory. This effort to exclude Soviet missiles aimed at Western Europe was a ploy to expose rifts within NATO, whose European members doubted that American cities would really be sacrificed for the sake of Western Europe. Then another dispute arose: the United States wanted to include offensive weapons while the Soviets preferred to discuss only defensive anti-ballistic missiles. That SALT gained any momentum at all was quite a triumph. There were disagreements within both the US and Soviet governments as well as the arguments that arose between American and Soviet negotiating teams. Nevertheless, SALT appealed to both sides and was associated with the concept of strategic parity. 'Parity' rested on the fact that both sides had the ability to respond to a first strike with a devastating counterattack. Yet 'parity' did not mean equality, for the United States and Soviet Union had different types of nuclear weapons, and SALT did not rule out nuclear war. In the late 1960s, the United States' nuclear arsenal was still larger than that of the USSR, but the Soviets were catching up. Both sides continued to develop weapons. America's offensive power was enhanced through the multiple independently targeted re-entry vehicle, or MIRV, and SALT did not cover weapons that were being built and tested. The Soviets did not test their first MIRVs until 1973. By 1969, though, they had overtaken the United States in ICBMs, while the Americans were still ahead in strategic bombers and missile-launching submarines. New anti-ballistic missiles gave American and Soviet leaders the capacity to shelter their civilian populations from retaliation, leaving them free to strike first if they chose. Offensive weapons created instability, but so did defence systems, because a stable deterrent relationship required that civilians on each side were hostages against an attack by the other.[1]

One of the Soviets' main concerns, as the negotiations progressed, was that an agreement would not be concluded. A blow to US-Soviet détente was likely to help China, and Moscow wished to prevent a further extension of the contacts between America and China and to limit the influence that China had over the course of US-Soviet relations. Washington DC was also concerned about China's military strength. A related goal for Moscow was a thaw in Europe. Brezhnev saw that if peaceful change in Europe could be promoted alongside a direct dialogue between the USSR and the United States, Moscow was bound to reap some benefits.[2]

The British press welcomed the opening of the SALT conference in Vienna in 1970. *The Times* reported on a 'hopeful start' but noted that US domestic politics could delay progress. Though some members of the administration and Congress wanted to avoid an arms race, others warned about the USSR's 'missile superiority'. In view of the advent of more destructive weapons and better defence systems, along with China's nuclear ambitions and the rise of nuclear-related fears in Western Europe, the *Observer* considered a quest for 'balance' to be entirely appropriate, while American newspapers emphasized that a SALT agreement would not be quickly or easily arranged.[3]

Originally, the Americans envisaged a comprehensive deal that included offensive weaponry. The Soviets blocked this. They wanted to focus on anti-ballistic missiles and to leave offensive systems for SALT II. While the Soviets sought broad restraints that would have maximum political impact, moreover, the Americans wanted specific, functional measures that would stabilize the strategic balance. The Soviets also liked to have agreements in principle before proceeding to precise terms, while the Americans wished to negotiate on the basis of a detailed package of proposals. Another complication was 'linkage', the effort by Nixon and Kissinger to use SALT to achieve other things. According to one member of the American negotiating team, Paul H. Nitze, a former deputy secretary of defence, Nixon was not deeply committed to arms control and only pursued it to gain more leverage in international affairs and to impress Congress. Nitze did not believe that the prospects for a meaningful SALT agreement were good. There was no consensus within the US government. The American and Soviet delegations wanted no 'linkage' with other issues, but Nixon and Kissinger thought otherwise. The White House accepted certain Soviet demands in SALT in order to get Moscow's assistance with Vietnam. Brezhnev had his own agenda: to restrain Peking; to obtain economic help, technology and credit from the West; to establish a system of crisis management and influence Washington DC's response to Soviet actions in different parts of the world; to open up rifts between the Americans and Western Europe; to encourage governments in the West to reduce their military spending; and to assist pro-Soviet leaders in developing nations. Brezhnev and his colleagues believed that arms control could be used to enhance Soviet power and limit the West's ability to prevent the growth of that power.[4]

Flexible policies, European agreements and SALT I

Representatives from the United States and Soviet Union engaged in covert conversations alongside the SALT talks, and eventually an agreement was worked out. There would be a limitation of anti-ballistic missiles and a freeze on the development of offensive nuclear weapons. There was another advance in September 1971, when the Americans, Soviets, British and French signed a new treaty regulating the status of West Berlin, expanding its links with the FRG and providing for easier access from the West. Cold War rivalry appeared to be easing and it was hoped that further agreements would follow, especially between the superpowers. There were hitches, however, as when war broke out between India and Pakistan late in 1971. This war underlined the fact that Britain was no longer the West's peacekeeper in the Indian Ocean and Persian Gulf, and it indicated that American leaders were still thinking in Cold War terms. To them the war resulted from Indian aggression, backed by the USSR, when in fact the war had more to do with local tensions that had mounted since India's partition in 1947. Notwithstanding these problems, neither the United States nor the USSR wanted their thaw to end. Nixon went ahead with a visit to Moscow in May 1972.[5]

The Berlin agreements of 1971–72 appeared to end some of the quarrels that had most impeded the development of stability and harmony in Europe since the Second World War. The FRG and GDR were involved in the talks, and for the first time the United States offered diplomatic recognition to the GDR. The British government worked hard to secure a settlement. *The Times* celebrated the fact that the West and the USSR 'have now managed to settle the last dangerous outstanding issue between them', and the *Observer* welcomed an official statement from Bonn that the FRG would continue its thaw with the USSR and seek promptly to improve its relations with Poland, Czechoslovakia and other bloc countries. The *Economist* pointed out that the German question was a long way from being solved: 'So long as the East German leaders continue to fear the consequences of unhindered intra-German communication, their negotiators will try to avoid being pinned down to precise commitments'. In America the press focused more on the improved prospects for East-West détente in general.[6]

The Soviets were satisfied by the Berlin agreements. In 1970, through a treaty with the FRG, Moscow had gained Bonn's acceptance of post-1945 frontiers, and in September 1971 the Soviets secured the implicit recognition of East Berlin as the capital of the GDR, the reduction of the western military presence in West Berlin and a formal statement that West Berlin, though it had 'ties' with the FRG, was outside the FRG's 'constituency'. By 1973 the FRG was the USSR's most important trading partner in the West. The Soviets were also pleased, though with caveats, about SALT I. The treaty was signed by Nixon and Brezhnev on 26 May 1972. Some of the arrangements were of an interim nature, which ensured that talks would carry on. A trade agreement was also signed. This facilitated Soviet purchases of American grain. On Vietnam, Washington DC and Moscow had to agree to disagree. Moreover, the Soviets drew up a document entitled 'Basic Principles of Mutual Relations', which stated their wish for peaceful coexistence while confirming that they would continue to defend their interests by all means short of war. Neither side expected SALT I to make a huge difference. The arms race continued.[7]

Although Brezhnev could stress that the Americans were treating the Soviets as equals, and that this would be useful both in addressing Soviet-Chinese relations and in increasing Soviet involvement in the developing world, he saw that SALT I was far from perfect. It did nothing about US bases that were close to the USSR's borders. Nor did it cover the nuclear forces of Britain and France. This explains Moscow's unilateral declaration that if America's allies increased their nuclear forces, the USSR would match the increase. If SALT I represented an important stage in détente, therefore, it was accompanied by indications of ongoing rivalry. SALT I included the Anti-Ballistic Missile Treaty, which was of indefinite duration and restricted the deployment of anti-ballistic missile systems by the United States and USSR, and a temporary agreement for a five-year limitation on certain types of offensive weapons while negotiations continued for a more comprehensive arrangement. The Americans and Soviets went on talking to each other but this did not mean that all disagreements would be resolved, as soon became clear in SALT II, which was expected to replace the interim agreement with long-term limits on strategic offensive weaponry. In public Nixon and Kissinger lauded SALT I, but in private they expressed doubts about its value. It mattered to them primarily because it was politically convenient.[8]

London was suspicious not only of Moscow but also of Washington DC, for the notion that the Americans might enter into agreements that had negative consequences for Britain was ever-present. In parliament, MPs who demanded to know what effect SALT would have on British security were reminded that Britain was not part of the SALT process. Therefore defence expenditure would not be directly affected, which annoyed those who advocated further reductions in the defence budget. Questions were raised about the amount of consultation between the United States and its allies. Britain had been adequately informed about SALT by the Americans, said Home in June 1972, and one of his deputies at the foreign office, Joseph Godber, subsequently maintained that the Americans 'have been in close touch with their allies throughout the course of the Strategic Arms Limitation Talks'. This was an exaggeration, and it shows how sensitive the British government had become on the matter.[9]

There was no unanimity among British newspapers about SALT I. Its significance was recognized, but so were its shortcomings. The *Guardian* noted criticism of SALT in the United States, while the *Economist* predicted the further proliferation of nuclear weapons, because US-Soviet limits on missile defences would 'reprieve the inferior nuclear armouries of Britain, China and France, which stood to lose much or perhaps all of their deterrent value'. This would encourage other states to go nuclear. The *Economist* made much of the fact that neither the Americans nor the Soviets would have to relinquish any weaponry they already possessed. *The Times* was more optimistic, arguing that SALT I would lead to agreements on Vietnam, the Middle East and other international problems: 'the structure of power in the world has been given a different look'.[10]

During Heath's premiership détente was seen as necessary and beneficial. There was also a determination to carry the process in a certain direction. Willingness to work with the United States was combined with the idea that Britain should take its own path when necessary. As Heath later wrote, détente 'accentuated those areas in which our interests and those of the United States could diverge'. In particular, 'European countries acutely felt the need for continuing bilateral contacts and negotiations with the Soviet Union, whatever the prevailing temperature of US-Soviet relations'.[11] Heath was concerned when negotiations were interrupted by crises: he thought that Washington DC had a tendency to overreact. The war between India and Pakistan in December 1971 was one example of this.

The India-Pakistan War of 1971 and its significance

Trouble had been brewing for some time. Unrest in East Pakistan, where a movement for self-rule had been gaining support, prompted the Pakistani government to take military action in the spring of 1971. Many refugees crossed the border into India. Britain gave £14 million in aid while disavowing any intention of interfering in the domestic affairs of Commonwealth countries. The Americans saw the situation differently. India and the USSR concluded a treaty of friendship in August 1971, and Washington DC assumed that Soviet influence in the region was increasing. London did not accept this analysis and suggested that India wished only to counteract the growing links between Pakistan and China. Tension between India and Pakistan led to war in December. Heath expected to mediate, but American support for Pakistan complicated his plans enormously. Washington DC saw India as a Soviet-backed aggressor. By helping Pakistan the Americans hoped to prevent the USSR from dominating the region while also assisting the thaw between the United States and Pakistan's protector, China. Heath's government favoured non-intervention, while Kissinger and Nixon warned that India was dangerous and complained about Soviet manoeuvring at the UN, where meaningful action was delayed until India had completed its military campaign and recognized East Pakistan as an independent country, Bangladesh. Home sympathized with the American line and regretted that Heath did not. The prime minister had been trying to improve Anglo-Indian relations, which shaped his opinion of the war, but Home agreed with Nixon and Kissinger that India was guilty of aggression. India protested about America's policy, alleging that Nixon and Kissinger could have prevented the war by promoting a solution to the crisis in East Pakistan. India's declaration received a lot of coverage in American newspapers, as did a rejoinder issued from the White House.[12]

Among British newspapers, the *Observer* suggested that tension was likely to grow: Moscow was attempting to limit the role of the Americans and the Chinese while China was increasing its support for Pakistan and the United States was threatening to stop aid to India and proposing a military balance between India and Pakistan. *The Times* argued for a speedy resolution of outstanding issues, including Bangladeshi independence, so that a peace settlement could be worked out, and lamented the unhelpfulness of the Americans, who had 'misunderstood the political tensions at work in the sub-continent' and 'mistimed almost all their interventions'. Allegations about Indian atrocities in East Pakistan increased the controversy. As the UN finalized arrangements for the withdrawal of opposing forces, Home assured the leaders of both Pakistan and Bangladesh of British friendship and promised that substantial reconstruction aid would be provided.[13]

This crisis was remarkable for misunderstandings and lost opportunities. The Americans had believed that Moscow would tolerate limited US support for Pakistan rather than have India dominate the region. Although China's friendship with Pakistan inclined Moscow towards India, the Soviets were reluctant to commit themselves. Nixon's thaw with China changed things, and the treaty of friendship concluded by India and the Soviet Union released India from the fear of great power intervention. The Nixon administration was condemned in Congress and in the American press, meanwhile, for its relationship with and arming of Pakistan (in March 1971 the military had taken over the government of Pakistan and refused to abide by the outcome of free elections). China did not welcome the prospect of an Indian success, backed by the Soviets, and wanted Nixon to act firmly. Moscow sought to show the world that the Soviet Union could do more for its allies than Peking could do for the allies of China, and knew that Kissinger's trip to China for talks in July 1971 had been facilitated by Pakistan, India's enemy. India shared the Soviets' concern about the possible consequences of US-Chinese détente, and the USSR had necessarily to move closer to India in order to gain influence in the region and prevent China from taking advantage of the instability there. When war broke out, America and China backed the losing side and Moscow's potential client, India, won a convincing victory. In fact, India never accepted client status, although Soviet influence in the country did increase.[14]

The Americans were victims of their own 'linkage' approach. They supported Pakistan because they knew that the Soviets were helping India. Peacemaking in Vietnam, the opening to China and détente with Moscow were all connected together. It was hoped that US-Chinese contacts would restrain the USSR, that US-Soviet contacts would restrain China, and that these dealings would in turn bring stability to the disturbed parts of Asia. William Bundy, who had been a senior White House adviser in the 1960s, described America's response to the India-Pakistan war as a 'fiasco'. Raymond Garthoff, an adviser on Soviet affairs at the US state department and the executive secretary of the SALT negotiating team, also wrote that US policy was flawed. It made little difference to the Soviets, or China, or Pakistan; it alienated India; and all of these states did what they wanted irrespective of Washington DC's wishes.[15]

Nixon was not greatly damaged at the time, however, because SALT I enhanced his prestige, and his overtures to China and the USSR made it easier to step up the US military effort in Vietnam, in order to obtain a settlement there. The air of diplomatic success assured his re-election in November 1972, which had been his principal goal all along. The Soviets stayed in the SALT process because they needed an accommodation with the United States. At the same time, they had a fixed idea about Europe. Here they wanted an assured advantage, which meant maintaining conventional forces that could make rapid advances, intermediate nuclear forces to counter NATO's 'flexible response', and enough missiles to match those of the western alliance. One of the main reasons why MBFR did not get far was that Soviet security doctrines entailed a decisive conventional superiority in Europe. The West did not offer enough to get Moscow to compromise on this. The Soviets resented the fact that British and French nuclear forces were not included in SALT. When they asserted a right to increase the USSR's forces in line with those of Britain and France the Americans objected, but the matter had to be left open, and it was not resolved in SALT II.[16]

British concerns about the changing international order

In September 1972 Brezhnev and Gromyko urged Kissinger to make a secret accord under which the USSR and United States would target their weapons only at each other's allies. The possibility that such arrangements might be made continually vexed the leaders of Western Europe. Britain was not immune. Although the Heath government welcomed negotiations between the superpowers, it disliked being excluded and feared the undermining of America's commitment to defend Western Europe. This attitude was shaped by a broader concern about détente. While he was defence secretary, Lord Carrington maintained that Britain could not focus on détente at the expense of national security. Carrington disliked the element of competition in détente, as western governments scrambled for access to markets in the Soviet bloc. The British also insisted, repeatedly, that the USSR should not be allowed to have the benefits of détente without making concessions, especially on human rights.[17]

This was the opinion of the Labour governments of the 1970s, and, as for the problem of competition in détente, Wilson also had cause to complain about it while he was prime minister between 1974 and 1976. When an Anglo-Soviet trade agreement was being arranged, British negotiators were frustrated by Moscow's insistence that they should offer more credit. The Soviets made much of the fact that France had been generous in this respect. They argued that Britain should be just as liberal, but they would not reveal the terms the French had offered, and neither would Paris. Wilson found this situation deplorable.[18]

In SALT, the Americans and Soviets were discussing matters that directly affected Britain. But having abandoned their own missile programme in the late 1950s, relying since then on American technology, the British could not expect to participate in SALT. There were wider implications here for Britain's role in détente. The superpowers had less need to use Britain as an intermediary, and Britain – which had long acted as the bridge between the American and European pillars in NATO – increasingly saw the FRG dealing with Washington DC on behalf of Western Europe. It looked as if superpower détente would further marginalize Britain. After SALT I British leaders pressed for a comprehensive test ban. The Americans favoured a smaller agreement, and President Carter declared in June 1979 that if the British did not cooperate the United States and USSR would arrange a test ban without them. In fact, he and Brezhnev had already decided that SALT II would take priority over a test ban treaty.[19]

Difficulties with SALT led the British to think that they had been right to view détente with caution and to preach restraint to their allies. The United States and USSR did not find it easy to tie up SALT I and there was little surprise in London at the failure to follow it quickly with a SALT II agreement. Still, SALT I was important to the British. They had to make a decision about the future of Britain's deterrent, and instead of having to replace Polaris completely they were enabled by SALT I to take a cheaper option, the updating of Polaris. Had the deployment of anti-ballistic missiles not been restricted, the ability of Polaris to penetrate Soviet defences would have been reduced. London continued to take a keen interest in the SALT process, making sure that Britain's nuclear forces were excluded and scheming as necessary to prevent the obstruction of Anglo-American strategic cooperation.[20]

London also knew that if détente resulted in the withdrawal of US forces from Western Europe, Britain would be expected to do more for collective security. The Conservative and Labour governments of the 1970s did not see how they could greatly increase the defence budget, but it was obvious that Britain's European partners would refuse to do more unless an extra British contribution was forthcoming. Such difficulties hampered Heath's plan to work more closely with the Europeans and simultaneously to reduce the importance of the 'special relationship'. In practice he objected to American policy only when it got in the way of his efforts to cooperate with leaders in Western Europe. Nixon was not strongly for or against European integration, though he was determined that European détente should not interfere with superpower relations, while Kissinger was dubious about EPC and wanted to bring it under NATO supervision. Heath complained that this amounted to an attempt to control Western Europe, so as to give Washington DC more sway over Moscow.[21]

Crisis in Chile

They spoke of flexibility and negotiation, but Nixon and Kissinger were generally unwilling to compromise for the sake of détente: hence the equivocal attitude towards Europe and the idea that Pakistan was a barrier against the Soviets. Washington DC also remained sensitive about communism in Latin America. In the early 1970s attention was focused on Salvador Allende's regime in Chile. Allende, a Marxist, had been elected president of Chile in 1970. In September 1973 he was overthrown by army officers. Kissinger insisted that the US government had 'nothing to do' with the coup, yet Allende's opponents had covert American backing, and with Allende gone Chile received substantial economic and military aid from the United States. The brutal right-wing dictatorship of Augusto Pinochet was to last for 17 years. Nixon's policy was briefly reversed later in the 1970s by Carter, who withdrew US support for the Chilean government and for other repressive regimes in Latin America. In the 1980s the former pattern was restored.[22]

The British had not been unduly concerned about the election of Allende. After the coup of 1973 they grumbled about US policy, and the Labour governments of 1974 to 1979 were unfriendly towards the Pinochet regime and imposed sanctions against it. Thatcher's government was of a different stripe, for it resumed diplomatic relations with Chile, encouraged Anglo-Chilean trade and lifted Labour's arms embargo. Thatcher justified all this with the claim that the human rights situation in Chile was improving. Evidence collected by the UN, Amnesty International and other bodies suggested otherwise, but Thatcher regarded Chile as an important ally in Latin America. In some respects her policy resembled that embarked upon by the Heath government shortly after the coup against Allende. There was a Commons debate on Chile on 28 November 1973, during which Labour MPs maintained that Britain should not recognize the new regime or offer it credit and aid, while the minister of state for foreign affairs, Julian Amery, outlined the government's case that what had happened in Chile was 'essentially a Chilean dispute settled by Chileans' and that ministers 'do not regard it as their duty to pass judgement'. *The Times* was more in line with Heath's government than with the Labour opposition. The *Guardian* had some sympathy for the 'Allende experiment' and argued that the coup did not prove that radical reform by democratic means was impossible. The *Economist* found Washington DC's professions of non-involvement in the coup unconvincing.[23]

In Moscow there was outrage at the coup against Allende. Washington DC was held responsible, yet the Soviet response was muted. Brezhnev had recently visited the United States, Nixon was expected in Moscow in 1974, and there was no desire on the Kremlin's part to forgo the benefits of détente. The Soviet Union did break off relations with the new government of Chile, but it had been careful not to become closely identified with Allende and had offered him only limited aid. Chile was too far away for the Soviets to prop up a left-wing government there. Allende's fall probably dented Soviet confidence. It was some time before Latin

America offered further opportunities for communists to gain power, whether peacefully or by force.[24]

The Middle East

Negative reactions to the coup in Chile embarrassed the US government. Even greater difficulty was to follow with the Arab-Israeli war of 1973. Egypt's president, Anwar Sadat, had in mind a limited war to regain the territories lost in 1967. The attack came on 6 October 1973, during the Jewish festival of Yom Kippur, and Israeli forces were initially pushed back. The United States assisted Israel. When the tide turned against the Arabs, Nixon and Kissinger pressed for a quick ceasefire. The Soviets threatened to help Egypt and Syria, however, and Arab governments cut oil supplies. Kissinger went to Moscow, then to Israel, and the United States and USSR cooperated to pass a ceasefire resolution at the UN, but the Israelis now had the upper hand and decided to launch a new offensive, increasing the danger that the Americans and Soviets would be dragged into the war. As Soviet naval and air force activity was heightened, US forces were suddenly placed on alert. This was Kissinger's way of keeping the Soviets out of the Middle East. The USSR had already moved quickly to supply Egypt and Syria, replacing arms and equipment lost in battle, and the prevalent view in the US Congress and among the American public that Israel was the victim of aggression reinforced Kissinger's sense that Israel had to be protected. Kissinger was determined that the Soviets should not be allowed to intrude. During the crisis America's aid to Israel far exceeded Soviet aid to the Arabs. When Moscow pressed for a ceasefire, Kissinger saw an opportunity. The oil embargo was worrying and it was not in America's interest to have Israel win a crushing victory or for Egypt to be humiliated, but Israel did not wish to end the war until Egypt had been decisively weakened. Kissinger told the Israelis that unless they desisted, American supplies would be withheld. Brezhnev's suggestion that a joint US-Soviet force should be sent in to separate the belligerents, and that the Soviets might act alone if the Americans refused to participate, was the main cause of the US alert. The alert was called off on the understanding that a UN force would be put together, composed of contingents from non-nuclear powers.[25]

At the time and afterwards the Americans were denounced. In the UN the weight of opinion was against them and their support for Israel. The General Assembly held an annual debate on the Middle East and many countries, including Britain and France, were losing patience with Israel, while the Americans isolated themselves further in 1973 by using their veto in the Security Council to block a resolution against Israel's occupation of Arab land. Heath publicly refused to endorse the US alert, the French tried to bolster anti-Americanism in Western Europe, and within NATO there arose a greater willingness to object to US initiatives. Kissinger hardly consulted America's allies as he worked for a Middle East peace accord. His main tasks, he thought, were to persuade Moscow to allow him a free hand and to persuade Israel to enter into discussions with the Arabs. A settlement was worked out in stages during 1973 and 1974. Egypt and Israel came to an understanding on the Suez area, and the Israelis gave up some of their gains from 1967 in return for an American guarantee of their security. A deal between Israel and Syria was more difficult to accomplish, because Israel refused to withdraw from the strategically important Golan Heights. President Hafez al-Asad of Syria decided that despite the promises that had been made, the Americans never had any intention of coercing Israel to accept its 1967 borders or respect Palestinian rights.[26]

During the crisis Kissinger repeatedly praised the Kremlin for acting responsibly, because he wanted détente to resume once the war was over. As for leaders in Western Europe, they disagreed with each other and with Washington DC. They could not pursue an independent common policy, and they reinforced the American view that they were not doing enough to sort out their own problems. The fixation with Arab oil, it seemed to Kissinger, meant that they did not think clearly enough about the consequences of alienating the US government. They complained that they were not being consulted, yet they had no agreed position themselves. Nevertheless, they questioned what Kissinger was doing, even if his diplomatic achievements did in time earn their respect. Kissinger's conduct did not go down well in Moscow, and a senior figure in the Soviet foreign ministry later looked back on the Yom Kippur War and suggested that there were no winners. Victor Israelyan could not see how Israel, or the Arabs, or either of the superpowers could be satisfied. The superpowers had not wanted war in the Middle

East, but failed to prevent it, and the next problem was how to bring about a settlement. Moscow preferred a peace that disadvantaged the United States. The Americans wanted a peace that damaged the Soviets. Israelyan thought that a good opportunity to stabilize the Middle East was lost because the Americans and Soviets did not work together, even though the international community would have backed them had they done so.[27]

If anger grew in Moscow as Kissinger eased the Soviets out of the Middle East peace process, there was an indication that the Kremlin was not going to tar Britain with the same brush. Soviet leaders were still suspicious of Britain, but they did not consider British policy to be as negative or dangerous as that of the United States. Indeed, Home's visit to Moscow in December 1973 added an air of reconciliation, rebuilding some of the bridges that had been burned in 1971 with the expulsion from Britain of suspected Soviet spies.[28]

Détente and SALT II

Due largely to Kissinger's efforts, Nixon was well received in the Middle East when he arrived for a tour in June 1974. Embroiled in the Watergate affair, the beleaguered president hoped that an active foreign policy would help him to recover support at home. The SALT II negotiations had been going on for over a year, and their slow progress added to Nixon's eagerness to make another high profile visit to Moscow. He arrived there at the end of June 1974. The Soviets expected him to make concessions in order to achieve the breakthrough he needed to save his presidency. In fact, neither on the Middle East nor on SALT was Nixon able to make an impact. His political weakness, along with Arab and particularly Israeli intransigence, meant that there was little the president could do to promote long-term peace in the Middle East, while the US government was internally divided on SALT II and the Soviets realized that Nixon's proposals would be scrutinized unsympathetically in America. Brezhnev had no incentive to bargain constructively. He said he wanted détente to continue but seemed not to care about expanding the existing framework. He saw little point in making a deal with a discredited president and only agreed to continue top level discussions because he hoped for a joint US-Soviet front against China. Though several new agreements were signed by Nixon and Brezhnev in Moscow, they only dealt with peripheral matters, not those that were central to SALT II. There was no bargain on offensive systems to replace the interim agreement of 1972 or on the deployment of MIRVs. This period saw the revival of old thinking in Washington DC. Things appeared not to be going America's way; the USSR had to be 'contained'. Vietnam and Watergate played a part in this, and opponents of Nixon and Kissinger warned them against offering undertakings, especially on SALT, that might disadvantage the United States. In the event, the Moscow summit of June 1974 did not bring a SALT II agreement much closer, though it did help to sustain superpower détente.[29]

Kissinger stopped in London in July 1974 on his way back to the United States from Moscow. He met with the British foreign secretary, Callaghan, and SALT was the main topic of conversation. Callaghan was struck by the 'stupefying complexity' of the issues involved and gained the impression that SALT was about to break down. Before and after his talks with Kissinger, Callaghan was challenged in parliament about US-Soviet relations, the SALT stalemate, and the difficulties involved in balancing Britain's membership of European bodies with Britain's cooperation with the Americans. Callaghan admitted that moves for political unity in Western Europe would affect 'consultation with the United States', but he insisted that the British government was free to work with the Americans 'at any stage' it liked. When discussion turned to nuclear issues, Callaghan said that Nixon and Brezhnev had agreed a limited ban on nuclear testing. He was sure that they both wanted a comprehensive ban, as he himself did, but he sidestepped the question of whether Britain should take the initiative. Callaghan subsequently had further opportunities to discuss SALT with the Americans and with Britain's other allies, as in November 1975 when the heads of government, foreign ministers and finance ministers of the United States, Britain, France, the FRG, Italy and Japan met for a conference at Rambouillet, near Paris.[30]

In *The Times*, the summit in Moscow in June 1974 was presented as an anti-climax: the agreement that the United States and USSR would limit themselves to one anti-ballistic missile system each merely confirmed decisions that had already been made, and the restrictions on underground testing were not stringent and would therefore do little to stop the arms race. Watergate had overshadowed the Moscow talks, declared the *Guardian*, and the *Observer* lamented a setback for détente. The *Economist* reminded its readers that the agreements signed in 1972 rested on 'a rough equality': America had accepted the Soviet lead in the destructive power of its weapons and the USSR had accepted America's lead in the number of individual weapons. This was no longer enough for either side, and future progress would depend on 'a reasonably precise formula' covering number of warheads and missile capacity and accuracy.[31]

The leaders of Western Europe regretted the deterioration in US-Soviet relations. They wanted superpower détente to carry on alongside the thaw in Europe, although with respect to the latter they had to own up to ongoing difficulties over human rights and trade. Economic agreements did not work out as they had hoped, because trade did not at first provide much political leverage. Eastern bloc countries began to borrow large sums from the West, but the West did not buy Eastern Europe's products in large quantities. In Western Europe the desire for a thaw remained strong, and it was hoped that economic disappointments and the lack of a breakthrough in SALT II would not matter. Europeans wanted CSCE to continue, for instance, because they had security concerns and had not been involved in SALT or MBFR. The British, as before, went along with their allies while doubting that much would be achieved.[32]

This was an anxious time for the British defence establishment. Unease was growing about the long-term impact of SALT on the Anglo-American nuclear relationship. It seemed that access to US technology would be affected by the agreements the Americans were making with the USSR. American military chiefs did not see the need to help Britain on the same scale as before, and Kissinger had doubts about nuclear cooperation with Britain because he thought it might alienate Moscow and interfere with SALT. Weapons researchers at Britain's specialist facilities recommended the development of MIRVs, which they suggested would help to preserve the link with the Americans and enable Britain to respond to improvements in the USSR's defences. The Royal Navy argued that money would be better spent on the expansion of Britain's conventional forces. In fact, SALT did not greatly affect Anglo-American nuclear cooperation, but this did not end the quarrelling in government, parliament, press and the armed services about Britain's weapons programme. Defence experts argued about how best to upgrade the deterrent. Penetration power and cost continued to be hotly debated. The Americans insisted that there was no reason to worry about the credibility of Britain's nuclear forces, because the Anti-Ballistic Missile Treaty of 1972 had prolonged their usefulness, but Washington DC was determined to prevent the British from hindering further progress in SALT, and London was aware that the Americans were not prepared to subject their SALT policy to a commitment to renew the British deterrent.[33]

Summary

If the SALT process, superpower détente and thaw in Europe began to fashion a new international order, the task for Britain was to find a place in that order. As had happened before, Britain needed to adjust to changing circumstances. There were political and economic problems, and some influence had been lost, but the British endeavoured to remain important, especially to the United States and Western Europe. They defended their interests, creating and using situations in a way that would help to preserve prestige and status. Even so, it could not be denied that key goals were now more difficult to accomplish. How long could Britain remain a great power with limited resources, relationships that were becoming less advantageous, and internal disputes about defence posture and foreign policy? It was fortunate for Britain that the changes in the world in the 1970s turned out to be less extensive than they first appeared. The global Cold War was moderated in some respects, but despite all the negotiation and flexibility it was not radically transformed. The need for Britain to adjust, therefore, was probably not so urgent after all.

4   Quarrelling with Allies

However virulent the enmity and discord between East and West during the most difficult periods of the 1970s and 1980s, divisions within the West were sometimes just as pronounced. Britain was both a participant in these disputes and a would-be reconciler. Western leaders found a lot to argue about. The slow progress with SALT II was a concern; the Helsinki process, the pros and cons of East-West trade and the human rights agenda were much debated; and superpower détente and the thaw in Europe presented problems, as states and peoples struggled to find an eligible way forward. How could East-West links be stabilized when the two sides also saw the need to go on competing with each other? Outside Europe there was continuing unrest and violence, especially in the developing world. Inside Europe tension increased, primarily as a result of the political and economic rise of the FRG and the many points of friction in US-European relations.

The Cold War: back to business as usual?

The Watergate scandal and Nixon's resignation inevitably had an impact on international affairs. Edward Heath thought it a pity that Nixon's achievements would be overshadowed by what had happened. Chinese leader Mao Tse-tung subsequently told Heath that he had known where he stood with Nixon and that, whenever the USSR made trouble, Nixon could be relied upon to respond. Mao was less impressed by Nixon's successor, Gerald Ford, who was appointed in August 1974. Kissinger remained as secretary of state and enjoyed prestige at home and abroad, but this was a declining asset as opinion in Congress and in the nation turned against détente and as America's allies continued to question aspects of US policy. Ford and Kissinger realized that a SALT II agreement was needed if détente was to be saved. Brezhnev concurred, and hosted the Americans at a summit in November 1974 at Vladivostok, but there was no dramatic breakthrough.[1]

Antagonism was rising again, not only over SALT but also over the Middle East peace process and other questions. Ford and Kissinger wanted to complete SALT II. Their hopes were dashed largely because of US domestic politics. Vladivostok established a principle of equality. Each side was to observe a limit of 2400 missiles and bombers, including no more than 1320 MIRVed missiles. This framework was incomplete because it did not cover the Cruise missiles of the United States or the Soviet 'Backfire' bomber. Nor did it lead quickly to a SALT II treaty. Kissinger claimed that an agreement was close. He went to Moscow early in 1976 to provide new impetus, but he failed, in part because his domestic support had dwindled even further. Ford, worried that opposition to SALT would affect his electoral prospects, hardly mentioned détente at all in 1976. Meanwhile, Brezhnev's planned visit to the United States in 1975 never took place. A US-Soviet trade agreement was cancelled by Moscow when Congress brought up the question of Jewish emigration from the USSR. In April 1975 the government of South Vietnam collapsed and North Vietnamese forces reached Saigon. This turned American opinion even more firmly against the idea of bargaining with communist regimes.[2]

The British had doubted that détente would achieve all the things expected of it. With no SALT II agreement and the cooling of superpower relations, they were vindicated. To the foreign office, the Kremlin saw itself in a continuing contest, with thaw a matter of tactical manoeuvre. Though Kissinger and Ford presented Vladivostok as a modest success, British newspapers saw it differently. So many details had not been settled at the summit, and there was such sharp disagreement about it, especially in America, that the *Guardian* feared for the future of arms control. *The Times* was disappointed by Vladivostok and assumed that animosity in one aspect of US-Soviet relations would affect all the others. *The Times* was confident that both sides would seek to slow down the arms race if they could, and that Vladivostok had at least opened the way for further negotiation. Still, *The Times* wanted the West to view SALT as part of a bigger picture: 'Détente is indivisible. Russian intentions must be tested not only in SALT but in the Middle East, in central Europe, and in the food and energy crises. There is an obvious interaction in all these areas'. The

Economist found American and Soviet claims about the importance of Vladivostok somewhat feeble.[3]

Ford looked upon the Vladivostok summit as a 'working meeting' and explained afterwards that greater effort would be needed to convert the agreed framework into a comprehensive deal. Five years after the summit, when a SALT II agreement was finally signed, arms control advocate Wolfgang Panofsky, a physics professor at Stanford University, California, wrote that Vladivostok had been pivotal because it laid down the basic ingredient for the SALT II treaty: an equal overall limit on offensive forces. Yet Brezhnev's criticism of US policy grew more insistent after Vladivostok. Indeed, in the mid-1970s détente seemed to halt while the development of weaponry continued apace. Three new warheads were added each day to the MIRV stockpile. The SALT process accelerated the arms race instead of stopping it, and there was no great change under Ford's successor, Jimmy Carter. Nuclear arsenals continued to expand, and America's arms sales abroad actually increased during Carter's presidency. Soviet leaders accused Ford of giving up on the thaw in order to appease right-wingers in America. The Kremlin also objected to the American tendency to connect trade and credit with human rights. Brezhnev focused on those parts of the Helsinki Final Act that most suited the Soviet Union. Eager to reap economic benefits, he resisted efforts to turn humanitarian provisions into a precondition. After Ford, he hoped that Carter would be more cooperative, but Carter began to focus even more on human rights.[4]

In Britain there was a sense of gloom, especially in the Labour Party. Wishing to demonstrate that he could still play a part in world affairs and that his government was committed to arms control, Harold Wilson took some interest in SALT II during his premiership of 1974 to 1976. He met with American and Soviet leaders on several occasions and was able to make a case in favour of détente, but as US-Soviet relations soured there was little that Wilson could do.[5]

The SALT II agreement was not ready until June 1979, and following the Soviet invasion of Afghanistan the Americans decided not to ratify it. Britain's main concerns were unchanged: to keep its nuclear deterrent out of the talks and to make sure that any restrictions on information and technology did not affect Anglo-American nuclear cooperation. The European allies of Britain and the United States did not care about non-transfer clauses and pressed Ford and then Carter for more consultation on what should be included in SALT II. NATO meetings on the matter became highly confrontational. When Margaret Thatcher became Britain's prime minister in May 1979 she endorsed SALT, despite reservations, because she expected technology transfers to go on and Washington DC to be generous when it came to negotiating the deal to replace Britain's Polaris force with Trident.[6]

London's belief that the East-West thaw would be limited, in view of the nature of international relations and the permanent threat posed by the USSR, gained ground in America as the idea spread that the Soviets were using détente to strengthen themselves. Washington DC and London were alarmed by Soviet involvement in Africa, especially Angola in 1974–75 and Ethiopia in 1977–78, and the rise of the left-wing Sandinistas in Nicaragua in 1978–79 was also a worrying development. Soviet assertiveness was underlined by the massive expansion of the USSR's navy and the establishment of Soviet bases in South Yemen, Somalia, Vietnam and Ethiopia. The Soviets had also maintained their superiority in conventional forces in the European theatre. Balance and stability seemed easier to achieve in Europe than elsewhere, though, and Kissinger's chief adviser on the Soviet Union, Helmut Sonnenfeldt, told US ambassadors in Europe in December 1975 that the unity of the USSR and Soviet bloc was advantageous and that equilibrium mattered more than trying to win the ideological and strategic battle, or at least, this was how Sonnenfeldt's remarks were reported. At the same time, it was thought that Soviet economic inefficiency should be exposed through East-West trade, so the model of stability did allow for elements of change. Kissinger was annoyed about the use that was made of Sonnenfeldt's remarks, especially in the United States. Détente, Helsinki, US-Soviet relations and America's dealings with Western Europe were growing more complicated, and Kissinger disliked the way discussions about these topics were going. One of the reasons for his scepticism about CSCE was what he took to be the unhelpful attitude of the European allies. They were more regularly challenging US policy. They wanted to agree things between themselves before taking them up with Washington DC, which would eventually mean that America could not deal individually with any of them, yet they were not modifying their relations with anyone else in this manner. Kissinger saw turmoil ahead if America and its allies failed to work together, especially when détente was losing support in the United States. Ford's attendance at the Helsinki conference had raised a storm of protest at home and probably weakened his chances at the presidential election of November 1976, which he lost.[7]

The Helsinki process proved to be more useful than Kissinger had expected. In his view, the 'Brezhnev Doctrine' had been contradicted because the Helsinki Final Act obliged all its signatories to respect each other's freedom to develop their own political, cultural, social and economic systems. Moscow went on arguing that human rights were an internal matter for each individual state, but this did not stop the dissidents and reform movements in the bloc or the many 'Helsinki Watch' groups in the West. Nevertheless, the Americans never attached the same importance that their allies did to the Helsinki Accords, and though for a time the Soviets made positive declarations about CSCE, they did not accept the West's position on human rights. In the later 1970s the Soviets appreciated Helsinki's role in reducing tension, but complained about the slow progress on the military side of détente and accused the West of interfering in the affairs of communist countries. In the United States, supporters of détente maintained that the Helsinki process would be helpful and many of their opponents, though they disliked CSCE, admitted that it could be turned to the United States' purposes.[8]

Throughout these transactions the British remained vigilant and pragmatic. It was relatively easy for them to take a consistent line on CSCE because the relevant issues were less urgent for Britain than they were for the FRG, for example, and British governments did not have to contend with the ethnic lobbies, partisan rivalries, or moralizing over foreign policy that affected the White House. The British were encouraged by CSCE because having set themselves low targets they found that some of these were exceeded. They were conscious that the Helsinki Final Act embraced potentially contradictory tendencies. It covered interstate relations, and here the purpose was to reduce tension, which meant showing respect for the existing order in Europe, but it also covered relations between the individual and the state, and here the agenda was for change. In particular, Britain sought to advance human rights. The right matters had to be addressed at the right time, and publicity avoided, for experience suggested that Moscow was easily offended. The British looked for a middle way between acceptance of a political freeze in Eastern Europe and rejection of the Soviet claim to dominion there. In contrast, the Americans did not pursue a consistent line. Although Sonnenfeldt had suggested that the West should accept the existence of the Soviet sphere, at the CSCE review meeting in Stockholm in 1984 US secretary of state George Shultz declared that the USSR's position in Eastern Europe had no legitimacy whatsoever.[9]

For the British, détente could never be the main priority. They were ready to promote it, but because they saw it as dangerous (should America make a bilateral deal with the Soviets that affected Britain's vital interests, for instance) they continued to insist that the West must attend to self-defence as well as to thaw. Scepticism about détente was combined with awareness that Britain's ability to influence the international order was decreasing.[10]

The SALT II treaty of 1979 was to last until the end of 1985, and its main function was to limit the size of offensive arsenals. There were temporary limits on systems for which no long-term deal was possible, including mobile ICBM launchers, air-to-surface missiles and ground- and sea-launched Cruise missiles. Temporary arrangements were also made on matters such as testing, deployment and range, and the Soviets accepted limits on the production and upgrading of their 'Backfire' bombers. In general the treaty was warmly received, although there were those who maintained that SALT I and II had not mitigated strategic rivalry and that the situation at the end of the 1970s would not have been greatly different had SALT never happened. The signing of SALT II brought a revival of enthusiasm for détente, but reservations remained. In London there had long been an awareness of the gap between Soviet rhetoric and Soviet conduct. Efforts continued to ascertain the real capabilities and intentions of the USSR, for Moscow was amenable on some issues and not on others. Still, when James Callaghan was foreign secretary between 1974 and 1976 he had decided that Soviet policy was becoming less ideological and more organized around détente and trade.[11]

Equilibrium and contact were reserved mainly for Europe. They were less obvious elsewhere. In parts of Africa, Asia and Latin America these were years of war and revolution. Washington DC aided its friends and bullied its enemies in Latin America, backed anti-communist factions in Angola, and encouraged South Africa to intervene in Angola and Mozambique. It seemed that the tide was turning against the United States in the developing world, as Vietnam, Laos, Cambodia, Ethiopia, Angola, Mozambique, Nicaragua and Afghanistan either moved into the Soviet sphere or came under the control of left-wing leaders. Although the British were less worried about these regimes than the Americans were, they agreed on the need for a response and tended to support US diplomatic and military action.[12]

Change in Europe and tension in the western alliance

The Americans were disappointed by reverses in the developing world, and by the failure of détente as a method of restraining the USSR. Their dissatisfaction also increased because US influence in Western Europe seemed to be declining. The FRG and France had been pursuing their own thaw with the USSR and eastern bloc, and some American leaders feared the 'Finlandization' of Western Europe: though Finland was neither communist nor a member of the Warsaw Pact it deferred to Moscow on foreign policy. The Soviet invasion of Afghanistan in 1979 prompted Carter's administration not only to set aside the SALT II treaty but also to begin a rearmament programme and to announce (in what was dubbed the 'Carter Doctrine') that the United States would resist any Soviet intervention in the oil states of the Persian Gulf. Carter's successor, Ronald Reagan, went further, increasing the US defence budget and pursuing an assertive anti-Soviet policy. Gorbachev's reformist approach after 1985 opened the door for a new period of superpower negotiation, and the Intermediate Nuclear Forces (INF) Treaty was signed in 1987.[13]

Disputes between America and its allies were not uncommon in the Carter and Reagan years. Callaghan, for example, quarrelled with the Americans about détente and disarmament in the late 1970s, thinking that Carter was wrong to turn his attentiveness to human rights into a public policy of rewards and penalties and pressing for a tougher test ban than Carter deemed appropriate. President Giscard d'Estaing of France became a firm critic of American policy. He conceded that human rights were important and that Soviet activities in the developing world had to be condemned, but he questioned Carter's methods. Paris favoured a moderate line towards Moscow and wanted to safeguard the thaw even after the Soviet invasion of Afghanistan, on the basis that the West should not jeopardize the progress that had been made in recent years. During the 1980s there were serious disagreements over détente, with Bonn and Paris frequently taking a view that was distinct from that of Washington DC.[14]

The assertion that Britain had 'no hand' in the 1987 INF Treaty[15] ignores the regular and detailed discussions on nuclear matters between Thatcher and Reagan. The idea that Britain's exclusion from the SALT process was a sign of Britain's decline needs also to be qualified. The British deterrent was not included in SALT because London ruled this out. Washington DC agreed, and it made sense for NATO as a whole in that the British deterrent would continue to be available for western defence. It is true, though, that the Americans took the lead in negotiating on nuclear and security matters with the USSR and that after the 1963 Test Ban Treaty, which was put together by the United States, Britain and the USSR and for which the British were largely responsible, no third power was ever again to play so important a role in US-Soviet discussions. Leaders in Western Europe, and sometimes in Britain too, expressed doubts about America's willingness to look out for its allies' interests. This tendency was reinforced by moves for greater cooperation on defence and foreign policy in Western Europe. Britain involved itself mainly to prevent France and the FRG from taking control. The British valued the US military presence in Europe and rejected the notion that Western Europe should detach itself from America. At the same time, Britain also saw a need for collective thinking on European defence problems in the 1980s. As ever, the continentals were torn between their need for American support and their resentment against American influence. This double-mindedness was evidenced on other matters. Reagan's Strategic Defence Initiative was condemned in some quarters, yet there was a scramble for contracts.[16]

Hardliners in America and Britain supposed that the Soviet willingness to compromise from the mid-1980s was a direct consequence of the firmness of conservative leaderships in Washington DC and London. This version of events was quite persuasive at the time, but there were doubts. Tensions within NATO increased on INF and on the bilateral interaction between the United States and USSR. There were fears that NATO would be fatally weakened, and Western Europe left unprotected, as treaties were signed on intermediate range missiles and strategic nuclear capabilities. Thatcher declared that Britain's deterrent would not be included in any US-Soviet agreement on strategic weapons. Despite her respect for Gorbachev, she insisted that the Soviets were still dangerous. The Eurogroup looked for ways to reinforce NATO and compensate for the loss of American weapons under the INF Treaty. Meanwhile, America's allies continued to differentiate themselves from the United States when they saw advantage in doing so. They could negotiate on their own account, and CSCE was important in this respect. CSCE became a permanent feature in East-West relations (and, converted into the Organization for Security and Cooperation in Europe in 1994, it would play no small role in the ending of the Cold War). As for NATO, Britain probably had an influence equal to that of the United States in shaping what the alliance did. Between the late 1970s and the signing of the INF Treaty in 1987, the British helped to hold NATO together, to frame compromises that combined the preferences of Britain, Western Europe and America, and to keep the Americans involved in Western Europe's security system.[17]

From the mid-1980s Moscow paid more attention to Western Europe, not only in an effort to get the INF talks moving but also because of common initiatives in Western Europe, the possibility that these would make America less assertive, and Gorbachev's wish to improve the USSR's economy. Moscow was struck by the rise of the FRG. By 1970 the West Germans produced nearly 20 per cent of the world's manufacturing exports, more than the United States and double the share of Britain, and the FRG's armed forces were also larger than those of Britain. The FRG was taking the lead in the European Community and also had influence through membership of the G7 ('Group of Seven', the world's top industrial powers) as the most economically successful European country, ahead of both Britain and France. This economic, political and military strength made the FRG more important in international affairs and more independent. The French were worried, and it was with much relief that Paris reconstructed a positive working relationship with Bonn during the 1970s. West German chancellor Helmut Schmidt and French president Giscard d'Estaing both took office in 1974. Their friendship contributed to the revival of the Franco-German axis and resulted in such initiatives as the

European Monetary System, a controversial element of economic convergence about which Britain was unenthusiastic. The British were left to bemoan the gap that had opened up between the FRG and Britain in terms of economic power. 'The mistake we made', remarked Callaghan during a visit to Bonn in 1976, 'was to think we won the war', and in 1979, noting the FRG's ability to resist pressure from the Americans, Callaghan commented: 'the economic giant becomes politically adult'.[18]

The creation of a 'new Europe' was primarily the result of Bonn's 'Ostpolitik', which typified the changed international mood of the late 1960s to mid-1970s. It worked well politically and diplomatically, gave a boost to the West German economy, and confirmed that the FRG was taking the lead away from France in Western Europe. The French briefly tried to draw closer to Britain in order to balance the FRG's industrial strength and foreign policy. Primarily, though, Paris responded to 'Ostpolitik' by attempting to carry forward its own plans for a thaw with countries in Eastern Europe.[19]

By this time Britain had a long record of constructive, if limited, engagement with the Soviets. There were trade agreements and scientific, technical and cultural exchanges, and the Heath government extended contacts with Poland, Hungary, Czechoslovakia, Rumania and the GDR. London remained cautious but there was a readiness to take up opportunities when they arose. 'Ostpolitik' increased the pressure on Britain to participate in détente. The British had not been keen because their basic premise was that Moscow could not be trusted, but as détente gained popular approval at home and abroad and as the United States, FRG and France worked to improve their own relations with the USSR, no British government could afford to remain idle. New links were established between states and peoples on either side of the East-West divide, and the British joined in. They favoured a broader type of détente, one that involved economic, cultural and humanitarian agreements, not just arrangements to ease tension between the two military-political blocs. The broader détente, it was assumed in the foreign office, would encourage more cohesion in Western Europe and assist EPC. It would win the approval of non-aligned and neutral countries around the world. It would oblige the Soviets to negotiate on matters that they had not intended to discuss, notably human rights.[20]

London needed Bonn's support in European bodies and was unlikely to come out strongly against 'Ostpolitik', but there was a difference between faint praise and enthusiastic endorsement, and in Bonn it was sometimes thought that Britain was not doing enough to help. Although Britain and the FRG disagreed on European issues, however, London backed Bonn's refusal to recognize the East German state until more conducive circumstances brought this change closer in the early 1970s. Politically, relations between Britain and the GDR were strained. Trade between the two did increase, but it remained small. The British welcomed 'Ostpolitik' at the end of the 1960s, and the attitude towards it was favourable thereafter. Heath, committed to European unity, saw in 'Ostpolitik' new possibilities for joint action. Home was a seasoned Cold Warrior and condemned Moscow's 'iron grip' over Eastern Europe, but his Labour successor at the foreign office, Callaghan, was more tolerant. Callaghan consistently supported 'Ostpolitik' as expedient in itself and useful as a means of facilitating trade and other links between Britain and the eastern bloc. Callaghan was determined that Britain should not be left behind.[21]

It was widely thought that tension was receding in Europe during the mid-1970s, as symbolized by the Helsinki Accords. The Kremlin did not realize how much use the West would make of the human rights component of CSCE in subsequent years. The Soviet government resorted to persecution. So did leaders across the eastern bloc, especially in Czechoslovakia, the GDR and Poland. The West protested. Still, in the context of 'Ostpolitik', détente and economic problems across both the East and the West, neither side wanted the Cold War to carry on as before. As part of the Helsinki process and in other ways, the British pushed mainly for agreements on human rights and trade. It was often difficult for them to influence the course of events. Relative economic and military decline meant that during the 1970s Britain's requests and suggestions carried less weight than they once had. Nevertheless, London could turn certain developments to its advantage, particularly the USSR's economic difficulties, the gradual loss of cohesion in the eastern bloc, the moves for common policies in Western Europe, and the United States' internal problems. British leaders did all they could to uphold Britain's interests at a time when the balance between domestic and foreign goals and between the nation's resources and overseas commitments had been disrupted. As for the Americans, though they had concerns about it they continued to promote détente in Europe, but both the Ford and Carter administrations were divided on European policy, and the increasing focus on human rights became very contentious. For Britain the human rights aspects of détente were always a primary concern. Wilson had made this plain in his speech at the Helsinki conference in August 1975. The British believed that Helsinki would make a difference. To the foreign office, détente had much to offer provided the West pursued it with a combination of firmness and patience. If, as expected, the Soviets tried to use Helsinki to prevent change in Eastern Europe, it was up to the West actively to promote change. The human rights angle offered the best option.[22]

American newspapers suggested that limited reform was likely in several of the USSR's satellites, but probably not in the Soviet Union itself. The *Washington Post*'s chief diplomatic correspondent, Chalmers M. Roberts, stressed that America and its allies saw in diplomacy a means both to avoid nuclear war and to mitigate 'the harshness of communism'. In Britain, *The Times* described the texts agreed at Helsinki as inadequate but maintained that they would have been much worse had the West not participated in the conference. CSCE had to be seen as part of a wider effort to define the terms of détente, and as for the charge that Helsinki represented surrender, because it endorsed the political situation in Eastern Europe, *The Times* insisted that the West had long accepted this situation. There was no resounding victory for Moscow. The main importance of Helsinki was that it offered 'gradual change for the better'. The *Guardian* respected the principles upon which the Helsinki Accords were based, but advised readers not to forget the crises of recent years and hoped next for progress in MBFR. In the *Observer*, historian and writer Edward Crankshaw declared that the West 'may live to regret Helsinki'. Moscow had been given what it wanted with regard to its ascendancy in Eastern Europe, and 'insofar as Helsinki helped to dress up a hostile power in a cloak of respectability, it was not only a betrayal of the victims of oppression, it was self-betrayal too'. The *Economist* considered CSCE to be deeply flawed, in that there were no sanctions. It was not clear what could be done if the Soviets refused to do what the West required.[23]

Soviet and eastern bloc leaders had made hardly any mention of humanitarian issues in their speeches at Helsinki. They eschewed statements of principle and the identification of general standards by which states would be expected to abide. They wanted to confine humanitarian issues to bilateral agreements on specific cases and cultural, educational and other exchanges arranged by governments. While warning that pressure from the West on human rights would bring an end to the CSCE process, Moscow was prepared to tolerate a certain amount of criticism so that negotiations on security and political issues could proceed.[24]

When the House of Commons discussed Helsinki on 5 August 1975, Wilson spoke of 'new and more constructive relationships on the basis of an agreed code of behaviour and undertakings to advance co-operation of all kinds'. The prime minister hoped that people, ideas and information would flow more freely and that much would be done before the projected CSCE follow-up meeting in Belgrade in 1977. Wilson also looked forward to advances in SALT II and MBFR. For the Conservatives, Thatcher argued that Helsinki had not altered the 'underlying position' in Europe. She reminded the Commons of the Czech crisis of 1968 and the 'Brezhnev Doctrine', and asked if the prime minister could really be sure that Moscow would observe the terms of the Helsinki Final Act. Wilson opined that the crisis of 1968 would not have happened had Helsinki come first. Many MPs disputed this, but Wilson did not withdraw his remark.[25]

As a result of Helsinki the division of Europe was formalized and stabilized, yet Cold War arrangements were challenged because human rights became a central element in international relations, and the West never explicitly accepted communist totalitarianism in the USSR and eastern bloc as appropriate or legitimate. The Helsinki process affected Soviet conduct in Europe. People in the USSR and eastern bloc came to realize that elites and institutions could be questioned, especially if they could not deliver the living standards and personal freedom enjoyed in the West. All this was not necessarily foreseeable in the 1970s, however, and British scepticism did not die. In the FRG, meanwhile, the commitment to 'Ostpolitik', the Helsinki process and EPC was strong, and there was a desire for the West to continue talks with the USSR and eastern bloc. Chancellor Schmidt was insistent on the need to prevent conflicts in the developing world from interfering with the relative stability in Europe. By the late 1970s the American government was taking a harder line, but the leaders of Western Europe were unwilling to follow suit. On détente and disarmament, argument increased between Washington DC on one side and Bonn and Paris on the other, with London frequently trying to intercede. The West Germans and the French challenged American policies more energetically and during the 1980s only Thatcher of Britain attempted to buck this trend, but she could not break the influence in Europe of the Franco-German axis. The quickening economic and political integration of Western Europe was a Franco-German project, opposed primarily by Britain. As the FRG continued its rise to preponderance in Europe, Thatcher feared that the Americans might relegate Britain and make the FRG their principal ally.[26]

Division in unity

Her wish to show loyalty to the Americans led Thatcher's detractors to accuse her of weakness and deference. It appeared that she was ready to defend US policy even when it involved military aggression or collusion with regimes that terrorized their own people. She was aware that Britain's usefulness to the United States had been fading and set out to revitalize the 'special relationship'. While not prepared automatically to support the Americans on every issue, she insisted that without close ties between London and Washington DC Britain could not expect to be safe or successful.[27]

Thatcher disliked Helmut Kohl, chancellor of the FRG from 1982, and thought that moves to end the Cold War would be disastrous if they led to the withdrawal of US forces from Europe and the creation of a Europe in which the Germans were supreme. One of the prime minister's devotees, Nicholas Ridley, who served in Thatcher's cabinet from 1983, fancied that Kohl wanted to take over everything. In July 1990 Ridley reportedly declared that to give sovereignty to European institutions would be like giving it to Hitler. He had to resign, but his thinking on these matters was close to that of the prime minister. According to Geoffrey Howe, Thatcher *was* anti-German, the Bonn government knew it, and this was part of a bigger problem: the prime minister's reluctance to work constructively with Britain's European partners. From the beginning of her premiership, Thatcher had made a point of criticizing them. She complained that Britain was paying too much into the EC budget and eventually obtained a new financial agreement. Foreign secretary Lord Carrington thought that although she was right to make an issue of Britain's contribution, her stridency hindered efforts to achieve other goals. Carrington favoured European cooperation but wanted it to evolve organically and in its own time as leaders and peoples found common ground. The key was to move patiently and slowly. This pragmatism did not accord with the more ideological and emotional approach to Britain's relations with Europe that was evinced by Ridley and Thatcher, and in July 1990 the government was embarrassed not only by the Ridley affair but also by a leaked report about a meeting that had taken place at the prime minister's official country residence, Chequers, during which negative remarks were made about the German character. Controversy increased as news came through from Moscow, where Gorbachev and Kohl were discussing German reunification. *The Times* concluded that British politics were now dominated by the struggle between Europeanists and Euro-sceptics. In one sense Ridley was right, *The Times* suggested, because changes were in prospect that would make the Germans even more powerful. Ridley's 'verbal gatling-gun assault' on the Germans and Europe led the *Economist* to remark that Thatcher would have to try harder to balance Europhobic and Europhile elements in the government, her party and the nation. The *Guardian* considered her handling of the situation to be less than assured.[28]

One of Thatcher's main objections to German reunification was that it was bound to affect Gorbachev's dealings with the West and the stability of Eastern Europe. The people of East Germany would choose democracy by themselves, Thatcher thought, because communism was collapsing. Reunification was a separate issue. She appealed to Reagan's successor in the United States, George Bush, and to French president Francois Mitterrand, pointing out that the question of territorial adjustments had been addressed in the Helsinki Final Act: Europe's post-1945 borders were to be respected. When Kohl came out strongly for reunification, however, Washington DC gave cautious support, linking the matter with further European integration and the rise of the single market, which the Americans favoured, and once Kohl made it clear that he would defer to the French when it came to sorting out the future of the EC, Mitterrand abandoned the idea of a united front with Thatcher.[29]

Circumstances had changed remarkably in just a few years. In the early 1980s American fears about the 'Finlandization' of Europe and loss of US influence there had deepened as arguments broke out about economic policy. The US government imposed sanctions on the USSR following the invasion of Afghanistan in 1979, and within a year America's exports to the USSR fell by half, but in the same period British, French and West German exports to the Soviet Union increased by 30 per cent. Great importance was attached to a pipeline that would carry gas from Siberia into Western Europe. The Soviets needed energy markets, and Western Europe wanted to reduce its dependence on Arab oil and save manufacturing jobs by helping to build the pipeline. The Americans opposed the project, and at the end of 1981 the Reagan administration tightened the sanctions against the Soviets imposed after the invasion of Afghanistan because martial law had been declared in Poland. In June 1982 the Americans decided to include pipeline technology in these sanctions. Kohl, Mitterrand and even Thatcher insisted that the pipeline contracts should be observed, and the United States relented in November 1982. While Thatcher believed in the 'special relationship' with the Americans, she was prepared to resist them on this matter. Her boldness owed something to the fact that Reagan's sanctions ran counter to his removal of restrictions on America's trade with the USSR. The United States had a large grain surplus and a balance of payments deficit, but to Western Europe it was outrageous for Reagan to interfere with the pipeline project when he was selling food to the Soviets. Reagan's argument was that the Soviet Union could buy its food anywhere, whereas the pipeline was a strategic matter and only America could provide the necessary technology.[30]

In July 1982 Thatcher told MPs that a way would be found for the contracts won by British companies to be completed. The quarrel over the pipeline was covered extensively in the US press. The *Los Angeles Times* declared that Paris and Bonn would never join in an 'economic war' against the Soviets. The *Washington Post* noted that the Reagan administration, despite the 'accommodative vibes' given off at recent NATO meetings and in other negotiations between western governments, wanted to put an economic squeeze on the USSR and to demand more from the Soviets in arms control talks. Some politicians, bankers, academics and others in America considered this foolish. Trade with the USSR was necessary, they argued, while sanctions rarely achieved any-thing, and it was undeniable that Western Europe needed new energy supplies. Among British newspapers, *The Times* and the *Observer* regarded the pipeline dispute as one part of a bigger con-undrum, the looming trade war between the EC and the United States. The *Economist* reported that the Soviets would be able to make their own equipment within two years. Therefore sanctions could not prevent the building of the pipeline; they would just dis-suade Moscow from offering contracts to firms in the West. The *Guardian* warned that the 'potentially grave breakdown of trust' between the United States and Western Europe would, if not quickly addressed, lead to the crumbling of the western alliance. Thatcher seemed to be steering a middle course, toning down EC statements while insisting that the US sanctions were inappropri-ate, but beyond the pipeline dispute there were other disagree-ments between the allies involving trade and financial policy, how to deal with the international recession, détente, the Middle East, and the deployment of US missiles in Western Europe.[31]

Though Thatcher agreed with the Americans on Afghanistan and Poland, she maintained that the pipeline should not be brought into this: it was not directly relevant, it was an issue on which NATO might become divided, and it could not alter the situation in Afghanistan or Poland. She also considered the idea that the pipeline would make the FRG and France dependent on Soviet energy supplies and amenable to Moscow's wishes a little far-fetched. Thatcher was certain that the pipeline would benefit the British economy, and, in view of the loans made by Britain to Poland, she was anxious about America's threat to force the Poles to default on their debts. In her conversations with Reagan on the subject, she stressed that Bonn and Paris would help to build the pipeline no matter what Washington DC and London decided to do. She understood why the Americans were reluc-tant for the Soviets to get their hands on western technology and why they feared that Western Europe might one day become reli-ant on the USSR for gas, but she told Reagan that disputation over the pipeline would be more disadvantageous than allowing the deal to go ahead. Reagan's impression was that Washington DC's quarrel was with Bonn and Paris rather than with London, and Thatcher's arguments helped to soften the American atti-tude, although she was less effective than she liked to admit. She championed British business and doubted the usefulness of sanctions, but she could hardly risk alienating the Americans for any length of time.[32]

Before he left office in June 1982, the US secretary of state, Alexander Haig, concluded that although the gas pipeline was objectionable for strategic reasons, the Europeans wanted it so much and the necessary arrangements had gone so far that it would be unwise for the US government to block it. Thatcher liked Haig's analysis. She also relied increasingly on legal arguments, denying that the pipeline contracts came under US jurisdiction and denying that the United States had the right to impose sanctions that were extraterritorial and retroactive in nature. The results of all this were not as good or as bad as many had expected. Western Europe's fuel problems were not solved. The West's security was not seriously undermined. The pipeline did not create a dependency on the USSR for energy, and Moscow's earnings from the exportation of gas were lower than predicted. Nevertheless, the dispute was not insignificant. It made plain a fundamental divergence between America and Western Europe on East-West relations, and resentment persisted even after the pipeline crisis had passed. This tension was acute with regard to trade. External trade was important to Western Europe, where interconnection with the economies of the USSR and eastern bloc was deemed to be necessary. The American and communist bloc economies were not so complementary in nature, and interaction had declined as Washington DC turned against détente.[33]

The Soviets saw a chance to separate Western Europe further from the United States, and they stepped up their propaganda to this end. The pipeline deal was the largest ever between East and West, and the Soviets claimed that they did not need it as much as the West did because they were not reliant on trade with the West, not greatly harmed by Reagan's sanctions, and not incapable of building the pipeline themselves if the West continued to make difficulties. Despite the discord in the West, however, and the tendency for economic preoccupations to come to the fore at a time when key industries in the United States and EC were in recession, there was still broad agreement on the basic elements of defence and foreign policy and on the need for the western powers to cooperate. The assertion of national economic interests did not irreversibly damage NATO.[34]

Quarrels between the United States and Western Europe in the 1980s grew more intense than those of the 1970s. The Nixon, Ford and Carter administrations had all favoured a thaw in the Cold War. As such, they were willing to work with America's European allies on some issues and occasionally made concessions to them. This willingness to negotiate was in large measure a consequence of America's economic problems. Then, as détente faltered, more friction crept into the US-European relationship. In the late 1970s, as American annoyance with the French and West Germans increased, Callaghan acted as an honest broker. His dealings with Carter were productive. In particular, Callaghan gained American help with the modernization of the British nuclear deterrent. Opinion remained divided on how to boost trade and promote prosperity in the West. Britain's suspicion of Franco-German remedies was strong, but Callaghan was cautious because, as he told Carter in April 1978, if the disputes involving Washington DC, London, Paris and Bonn grew worse, the Europeans might decide to 'go it alone' on both defence and economic policy. Unity and confidence were hardly reinforced in these years by doubts about SALT. Helmut Schmidt thought that the Americans would ignore the wishes of their allies in order to conclude an agreement with the USSR. There was also much criticism in Western Europe of the Carter administration's 'aggressive moral tone', which, it was claimed, would mislead the Soviets and make for confusion rather than clarity in international affairs.[35]

When the détente of the 1970s gave way, the cry arose in the West that international agreements had allowed the USSR to gain military and nuclear superiority. In 1979 NATO adopted a 'dual track' policy: the Soviets would be pressed to remove intermediate range SS20 missiles aimed at Western Europe, and, if there was no deal on this, equivalent US weapons would be deployed in order to bring the Soviets to the negotiating table. The deployment of Cruise and Pershing missiles was controversial. The peace movement gained momentum and disarmament became a major political issue. Even in Britain, America's most reliable ally, there was both a strong anti-nuclear movement and a high level of popular disenchantment with US policy.[36]

In contrast to many observers, Thatcher thought that rather than overreacting to world events, the Americans before 1981 were insufficiently assertive: hence her relief when Reagan took over as president. She regarded Ford as 'a safe pair of hands' but 'not the kind of man to challenge accepted orthodoxies', and although she welcomed Carter's readiness to challenge the USSR on human rights, she found his policy naïve and his thinking 'muddled'. Carter offended pro-western governments around the world by lecturing them on humanitarian issues when, as Thatcher put it, 'there is no need to apologize for supporting an unsavoury regime which temporarily serves larger western interests'. Carter also forgot that focusing on human rights when dealing with the Soviets was not enough, 'for the simple reason that rights have ultimately to be defended by force'.[37]

Summary

The last year of Carter's presidency and the early part of Reagan's brought in more of the firmness that Thatcher wanted from the Americans, but in Western Europe there was little enthusiasm for the change. Differences of opinion between the Americans and the European members of NATO were nothing new. Indeed, European détente had made them more likely. When fear was not felt in equal measure by all the states in NATO, quarrels developed and the Europeans reconsidered their security relationship with America. This happened frequently in the 1970s and again at the end of the 1980s. The Americans were annoyed by leaders in Western Europe who spoke of unity while ostentatiously distancing themselves from US policies. In the late 1970s and early 1980s an open rift developed as these leaders accused the Americans of counterproductive behaviour on the world stage, yet the Europeans were themselves divided. Their own national interests often precluded joint action, and they had also to find a balance between the pressures to cooperate with the United States and their reluctance to follow America's lead.[38]

5 Confronting the Soviets

In London it was thought that, although it could rise and fall, the threat posed by the Soviet Union was ever-present. The danger had many manifestations: direct and indirect, European and extra-European, military and strategic, political, ideological, diplomatic, economic and even, to some observers, social and cultural. Within Britain, and within the alliances and organizations to which Britain belonged, there were differing answers to the question of how to meet this threat. Discussions took in NATO's 'dual track' policy and the relationship between defence enhancement and disarmament talks, the course of European détente and US-Soviet bargaining, the several elements of CSCE, the prospects for reform in the USSR and communist bloc, East-West trade, and what crises in Africa, Nicaragua, Afghanistan and elsewhere revealed about the nature of the international order and how it might evolve in the future.

NATO's 'dual track' policy

Anti-nuclear and peace campaigners in the West were disgusted by NATO's deployment of Cruise and Pershing missiles. It is possible that the SS20s were a convenient excuse and that NATO would have deployed new weapons no matter what the USSR was doing, as part of an ongoing effort to strengthen the West's defences. Western leaders could not present their decisions in this way, however, for they required a better justification to win the necessary domestic approval, so they pointed to the need to counter the Soviet threat, rather than to doubts about the US nuclear umbrella or NATO's military options. Had the USSR been willing to make a deal on the SS20s, military chiefs, arms manufacturers, hawkish politicians and other vested interests in the West would have faced more opposition, but as it was they were able to get their way because the Cold War competition between the West and the

Soviets was intensifying. The deployment of Cruise and Pershing became symbolic. It was a test of NATO's unity and resolve.[1]

The Soviets were aware of NATO's deliberations but did not think that deployment was inevitable and wished to avoid an increase in tension while there was still a chance that the US Senate would rat- ify SALT II. By October 1979, however, the Kremlin had run out of patience. Brezhnev condemned NATO and warned that détente was in jeopardy. He accompanied this with an offer to confer on nuclear matters and an announcement that the USSR would uni- laterally reduce the size of its conventional forces. This led some NATO members, notably Belgium and the Netherlands, to argue that deployment should be postponed. Chancellor Schmidt also came under intense pressure domestically, though in December 1979 the FRG joined Britain and Italy in formally agreeing to par- ticipate in the deployment of Cruise and Pershing. The Soviets did not initially seek to take advantage of popular unease about the missile deployments in the FRG and elsewhere. Instead, they focused on SALT III and pressed for a speedy resumption of nego- tiations. Perhaps Moscow made a mistake here, and an opportun- ity to interfere with the deployments slipped away. On the other hand, even if Moscow had offered concessions it is unlikely that NATO would have halted the deployment side of 'dual track', for this was a political as well as a military decision.[2]

Lord Carrington later insisted that leaders in Western Europe never doubted the need to deploy Cruise and Pershing, that this was purely a response to the SS20s, and that the importance of nuclear balance between NATO and the Warsaw Pact was gener- ally accepted, despite Soviet propaganda about the arms race. The commitment to deploy by the end of 1983 was probably necessary if there was to be a joint NATO position at all, Carrington thought, but it did mean that in the intervening four years Moscow had the chance to stir up public opinion in the West, which in turn affected some policy-makers. Once the deployment began, how- ever, there was less quarrelling between NATO members and the USSR took arms control talks more seriously.[3]

The Times came out strongly in favour of NATO's decision. The Soviets were attempting to prevent NATO from moderniz- ing its medium-range capabilities, but NATO had to hold to the 'dual track' and seek an agreement with Moscow while simultan- eously improving Western Europe's defences. The new weapons in development might be rendered unnecessary, suggested *The Times*, if Moscow made a bargain before they became operational. In the meantime, NATO should proceed with deployment. Brezhnev was not offering enough to justify postponement. Although SALT III, CSCE and MBFR were all important, NATO had to 'plug the gap in its defences'. The *Economist* also wanted talks with the Soviets to proceed alongside NATO missile deployment, as did the *Observer,* and the *Guardian* argued that, notwithstanding NATO's decision, the diplomatic and political advantage was with Moscow. In America, the *New York Times* noted the problems caused in Western Europe by 'unusually sharp' pronouncements from Moscow, and the *Chicago Tribune* reported demonstrations in the eastern bloc, especially the GDR, where 13 million people signed a petition against NATO's policy. There was a question as to how genuine this petition was, as an expression of popular opinion, and the *Chicago Tribune* suggested that the GDR's rulers were manipulating protests about Cruise and Pershing to prepare the way for a diversion of money from social programmes to defence.[4]

The 'dual track' entailed negotiation as well as deployment, and it was natural for governments and peoples to attach great importance to negotiation in the context of 'Ostpolitik' and détente, CSCE, the SALT process and MBFR. Washington DC could hardly disappoint leaders in Western Europe in their desire for meaningful talks, moreover, if it wished to restore confidence in US security guarantees. Schmidt was not alone in thinking that progress with arms control would make new Soviet deployments less likely, and all interested parties knew that if the effort was not made, Cruise and Pershing would not be politically acceptable in Europe. At the same time, it was assumed that arms control would not happen without modernization and that Moscow would have no incentive to negotiate unless NATO deployed Cruise and Pershing.[5]

Arms control and the arms race were linked, because weapons were bargaining tools and arms control talks tended to encourage weapons development and deployment. At the time of the December 1979 decision to deploy Cruise and Pershing, some NATO members expected the Soviets to make concessions that would be matched by NATO, and they expected this to happen quickly. Moscow was also thinking about an accommodation. Previously, the purpose of the SS20 was to replace older missiles, but from 1979 older missiles were kept in service so that they could be included in talks. Neither the Soviets nor NATO envisaged the complete abandonment of whole classes of weapons. This is unsurprising in view of the political and technological efforts and all the time and money that were needed to develop new weaponry. NATO leaders had sanctioned the development of Cruise long before they knew that the USSR would be deploying SS20s.[6]

In Britain and in Europe there was mounting resistance to the deployment of Cruise and Pershing. Unmoved by all the criticism, Thatcher was insisting by 1987 and the signing of the INF Treaty that NATO was victorious, since the Soviets had finally agreed to withdraw their SS20s. Back in December 1979 she had rejected the case against the decision to deploy. She was unimpressed by Brezhnev's offer to negotiate because she knew he would hang on to the SS20s, the most up to date weapons of their kind, to which NATO did not yet have an equivalent. As she said in an interview on Dutch television in February 1981, the Soviets were producing SS20s at the rate of more than one a week, and Moscow could render the NATO deployment unnecessary simply by removing the SS20s from the European theatre. Thatcher declared that though she personally disliked nuclear weapons, they were essential if freedom was to be preserved.[7]

Differing attitudes towards the Soviet Union

This view of missile deployment and arms control did not go uncontested. Attitudes in Britain, Western Europe and the United States towards the Soviet Union and the Cold War in the 1970s and early 1980s were rarely the same, and on problems outside Europe there were many clashes. There was no common policy, for instance, on recognition of the left-wing regime established in Angola in 1975, which was backed by Cuba and the Soviet bloc. The process of European Political Cooperation did not produce unity on Afghanistan. When the Soviets invaded there was a delay before an emergency meeting was convened. The Americans expected support for their policy of suspending East-West dialogue and imposing punitive measures upon the USSR, but most members of the European Community were unwilling to furnish such support. They hoped to salvage elements of détente. Western Europe's initial reaction to the invasion of Afghanistan was confused. Eventually the British foreign secretary, Carrington, went to Moscow to present a plan for a neutral and non-aligned Afghanistan. The Soviets were not convinced by the show of western unity on Afghanistan, much to Washington DC's frustration.[8]

Paris and Bonn would not give up hope for an end to the Cold War. They were now acting much more independently of Washington DC. In both the Carter and Reagan administrations, indeed, there were frequent complaints that Western Europe was getting out of control. Against American wishes, French president Giscard d'Estaing met with Brezhnev in Warsaw in May 1980 and tried to persuade the Soviet leader not to get drawn into Afghanistan. Giscard d'Estaing wished to improve Franco-Soviet relations and avoid charges of pro-Americanism. The meeting surprised many in the West. Washington DC was offended, and Bonn even more so, because Giscard d'Estaing had previously advised Schmidt to cancel a proposed visit to Moscow. Despite his anger, Schmidt continued to argue that the main point was not to allow events outside Europe to interfere with the thaw in Europe. The British, meanwhile, were shocked by the French action. Carrington was amazed that there had been no consultation. Still, apparent concord was restored and this provided the context for Carrington's trip to Moscow, where he told Soviet foreign minister Gromyko that the EC wanted an international conference on Afghanistan. Was it not appalling, Carrington asked, that the Soviet invasion had prompted over three million refugees to flee across the border into Pakistan? Gromyko replied that 'the Afghans have always been a nomadic people'.[9]

The Warsaw meeting between Giscard d'Estaing and Brezhnev, and the indications of tension within NATO and the EC, did not go down well in the British press. *The Times* considered the Warsaw meeting a gift to the Soviets, making more credible their claim that they still cared about détente and suggesting that leaders who defied the United States could gain diplomatic and other rewards. Brezhnev was ready to talk to anyone if he thought this would drive a wedge between Western Europe and America, and the French president had played into his hands. The *Guardian* was at a loss to know why Giscard d'Estaing decided to court such controversy at home and abroad. American newspapers noted the French retort to US criticism, to the effect that Paris had a right to maintain relations with Moscow without approval from others, and suggested that the main problem with the Warsaw meeting was that it 'gives the impression that something is happening on the diplomatic front when it is not'. In addition, NATO was now looking like 'an alliance in disintegration'.[10]

The Thatcher government did not find it easy to reconcile differing needs and goals in the early 1980s, and the situation in Afghanistan made matters worse. The prime minister wanted to show her support for Washington DC's hard line, but she also wanted to cut Britain's defence budget and wondered if détente might still benefit Britain. While he was foreign secretary, Carrington had no doubt that détente could be saved. He found American leaders too confrontational. On Afghanistan, Carrington thought, the United States and its allies should keep tension to a minimum. At the same time, it was important for the West to make clear its disapproval. Some punitive measures were appropriate, but it was also necessary to offer the Soviets a way out. London was frustrated, no less than was Washington DC, that the EC's unity on Afghanistan was temporary and limited. The French liked to take their own path in international affairs, while Thatcher saw the invasion of Afghanistan as proof that the USSR had used détente to strengthen itself militarily. Thatcher wanted a strong response and tried to get the EC to back the United States. What was needed, she claimed, was a 'fundamental rethinking' of the West's relationship with the Soviet Union and eastern bloc, but a full year after the invasion she complained that this had 'barely begun'. Clearly the leaders of Western Europe were not going to abandon measures of détente just because Britain or America said they should. They did not regard the invasion of Afghanistan as a final straw. They thought that détente was working and did not see why trade with the Soviets should be curtailed. They did not think that Washington DC had been consulting them properly for years, and they had no reason to link Afghanistan with European questions. London was not entirely unsympathetic to these arguments, which came primarily from Paris and Bonn.[11]

The intensification of the Cold War in the late 1970s and early 1980s therefore put some distance between the Americans and their allies. Governments in Western Europe did not wish to adopt the harder line towards Moscow that Washington DC was advocating. Quarrelling increased. In 1981, when the Americans told their NATO partners that détente should be suspended, the latter refused and the Americans had to agree to carry forward the INF talks with the Soviets. NATO's position was that détente should be promoted when Moscow's behaviour allowed. As for the other side of 'dual track', deployment of Cruise and Pershing, many people in Western Europe saw these missiles as an American imposition. Washington DC, it was alleged, was scheming to confine nuclear war to the European continent. Carter was disappointed by the fate of superpower détente and the wrangling in NATO, but he was also certain that a harder line had become appropriate. Reagan made even plainer the United States' readiness to compete with the Soviet Union, while in Britain, as well as in the FRG and France, more questions were raised about US policy, collective security and nuclear deterrence. Whereas Carter had tried to explain that he had not really turned his back on détente and that America had presented the Soviets with a choice between cooperation and confrontation, the Reagan administration for a time repudiated détente even as an objective.[12]

Despite his robust response to the invasion of Afghanistan, Carter may have been partly responsible for the difficulties that arose as a result of the Soviets' aggression. He did not react quickly to evidence that the Soviets were going to invade and might have done more to make Moscow reconsider. On the other hand, Carter acted honourably and made political sacrifices. He called upon the UN to put pressure on the USSR. He withdrew SALT II from the US Senate. He imposed economic sanctions, which brought up a particularly difficult issue: a grain embargo. Carter knew that to stop grain exports to the USSR would be to let down American farmers, and he did not wish to damage his re-election bid in 1980. Even so, he decided that the invasion of Afghanistan was an emergency and hoped that American farmers would understand. Carter also saw in the embargo a way to galvanize other world leaders. 'How am I going to lead the West and persuade our allies to impose sanctions against the Russians if we aren't willing to make some sacrifices ourselves?' he asked his aides. 'What can I say to Margaret Thatcher or Helmut Schmidt if we fail to exercise the single option that hurts the Russians most?'[13]

Brezhnev claimed that US-Soviet relations were ruptured not because of Afghanistan but because there were powerful groups in the United States and in NATO that opposed détente and were ready to take any opportunity to disrupt it. Such rhetoric was not without effect in Western Europe, where governments and peoples disliked the direction US policy was taking, but it was also noted that for the Brezhnev regime, a thaw abroad did not entail reform at home. During the 1970s the Soviets appeared to be confident and strong. By 1971 the USSR had more strategic land-based and submarine-launched missiles than the United States, and foreign minister Gromyko declared that no significant issue anywhere in the world could be decided without Moscow's approval. Inside the Soviet Union the Brezhnev government was firmly entrenched. It brought stability and predictability, with authority consolidated in the hands of the communist party elite. Armaments remained a flourishing sector, and in relation to resources the USSR spent twice as much on defence as the United States between 1964 and 1974. The Soviet economy grew more slowly than America's, however, and Brezhnev did little to mitigate the USSR's social and economic problems. Détente brought opponents of the regime into the open. They were subjected to imprisonment and persecution. A new Soviet constitution adopted in 1977 reinforced the totalitarian system and prescribed harsh penalties for dissent.[14]

The expanding humanitarian framework

This increased the importance to the West of the human rights aspects of CSCE. Repression in the USSR and eastern bloc featured ever more prominently in the diplomacy and propaganda of the West, and what had been said about the Helsinki Final Act, that it would open a door that Moscow would rather have closed, proved to be correct. For the CSCE follow-up meeting in Belgrade between October 1977 and March 1978, the EC agreed a joint platform on human rights. The idea was to persuade the Soviets into concessions without criticizing their record or demanding too much. Problems arose at Belgrade because the American delegation was less restrained, and Soviet delegates baldly declared that Moscow would not yield. The British verdict was that the Belgrade meeting had not been worthless, even if Soviet intransigence on human rights had put a limit on what could be achieved. At least Moscow had not outmanoeuvred the West by making an offer which some, but not others, could have accepted. The document produced at Belgrade reaffirmed the shared commitment to the Helsinki Final Act, including, by implication, its humanitarian features. Nevertheless, there were open disagreements about the

extent to which the Final Act had been implemented. The next
follow-up meeting was to be in Madrid in 1980.[15]

After Belgrade, the Soviets continued to complain that détente
was being undermined. The West maintained that all parts of the
Helsinki Final Act were interdependent and that Moscow should
prove its willingness to live up to the obligations it had entered
into. 'Helsinki Watch' activists in the West were in touch with
groups in the USSR and eastern bloc, and the Carter administration put human rights at the forefront of American foreign policy.
Moscow became worried because the West's influence in the bloc
seemed to be growing, with more trade and cultural links. The
Kremlin was sure that order could be preserved inside the Soviet
Union but was less certain about the USSR's satellites. To counter
pressure from the West, Moscow repeated the principle of non-
interference in the internal affairs of sovereign states and insisted
that the Soviet constitution of 1977 guaranteed a range of rights,
but there was a problem here in that rights could be defined in
different ways. The Helsinki process made the USSR's internal
affairs the subject of unprecedented attention and comment. This
was much more threatening than the Nixon-Kissinger approach,
which had focused on the Soviet Union's external policy.[16]

In the West there were disagreements about the likelihood of
reform in the Soviet Union and about how to reduce Cold War
tension. Writing in the early 1980s, a Princeton, New Jersey, professor named Robert Tucker insisted that the USSR was facing
economic and social failure and that, as a result, internal pressure for reform was building up. The influential dissident and
recipient of the Nobel Prize for literature in 1970, Alexander
Solzhenitsyn, argued in an essay dated February 1980 that the
West was wrong to think that the Soviet system could be made
'better' or 'kinder'. Solzhenitsyn opposed détente. He was amazed
that the West was still pursuing it after Soviet military intervention
in Czechoslovakia, Angola and Afghanistan. He urged the West
to help reformers inside the USSR. Instead of treating ordinary
Russians as 'lost' to communism, the West had to view them as
friends, co-workers for humanitarian causes, and people who were
looking to the West for their liberation. In fact, the late 1970s and
early 1980s were not encouraging times for reformers and dissidents in the USSR and eastern bloc. State repression was generally
effective and sometimes worse in the bloc than it was in the Soviet

Union. The dissident and historian, Roy Medvedev, doubted that pressure from the West, by itself, could bring democratization. Something had to happen *within* the communist countries. In his account of the Soviet constitution of 1977 Medvedev was scathing: it mentioned rights that did not really exist; it allowed for arbitrary rule and abuses of power from above and encouraged political apathy below. Long before she became British prime minister, Thatcher had decided that détente and the Helsinki process had brought more trouble than they were worth. She regretted their 'corrosive' effect and claimed that the West was becoming complacent. The tendency was to assume that pressing Moscow on human rights was having a positive impact, when in truth persecution was increasing in the USSR and eastern bloc, not decreasing.[17]

When Brezhnev defended the 1977 constitution his remarks were scrutinized by the western media. Among British newspapers it was *The Times* that offered the most detailed assessment, explaining that the constitution prescribed no limits on state power and no protection for the people. There was a 'dazzling' list of rights, but the individual could not act against the state, and rights in the Soviet Union had more to do with obligation than freedom. Soviet expert Dr Archie Brown, of St Anthony's College, Oxford, made a similar point in the *Observer*: the constitution provided for continuity and reinforced Brezhnev's position and the authority of the Soviet government. American newspapers were equally negative in their comments.[18]

Rising Soviet assertiveness

The Kremlin was bothered but essentially unmoved by all the talk of human rights. Soviet leaders considered that they had no option but to maintain order and discipline. Stability at home was a platform for growing influence abroad, and one of the key developments here was the rapid expansion of the navy. Soviet strategists knew that operations outside Europe required a larger navy. Soon Soviet vessels were covering larger areas of the Mediterranean, the Atlantic, the Pacific and the Indian Ocean. Naval strength meant that the Soviets were better able to get involved in Africa. For African operations it was useful to employ Cuban troops. Dependent on Soviet aid, Cuba was a willing accomplice. The intervention of Soviet troops in Africa was potentially problematic because they were white, and Africans might easily decide that they had the same imperialistic designs as other outsiders. There was also resentment because the Soviets gave their African friends old machinery and equipment and took raw materials as payment, often selling these on to the West at below-market prices. In view of all this it was better for Moscow to send in Cuban troops, who could pose as non-aligned and were neither white nor imperialists. The Cubans played a prominent part in the war in Angola. Several African states became Soviet allies and provided bases, diplomatic support, favourable propaganda and economic preference. In 1979 Nicaragua came under Cuban influence, so there was now also an opening in Latin America.[19]

Soviet activity in the developing world was not only an expression of expansionist impulses or a design against the security of the West. It had a lot to do with political change in the developing nations themselves. Black Africans, for example, wanted to eliminate the remnants of colonialism. If they needed help and applied for it, Moscow was unlikely to refuse. It made sense politically and economically for the USSR to establish relations with new independent states. For the commander-in-chief of the Soviet navy in the 1970s, Admiral Sergei Gorshkov, the chief goal was to promote the USSR's global interests. Allies could be assisted and the measures of Washington DC and Peking counteracted. The navy was to be used to support peacetime foreign policy, protect trade routes, add to Soviet influence and prestige, and provide more strategic options. Naval expansion became a crucial component in Moscow's competition with the West. So did intervention in Africa. As for Nicaragua, the prospect of a success for socialism there prompted the Soviets to offer substantial aid, and this coincided with a bolder policy on the part of Cuban leader Fidel Castro. Moscow, regarding Cuba as a valuable link to the developing world, encouraged him. Cuban forces would remain in Angola for 15 years. The economic costs were seen by Castro to be less important than the political goals he had in view, and involvement in Africa demonstrated Cuba's commitment to socialist revolution and gained for Castro more room to manoeuvre in international affairs, which set the scene for another plan to pressurize the United States, this time in Nicaragua.[20]

To Washington DC, Nicaragua became a thorn in the side. The US government had been supporting right-wing dictator Anastasio

Somoza. After he was overthrown a political, economic and military struggle was carried on against the socialist Sandinistas, beginning under Carter and greatly intensified by Reagan from 1981. The Conservative government and press in Britain backed US policy. American and British leaders opposed the Sandinista regime and refused to accept it even when it won elections. The United States and Britain were the only major donors of aid in the world that gave more to Nicaragua in the last seven years of the Somoza dictatorship than in the first seven years of the Sandinistas. American policy went back and forth. Having supported Somoza since the late 1960s, the United States became increasingly unsympathetic in the Carter years and insisted on reforms in return for aid. In 1978, having decided that Somoza had to go, Carter tried to make sure that the regime that replaced him would not be dominated by the Sandinistas. This effort failed. Then the Reagan administration, conceiving of Nicaragua as a potential launch site for a communist takeover of the wider region, imposed stiffer sanctions and provided backing for anti-communist insurgents.[21]

On the political right in Britain were some who thought that the Americans had made a mistake in allowing Somoza to fall. The *Daily Telegraph*, for instance, suggested that Somoza, though 'certainly a deplorable figure' whose 'monomaniacal greed' had led him to amass huge wealth at his people's expense, had cause to feel aggrieved at US policy. For years the Americans had sustained him. More recently, Carter had cut the aid, encouraging the Sandinistas to step up their destabilizing efforts. While Carter could not be faulted for his aversion to 'morally undesirable foreign dictatorships', this situation had been badly handled: 'Baby *and* bathwater have been thrown out. Nicaragua is now almost certain to set course on a communist, pro-Castro, pro-Moscow road'. Britain recognized the new government of Nicaragua on 3 August 1979. What would the United States do? Moscow regarded Latin America as a US sphere: Soviet leaders knew they could do little about the enmity between the United States and Cuba, and they had not prevented or tried to reverse the overthrow of Allende in Chile in 1973. Still, Moscow hoped that the Sandinista regime would survive. For Reagan and his supporters, meanwhile, the United States had to save Nicaragua from communism.[22]

Greater involvement in Nicaragua was designed to combat Soviet assertiveness. Even if Moscow was reluctant to get drawn into Latin America, Washington DC could not be sure that this would remain the case. There was no choice but to accept Cuba's alliance with the USSR, but anything more had to be forestalled, not because the Soviets posed an immediate threat in the region but because they might come to pose a threat in the future. Latin American countries were interested in agreements with the Soviet Union because they saw a chance to strengthen themselves politically and economically. For some, the real goal was to gain advantages in dealing with the United States. In Moscow it was thought that contacts with Latin America would enhance the USSR's international status, its position at the UN and in the developing world, and its trade. The Soviets were cautious, however, because they did not want links with Latin America to interfere with goals related to détente with the United States. Into the mid-1980s Nicaragua received substantial aid from the USSR, Bulgaria and the GDR, but Moscow did not intend to create another client, like Cuba, and offered no security guarantee to the Sandinistas. Facing economic problems at home and already shouldering considerable burdens in Vietnam, Africa, Afghanistan, Poland and elsewhere, there was a limit to what Moscow could do in Latin America.[23]

American support for the insurgency against Nicaragua's left-wing regime had an impact in Western Europe. For years the allies of the United States had been less alarmed than the Americans about communism in the developing world. Now, Nicaragua became a sign of how Washington DC viewed the wider contest between the West and the USSR. The question of how to deal with Nicaragua merged into the question of how to deal with Moscow. Western Europe preferred diplomatic to military methods. On the other hand, since Britain and the other European members of NATO had little at stake in Nicaragua, they saw no point in risking an open breach with the United States. This is not to suggest that they were oblivious to Soviet designs. Concern did grow about Nicaragua and Africa and about Soviet naval strength. Thatcher described the late 1970s as a time when the Kremlin 'displayed less and less caution in dealing with internal dissent or planning foreign adventure'. In addition, the Soviets were competing well in the international arms trade. By 1980 the USSR was the biggest seller of arms in the world. France was second, the United States third and Britain a distant fourth.[24]

A lot of these weapons were exported to developing countries. In 1988 the main arms suppliers to developing countries were the

USSR, with 43.4 per cent of the total in value; the United States, with 19 per cent; China, with 8.6 per cent; France, with 7 per cent; and Britain, with 6.4 per cent. The Soviets also built up a clear lead in arms exports as a share of total exports. The proportion in 1976 was 10.1 per cent, and it had risen to 20 per cent by the early 1990s. Over the same period the United States' figures fell from 4.5 to 4 per cent. China's went up from 1.6 to 4 per cent. For France and Britain, arms exports as a share of total exports rose from 1.5 to 2 per cent and from 1.4 to 2 per cent respectively.[25]

In the 1970s there was some talk of limiting international arms transfers, yet the global demand for armaments quickly expanded. For everyone who argued that arms sales made wars more likely, there was somebody else who insisted that every country had the right to determine its own security needs and to purchase weapons if it so desired. Moscow and the political left in the West and across the developing world maintained that western governments were using the market for arms to increase their influence. They wanted to turn their customers into dependants and construct a 'new imperialism'. Yet the Soviets played the same game: they flooded the developing world with weapons. The USSR and the United States both sold weapons as part of their strategic competition. For other suppliers, including Britain and France, profits were a bigger motivation, and the economic aspects of the trade mattered no less than the political ones. Arms were often sold in order to open countries up to other types of business. Within NATO, quarrels broke out when the Americans tried to push their allies into buying US weapons. Economic problems in the West made matters worse, and, when governments reduced their defence budgets, weapons purchases by their own armed forces became more difficult. The sale of weapons to other states was essential to the profitability of a nation's armaments industry and had effects on employment and the balance of payments.[26]

The arms trade was a matter of no small concern to the British. In Britain's relationship with South Africa, for example, arms sales had come to play a key part. The Labour government appointed in 1974 reintroduced the embargo on sales that Heath had removed, which caused an outcry, since Britain was losing a good customer.[27] Soviet and Cuban involvement in Africa was relevant, too, because South Africa's leaders were steadfastly anti-communist.

During Callaghan's time as Britain's foreign secretary and prime minister, the Americans often consulted him about Africa. There was a shared concern about Soviet advances there. Callaghan and Kissinger discussed in detail the war in Angola, the establishment of a left-wing regime in Mozambique (which followed the revolution of 1974–75 in Portugal, the colonial power) and Britain's role in Africa, especially the effort to find a settlement in Rhodesia. Kissinger became more active on African matters, even holding direct talks with Ian Smith. The Conservative opposition in parliament accused Callaghan of surrendering responsibility to the Americans, but perhaps he was simply facing facts: Britain had been unable to reach an agreement with Smith and could do little alone to stabilize Africa. As for the USSR's fractiousness and ambition, Callaghan expected the danger to recede. He was confident that the Helsinki Accords would open up Soviet society and influence Soviet foreign policy. He did not consider reform within the USSR and Soviet bloc to be impossible. Although he knew that divisions in the West would encourage Moscow to be more demanding, he was sure that the Soviets would eventually drop out of the arms race with America through lack of money. Callaghan's successor as prime minister was rather more concerned about Soviet involvement in the developing world and about the USSR's military strength. Thatcher looked at the 20,000 Cuban troops in Africa, with the Soviets pulling the strings, and saw an attempt 'to further communist subversion throughout the Third World'. The Soviet invasion of Afghanistan in 1979 was 'part of a wider pattern'. In some respects, however, Callaghan was right. The USSR's economic growth slowed down, and by the time the West placed limits on trade in response to the invasion of Afghanistan the eastern bloc was heavily indebted to the West. Recession set in throughout the bloc and in the Soviet Union. Perhaps for the first time, Moscow began to see the satellites as a burden. Soviet agricultural policy, moreover, had been failing for years, making the USSR a major importer of food.[28]

Food: to sell or not to sell?

America's grain sales to the USSR, and the political uses to which they could be put, were the subject of much debate in the United States and across the West. In the early 1970s the Soviets tried to arrange a supply from American companies in the belief that privacy could be maintained and on the assumption that if they

approached the US government, the latter would demand concessions in return for food. Kissinger decided that the United States'
need for cheaper fuel, at a time when OPEC was raising its prices,
represented a sound basis for a bargain: grain in exchange for oil.
Kissinger was hampered by the opposition to détente. The idea
spread that America should not feed the USSR while the Soviet government was spending huge sums on weapons instead of making
sure that sufficient food was produced for domestic consumption.
Critics of détente also stressed that the United States no longer
needed Soviet friendship. American forces had left Vietnam and
SALT had stalled. In the event the Soviets refused to offer oil at
a discounted price, perhaps worried about how their Arab allies
might react, and Kissinger was unable to link the grain and oil
questions. Finally it was arranged that American grain would be
supplied, subject to a ceiling beyond which the US government
would have to give express approval. The US-Soviet grain agreement was signed in October 1975 and was to last for five years. It is
possible that Kissinger never expected the USSR to provide cheap
oil and that his main purpose was to distract Moscow. By keeping
the grain and oil talks going, he thought he would be better able
to continue his Middle East diplomacy without Soviet interference.
Early in 1976 the suggestion was made that the supply of grain
should be suspended to punish the Soviets for their intervention
in Angola, but President Ford announced that grain would not
be used as a political tool. If pushed, he said, the Soviets would
buy their food elsewhere and this would reduce US influence in
Moscow.[29]

The *Economist* noted that poor harvests in the USSR and eastern
bloc, and also in Western Europe, had coincided with increased
output from the United States and Canada (240 million and 33
million tons of grain respectively in 1975–76 compared with 198
million and 29 million tons in 1974–75). Prices would go up, but not
by much, and the Soviets would probably be most affected. Their
grain imports were rising quickly and they relied on the United
States for almost 60 per cent of the extra they needed to make up
for the domestic shortfall. The *Guardian* suggested that the USSR's
inability to feed itself would undermine the Brezhnev regime and
give America the chance fundamentally to change the Cold War:
'For America to become Russia's bread basket could do more than
all the missile building and weapon rivalry of the post-war era to

alter the balance of power'. The US-Soviet grain agreement was welcomed by *The Times*, which considered it economically and politically useful. Though 'experience has shown that attempts to link politics and commerce too closely can backfire', the Soviets had to 'understand the broader effects which their domestic and foreign policies are bound to have on the willingness of the West to do business with them'. According to one American observer, the idea that 'food is power' was a delusion, and governments that tried to use food for political ends held an exaggerated notion of their capacity to determine the behaviour of other countries. Another commentator, writing in 1977, argued that while it was appropriate to use food to further America's international objectives, this had to be done in the right way. As the world's largest producer of food for export, and the supplier of about half of all the grain that was traded internationally, the United States had a significant advantage, but it was important not to link food too closely with other matters. The task, rather, was to enhance US influence through interdependence in food. Washington DC had to show the world that it was aware of the food requirements of all countries and that it was promoting a reliable supply system. Interdependence would bring greater influence for the United States, whereas threats and embargoes were to be avoided.[30]

The grain issue needs also to be seen in its wider economic and political context. By the early 1970s the United States had a trade deficit, for the first time in the twentieth century. Once a leading exporter of raw materials, America had become an importer of copper, lead, zinc and oil and was also importing manufactures. Fortunately there were large agricultural surpluses in 1972 and 1979. Grain was sold to the USSR, and although the US government subsidized this trade it did ease the balance of payments situation. When Moscow's criticism of US foreign policy became less strident in the early 1970s, Nixon and Kissinger claimed that this was because of their political initiatives, but many commentators thought that the Soviet Union was becoming more agreeable because of its need for American grain. Though Carter and his secretary of state, Cyrus Vance, favoured a moderate policy involving 'positive incentives', including trade, the Carter administration suspended grain sales when the Soviets invaded Afghanistan. Reagan initially favoured economic sanctions against the USSR, but he had to contend with balance of payments problems and a grain surplus. Reagan reversed Carter's policy on the grounds that the grain embargo was having little impact. In 1982, therefore, the United States and the USSR concluded another five-year deal on grain exports, which helped Reagan to conciliate the American farm vote and reduce the trade deficit.[31]

Britain's role in East-West relations

The economic side of détente had for years been important to Britain. Even before the signing of the Helsinki Final Act, Callaghan had been confident that the CSCE process would stimulate trade with the USSR and Eastern Europe. In a circular he sent to all of Britain's overseas representatives in July 1975, he envisaged East-West cooperation on the world's economic problems, direct contact between businessmen, the exchange of commercial information, improved services for individual firms, and the gradual erosion of distinctions between the economic systems of the West and the communist bloc. Callaghan subsequently announced that the increase in Anglo-Soviet trade was exceeding expectations.[32]

Britain's commitment to détente declined after Thatcher replaced Callaghan as prime minister in 1979. As leader of the opposition, Thatcher had accused the Labour government of gullibility and distanced herself from the optimism that surrounded the Helsinki process. Strongly anti-communist in sentiment, she spoke of the ongoing struggle between 'freedom' and 'tyranny'. She opposed defence cuts, condemned leaders in Western Europe for their willingness to bargain with the Soviets, and emphasized the importance of the Anglo-American 'special relationship'. Thatcher took office at a time when détente had faltered, which suited her outlook. Britain's bipartisan consensus on most matters of defence began to break down. On arms control, Afghanistan and Poland, Thatcher rejected what she saw as the submissive attitude of some in Western Europe. She condemned the invasion of Afghanistan, called on British athletes to boycott the Moscow Olympics of 1980 and denounced the harsh treatment meted out to Polish reformers and trade unions. This period also saw the British government place greater emphasis on human rights, particularly through the CSCE review conferences. In various ways the Thatcher government sought to re-establish Britain as a world power, allied to the United States and opposed to the USSR. One of the reasons why a task force was sent to the South Atlantic in response to Argentina's invasion of the Falkland Islands was to show the communist bloc that Britain was strong. In Thatcher's Cold War agenda there was no room for retreat and loss of face.[33]

In the early 1980s the prime minister saw no need for overtures to Moscow. She did not attend Brezhnev's funeral in 1982. Though she was at the funeral of Brezhnev's successor, Yuri Andropov, in 1984, she did not speak or even shake hands with the new Soviet leader Konstantin Chernenko. At a lower level, normal diplomatic routines did mean that links with the USSR and eastern bloc were maintained, and in 1980–81 the foreign secretary, Carrington, visited Rumania, Hungary and Poland. Cultural exchanges between Britain and Eastern Europe at this time were limited, as was trade. In the mid-1980s only about 2 per cent of Britain's total trade was with the USSR and eastern bloc. The Thatcher government became a little more conciliatory after it was confirmed in office at the general election of 1983. A thorough consultation exercise over the summer led ministers to conclude that reform within the Soviet Union was possible. Thatcher began to listen more to foreign office advice, and, confident after victory in the Falklands War and her electoral success, she wanted to position herself to take advantage of new developments in international affairs. Other influences also guided her towards a more moderate line: the FRG was pressing Britain to be more constructive, and quarrels in NATO, hold-ups in the INF talks and resistance from Western Europe to US leadership on key issues indicated that the time was right for Britain to act.[34]

Britain's foreign secretary from 1983 was Geoffrey Howe, and he hoped for a thaw with Moscow. In talks with the Americans in July 1983 he found them full of objections, which reinforced his notion that Britain should make the running. He considered it perfectly reasonable to work for détente even while continuing to criticize the Soviet occupation of Afghanistan and the crackdown against reformers in Poland. Following Howe's visit to Hungary in September 1983, Thatcher arrived in the country in February 1984. This was the first time she visited the eastern bloc as prime minister. Anglo-Soviet contacts increased. During 1985 and 1986 several British delegations arrived in Moscow to discuss trade, energy and other matters, and Howe visited the GDR, Czechoslovakia, Poland and Yugoslavia. There were some quarrels. Though Gorbachev later described his first meeting with Thatcher (in December 1984) as 'a turning point towards a major political dialogue between our countries', he took the opportunity then and on later occasions to argue that Britain's policy would have to change if it was to promote stability. Gromyko accused the Thatcher government of giving unconditional support to the United States, which was bad for Europe and for the world. Tit-for-tat diplomatic expulsions went on in the mid-1980s. Nevertheless, the prime minister attended Chernenko's funeral in Moscow in March 1985, and she and Howe met with Gorbachev and Gromyko. Thatcher still found it difficult to trust the Soviets, and her public remarks remained censorious, but opinion polls indicated that the British public favoured a thaw. The growing likelihood of an arms control agreement also influenced British policy. The Americans wanted a deal, as did Gorbachev and his foreign minister (from July 1985) Edward Shevardnadze. In addition, the Thatcher government was under pressure from the Labour Party and the large anti-nuclear movement and peace lobby to make genuine efforts to improve East-West relations. Criticism of the Soviets was combined with agreements with them. Official visits continued, and in 1986 and 1987 there were arrangements for economic cooperation, an accord on finance and credit, and exploratory talks on the prevention of terrorism. Thatcher and Gorbachev met for a summit in Moscow in March 1987 and agreements were made on a range of diplomatic, cultural and educational matters. Thatcher's image as a strong and experienced world leader was further heightened in December 1987 when Gorbachev stopped in England for talks on his way to sign the INF Treaty in Washington DC. Thatcher's claim to be more than merely a European leader irritated Paris and Bonn, but here was Gorbachev, treating her as someone who had Reagan's ear and whose views really mattered.[35]

Thatcher's popularity ratings went up owing to the meeting with Gorbachev, but the *Guardian* pointed out that Britain's global influence still fell far behind that of America and the Soviet Union. The government had recently been embarrassed, moreover, by the revelation that there were more US missiles on British soil than had previously been admitted and by the growing sense, encouraged by the parliamentary opposition, that to modernize Britain's nuclear deterrent would be to hamper arms limitation and encourage the Soviets to respond in kind. *The Times* opined that Gorbachev was right to stop off in England. Not having been to Washington DC before, he would find his meeting with Thatcher instructive, and she had the chance to remind him that the INF Treaty would not lead to the denuclearization of Europe or to US disengagement from Europe and that it did not preclude a continuing search for security in which America's 'star wars' programme might play a part. Nor could Gorbachev be permitted to think that the human rights element in East-West relations had less importance now that an agreement had been made on arms limitation.[36]

The American and Soviet governments had both faced domestic opposition while negotiating the INF Treaty. Reagan was worried about annoying his conservative supporters. He was accused in some quarters of allowing himself to be tricked into thinking that the USSR was now safe and reliable. Gorbachev was also accused of giving up too much, and it is easy to see why. The USSR had deployed more missiles than NATO and had more to lose: for every warhead the Americans surrendered, the Soviets lost four. Gorbachev hailed the treaty as 'the first well-prepared step on our way out of the Cold War, the first harbinger of the new times', but he was frustrated in the course of the negotiations. He was very irritated, for example, by Thatcher's claim that nuclear weapons had kept the peace for 40 years and that some of them should be retained for deterrence purposes.[37]

British leaders had been in two minds about détente in the 1970s but had adapted well to the changes in East-West relations, and in the 1980s Britain's influence continued to exceed British power, measured in economic and military terms. Détente was viewed as a process in which the different parts had to be balanced together. Bargaining from a position of strength was essential, it was thought, and the West should not make concessions without gaining something from the USSR. In the early part of Thatcher's premiership she made her mark as a hard-line opponent of the Soviet Union. She subsequently adopted a more flexible approach. She prized Anglo-American cooperation, but neither the 'special relationship' nor the possession of nuclear weapons greatly increased Britain's role in the world. The closeness to America was frequently a disadvantage, in fact, because it offended Britain's allies in Europe, members of the Commonwealth, and many other countries besides. It fed anti-American sentiment within Britain. There were protests when the government sanctioned

British participation in SDI research projects in the mid-1980s, the takeover of Westland Helicopters by an American-led consortium in 1985–86, and the use of US bases in Britain for the American bombing of Libya in April 1986. Britain's withdrawal from the UN Educational, Scientific and Cultural Organization (UNESCO) was also controversial. The Americans, who provided about a quarter of its total budget, left UNESCO in 1984 complaining about its inefficiency and politicization. Britain followed suit in 1985. Washington DC and London had been disappointed by the unwillingness of leaders in the developing world to alter their economic policies or cooperate with the West in foreign affairs.[38]

Summary

London's determination to stay close to Washington DC meant that it was some time before a real effort was made to improve Anglo-Soviet relations. Neither Britain nor the USSR considered these relations to be of primary importance. Moscow focused more on Bonn and Paris in an effort to facilitate European détente, and although the Soviets occasionally thought of using London to gauge opinion in Washington DC, again, this was not a priority. Britain's influence in Moscow fell behind that of the larger states in Western Europe, and they were much more successful in expanding their trade with the USSR and eastern bloc. In London the older view, of trade as a political instrument rather than an end in itself, still had many supporters. Perhaps another old idea, of Britain as a mediator between America and Europe and between the West and the USSR, survived as well. It is possible that it hindered a clearer understanding of the limits on independent British action.[39] On the other hand, confronting the Soviets in the 1970s and 1980s was always a shared endeavour. London appreciated that it could not usually influence Moscow's policies by itself and that collaboration with allies to this end, inside and outside Europe, was advisable and necessary. The Heath, Wilson and Callaghan governments, to varying degrees, combined a readiness to seek agreements with the USSR and eastern bloc countries with a determination to act firmly on specific issues. Thatcher made much of her toughness and clarity in foreign affairs, but she also mixed accommodation with resistance. The British could not have everything their own way, and they struggled to find a comfortable role in the development of multilateral East-West relations. This did not mean that they were bereft of influence and respect, however, for they continued to pursue and to accomplish goals in the fields of NATO strategy, arms control, human rights, economic and political détente and crisis management.

6 Multipolarity and Nuclear Weapons

Among the many challenges facing Britain during the 1970s and 1980s were those connected with multipolarity and nuclear weapons. New diplomatic initiatives, a search for agreement, the vocabulary and practice of détente, and the rise of politically assertive and economically successful nations meant that Britain had to operate in a changing international environment. Superpower negotiations affected Britain, as did the internal dynamics and external impact of some of the organizations to which Britain belonged. Though the speed and extent of the move away from bipolarity in the world order should not be exaggerated, international relations *were* transformed in this period, and the British tried hard both to take advantage of the flexibility of others and to shield the national interests from new threats. Britain's status as a nuclear power became a particularly difficult issue. Antinuclear opinion gained support in parliament and in the country, but defence policy was premised on the maintenance of a credible deterrent. The modernization of Britain's nuclear forces and questions relating to NATO and collective security were increasingly contentious, and as arms control grew in international importance the future of Britain's deterrent was placed in doubt.

'An open world'

The emergence of 'new Europe', the vision of a multi-polar world and related changes in the international order in the 1970s meant that the influence of the two superpowers was not so dominant, and they recognized this. They knew they had to show more respect towards other powers. Nixon pursued détente partly because of the United States' economic problems, the oil shock, international criticism and the embarrassment in Vietnam. The United States still intended to be a major influence in the world, but its leaders realized that the bipolar configuration of the early Cold War was passing away and that stability depended on a balance between the United States, Europe, the USSR, China and Japan. The American rapprochement with China highlighted US security concerns in Asia and the Pacific and, equally important, Washington DC's desire to show Moscow that the world was changing.[1]

According to Percy Cradock, Britain's ambassador in Peking between 1978 and 1984, there was a difference between rhetoric and reality in China's foreign policy. Publicly, China disavowed any ambition to be a superpower. In fact, China intended to advance in order to gain more influence over Washington DC and Moscow and to match the 'rich' western states and Japan. This is why China improved its relations with Britain. The priority, though, was to reach an understanding with the Americans, who engaged in talks with Peking and Moscow simultaneously in the early 1970s and claimed that they wanted 'an open world' in which no state was isolated. Nixon was worried about appearing weak, however, and while seeking better relations with the USSR and China he tried to impress audiences at home and abroad by sounding robust. If the Soviets and the Chinese did not abide by the agreements they made with him, he said, he would turn on them 'like a cobra'. Moreover, the concessions made by Washington DC in order to draw China into an agreement were not as momentous as they first appeared. The Americans knew that there could be no thaw unless they made a gesture with respect to Taiwan, that pressure was growing for the representation of China at the UN and that Chinese help was needed to arrange the US withdrawal from Vietnam. Once these problems were addressed it was not clear what Washington DC and Peking could offer each other, although their thaw still had potential because both sides had in common a strong suspicion of the USSR.[2]

In Britain, an impression developed that the US-Chinese thaw was not developing satisfactorily and that this was America's fault. In August 1972, for instance, *The Times* pointed out that fighting in Vietnam had become more intense, the Taiwan question remained unresolved, tension between North and South Korea was as palpable as ever and the regional role of Japan had yet to be clarified. Leaders in Peking, Moscow, Hanoi, Saigon and Tokyo all seemed to be saying the same thing: there could be no lasting peace in the region unless the United States made substantial proposals. The

Guardian was more impressed by Nixon and Kissinger, and the *Economist* noted their boldness in promoting peace despite domestic criticism.[3]

Kissinger later explained that the thaw had a simple premise: 'Peking needed us to help break out of its isolation and as a counterweight to the potentially mortal threat along its northern border. We needed China to enhance the flexibility of our diplomacy... we had to take account of other power centres and strive for equilibrium among them'. The chief of staff in the Nixon White House, Bob Haldeman, wrote at the time that the president and his aides were convinced of the interdependency between the approach to China and the policy on Vietnam. In time, US-Chinese relations did improve. President Carter established full diplomatic relations with China in December 1978 and ended America's mutual defence treaty with Taiwan. During the 1980s there was a large increase in US-Chinese trade. Back in the early 1970s, however, predictions about a new world order were in some ways premature. Nixon and Kissinger used the language of conciliation and multipolarity, but their goal was American ascendancy.[4]

In the military sphere, indeed, it is difficult to detect a fundamental shift in the 1970s. The Americans and Soviets still had military supremacy, with their nuclear arsenals and large conventional forces. This ensured the survival of a bipolar structure of power, despite the growing political and economic influence of China, Japan and the FRG, into the 1980s. Each of the two superpowers had a military range and capacity that no other state or group of states could match. Their nuclear weapons inhibited any military challenge to their primacy, and they could use conventional forces anywhere in the world thanks to their large navies.[5]

Nevertheless, the general assumption was that bipolarity was giving way to multipolarity in many aspects of international relations. What were the implications for Britain? Multipolarity and détente were seen in London as mixed blessings. There was a need to make use of the advantages that might arise while combating the disadvantages. Heath characterized the early 1970s as 'a period of increasing fluidity'. He called upon the Americans and the Soviets to take more notice of other power blocs, including Western Europe, which he thought could have greater influence in a multi-polar world. The British were to exercise power as part of a united Europe. The friendship with America would continue, Heath assumed, but not in the form of an unequal 'special relationship'.[6]

Heath's wish to move away from reliance on the United States marked him out from his predecessors and successors, but he could only carry this project so far. Shifting patterns of collaboration and interaction did not bring all the changes that had been expected. Even so, there were more joint endeavours, and these were pursued through both choice and necessity.

Economic realities prompted cooperation, and the leading nations of the non-communist world, the G7 (the United States, Britain, Canada, Japan, the FRG, France and Italy), held regular summits on trade from the mid-1970s in search of a more coordinated approach to common problems. In time the G7 took up political as well as economic concerns. Under President Reagan, for example, the United States used the G7's influence to put pressure on the Soviets. So did Japan. Economic rivalry had always been part of the Cold War. Now, in the 1980s, economic help for the USSR could be withheld unless the Soviets made concessions on security matters (only in 1997, after the break-up of the Soviet Union and eastern bloc, did the G7 become the G8, with Russia as a member).[7]

The Reagan administration did not doubt that economic measures should be used against Moscow. Some leaders in Western Europe disliked this aspect of US policy and refused to support it, while fear of Soviet assertiveness led Japanese leaders to cast off their previous reluctance to involve themselves in security discussions. In 1982 and 1983 Japan's prime minister, Yasuhiro Nakasone, used G7 deliberations to press for a united front against Moscow. The Americans found that the application of economic pressure became more difficult and less effective. Notwithstanding Reagan's hard-line attitude towards the Soviet Union in the early 1980s, in some areas détente was not ended, and in the economic sphere Moscow was influenced less by America's actions than by other developments: the fall in the price of oil, the indebtedness of the USSR and its satellites to the West, and the pressure for economic liberalization created by the success of the FRG and Japan and by reforms in Eastern Europe. America's relative economic position deteriorated. Between the early 1980s and early 1990s, the United States went from being the largest creditor nation to the largest debtor the world had ever seen. Once the world's leading exporter of manufactured items, America was overtaken by the FRG, which had a much smaller workforce. The United States had the two largest banks in the world in 1980, but by 1991 the world's ten largest banks were all Japanese.[8]

The changing international situation was also reflected in the United Nations. By the mid-1960s the majority of UN members were from Africa and Asia. The body seemed increasingly anti-West in attitude. The G7 made this charge during the 1970s and 1980s, while calling for the UN to take on a bigger role in conflict resolution and international relief. By this time American dissatisfaction with the UN was a long-established fact.[9]

Some observers have suggested that the G7, UN Security Council, IMF and World Bank were all used selfishly and ruthlessly by the West.[10] Yet claims about the West's hegemony need to be qualified, because political, economic and military relationships underwent considerable change during the 1970s, 1980s and 1990s. Nevertheless, it is true that as the G7 increased its influence and coordinated the activities of the world's richest nations, other nations had to fit in with what the G7 decided. The head of the IMF regularly attended G7 meetings, where the United States, Japan and the FRG had the most sway. The framing of economic arrangements became the subject of ongoing disputation between the G7 and UN. Increasingly, the G7 countries planned their activities to suit themselves. This provoked loud protests, especially from the developing world. The tendency to make ad hoc and often bilateral deals instead of creating a multilateral system cut across the efforts to establish a viable body of international economic rules administered by the UN.[11]

Britain's experiences in the G7 were not particularly happy. A rift developed from late 1975 over energy policy, with Britain insisting that, as the EC's only oil producer, it had to speak for itself and not as part of the EC. A more promising development was the G7 conference hosted by Britain in May 1977, which resulted in agreements on aid for developing nations and policies to combat unemployment and stimulate economic growth. This conference was marred by tension, however, especially between the United States and the FRG. Britain's influence in the G7 was limited, and there was more trouble from 1979 as the Thatcher government moved away from the EC's position on key issues. Thatcher was critical of French and West German notions about how best to

promote economic and financial stability. As European integration picked up speed, the European members of G7 tended to side
with the FRG against America whenever there was a divergence.
London was unwilling to accept Bonn's leadership and sometimes
sided with Washington DC, but there was little prospect of guiding
the G7 in a chosen direction, and the British had to accept many
decisions with which they disagreed. The weakness of sterling and
Britain's economic decline relative to the rest of the G7 meant
that there were few opportunities to control collective policy.
Membership of the G7 probably did not increase Britain's importance to the Americans. On the other hand, there were occasions
when Britain clearly benefited from membership of G7, as in the
mid-1980s when there was joint action to deal with the overvalu-
ation of the US dollar and to limit the variability of exchange rates.
This helped the British economy by imposing some order in international trade. But involvement with the G7 continued for Britain
to be as frustrating in some respects as it was useful in others.
The G7's tendency to address political issues was confirmed at successive meetings during the 1980s. The Williamsburg summit of
1983 considered arms control and endorsed NATO's deployment
of Cruise and Pershing missiles in Europe (though France and
Canada had reservations). The Tokyo summit of 1986 discussed
international terrorism. The Venice summit of 1987 looked again
at arms control and was notable for quarrelling between Britain
and the FRG on the question of short-range nuclear weapons.[12]

British dissatisfaction with the UN increased, meanwhile, and
there was a link here with Britain's attitude towards developing
countries, some of which were members of the Commonwealth.
The overseas aid budget was cut under Thatcher, and disputes
arose over Britain's stance on sanctions against South Africa
and British withdrawal from UNESCO. Although many developing countries still looked to London for help and advice, the
Commonwealth and the developing world were not very important to Britain in the 1980s, and even if the British saw a need
to remain involved in parts of Africa and Asia in order to contain communism, the means and the will were declining. In the
mid-1970s Britain had joined with other advanced countries to
oppose reforms at the UN that were favoured by the developing
world. Discord continued into the Thatcher period. London and
Washington DC complained that the developing nations voted

together so that they could get their own way, which meant that UN bodies and policies were being improperly politicized. Thatcher greatly annoyed the developing world by condemning its promotion of collective agreements on trade and finance. The answer, she insisted, lay with 'domestic good housekeeping and the free flow of world trade and investment'. Divisions were evident at the time of the special meeting to mark the UN's fortieth anniversary, in October 1985. Thatcher suggested that the UN was in danger of becoming a mere talking-shop. There ought to be more action, she said, to deal with famines, the drugs traffic and terrorism: 'We cannot do without the UN, but we can do a lot more with it'. These years also saw a change in the UN's peacekeeping efforts. Its activity as a peacekeeper had traditionally been limited in scope and objectives. In the 1980s and 1990s it was extended – and much criticized. Sometimes members of the Security Council acted for themselves, using vaguely worded resolutions as a cover for independent use of military force. Criticism of the UN also took in the nuclear issue, for another important development in international affairs was the spread of nuclear weapons. The major powers no longer had a monopoly. Despite arms limitation treaties, test bans and other efforts, nuclear proliferation was a serious concern. Among the economically advanced powers, Japan and the FRG were happy to remain non-nuclear because they had US security guarantees, but an increasing number of states had developed a nuclear capability, including China, India, Pakistan, Israel and South Africa.[13]

Nuclear proliferation and the British deterrent

By the mid-1970s it was clear that any power wishing to develop nuclear weapons would have to cover a huge financial cost. The expenditure would need to continue for many years as missile technology improved and as targeting and support facilities became more sophisticated. It was noted at the time that cost was the main determinant in a government's decision on whether to go ahead with a nuclear programme. Cost had to be balanced with the expected advantages. For those states that were considering these points in the mid-1970s, much depended on the relationship between the Americans and the Soviets. Certainly Japan, China and India assessed their own requirements in the light of the overall defence posture of the two superpowers. Tokyo was a particularly interested observer of Washington DC's negotiations with the USSR and China in the 1970s and the subsequent INF talks between the Americans and Soviets. Targeted by Soviet and Chinese missiles, Japan relied on the United States for protection and had no nuclear weapons of its own, preferring to devote its resources to economic development. There were quarrels with the Americans over the United States' trade deficit with Japan and Japan's desire to build nuclear energy plants.[14]

While Japan tried to steer clear of the nuclear arms race, Britain had taken a different course, looking to the Americans for weaponry and seeking the closest possible military and strategic cooperation with the United States.[15] As had earlier British governments, those of the 1970s were determined to preserve the nuclear deterrent and committed themselves to the necessary expenditure.

The Callaghan government of 1976–79 pursued two goals simultaneously: international disarmament and the modernization of the British deterrent. These were not considered to be contradictory, since a viable deterrent would be a useful bargaining tool in disarmament talks with the Soviets, but the British could not get very far without the Americans, and French and West German views also had to be considered. This made the four-power summit at Guadeloupe in January 1979 all the more significant. Attended by Callaghan, Carter, Giscard d'Estaing and Schmidt, the summit focused on security issues and disarmament. The four leaders agreed that the SALT II treaty should be completed as speedily as possible, but there were arguments on broader strategic matters. Schmidt was concerned that SALT II would create a stalemate between the United States and USSR, making Germany more vulnerable. He wanted a bargain with the Soviets for the removal of their SS20s but was reluctant for NATO to deploy the weapons that Callaghan and Carter thought necessary to affect Soviet policy. It was agreed that ground-launched Cruise missiles would be stationed in Europe, that Britain would accept them and that Schmidt would consider accepting them in the future. The possibility of a SALT III treaty was also discussed. Guadeloupe opened the way for NATO's 'dual track' approach, which involved the deployment of missiles while simultaneously negotiating with Moscow for the removal of all intermediate range weapons, including the SS20s.[16]

Guadeloupe was also important because Callaghan convinced Carter that the United States should renew Britain's nuclear deterrent. This was essential if Britain was to be a useful ally, the prime minister stressed, for it had implications for Britain's military and diplomatic strength, and the British deterrent would also have a bearing on international arms limitation agreements. Callaghan faced the same political problem that other Labour leaders had faced: a large section of the Labour Party opposed nuclear weapons. Indeed, some members of the cabinet suggested that instead of renewing the deterrent it would be better to strengthen Britain's conventional forces. The prime minister disagreed. So did Schmidt, on the grounds that France should not be the only nuclear power in the European Community. Carter decided that Britain should have a successor to Polaris and that this would enhance western security and assist with SALT. Talks were still in progress when Callaghan's government fell in May 1979.[17]

Although Britain's desire to preserve its deterrent was combined, as in previous years, with a desire to check nuclear proliferation and promote arms limitation, on these matters the lead was taken by the superpowers. The Test Ban Treaty of 1963, Outer Space Treaty of 1967 and Non-Proliferation Treaty of 1968 were followed by the SALT I agreement of 1972. SALT II was finalized by 1979, but the Soviet invasion of Afghanistan prompted the Americans to set it aside. At this stage the existence of the American and Soviet arsenals was probably less alarming than the development of marginal nuclear capacity by unstable Arab regimes and states that felt insecure or inadequately protected by alliances. The threat was perceived to be growing in the Middle East (most notably from Iraq), South America (Brazil and Argentina) and the Pacific area (South Korea, Taiwan and Indonesia).[18]

The Non-Proliferation Treaty had not halted the spread of nuclear weapons. By the time a review conference was convened in 1975, over a hundred countries had signed it and 87 had ratified it. A number of 'threshold nuclear powers' refused to adhere to the Non-Proliferation Treaty, however, and this made clear its inadequacy. The Americans often complained that governments in Western Europe were either failing to assist or, even worse, making nuclear technology available to 'threshold' states. It was repeatedly suggested that one way to restrain proliferation was for the main nuclear powers to issue guarantees that they would not use nuclear weapons against any non-nuclear state. Special meetings took place at the UN on this matter, but no firm agreements were reached.[19]

British leaders saw that stricter rules on non-proliferation might get in the way of the Chevaline project and related defence activity. Until certain programmes were completed, indeed, a ban on testing was not in Britain's best interests. Even if this changed, there was little point in pushing for new controls while the United States and USSR were sceptical. When he was prime minister, Callaghan was personally in favour of a test ban agreement, but he saw no easy way to resolve such matters as its coverage and duration and how to enforce it. Preventing the transfer of information and technology from civilian to military establishments also seemed impossible, and the British government was aware that no action taken unilaterally by Britain would have much effect on others. Quarrels went on about the exportation of nuclear technology. The Americans tried to persuade France and the FRG to discontinue these exports, but from the mid-1970s it was clear that American dominance of the global nuclear industry was slipping. Competition increased: the US and European nuclear industries went into recession and the struggle for exports became more intense.[20]

Britain's decision to purchase Trident appeared to some commentators at home and abroad to be incompatible with non-proliferation, but British leaders responded by pointing out that Trident represented continuity, in keeping with the established policy of modernizing the deterrent. There was no conflict between deterrence and non-proliferation because Britain was also committed to disarmament. These three elements, it was claimed, taken together, made Britain's position logical and consistent.[21]

In later years, the Outer Space Treaty, Non-Proliferation Treaty and SALT agreements were considered by many to rank among the most substantive and enduring accomplishments of détente. Less positive opinions were also expressed, however, and, at the time, the fate of SALT II was of special concern. By the end of 1977 the United States' European allies were agitated because there were signs that the two superpowers had goals in mind that would undermine Western Europe's security. It seemed that intercontinental weaponry would be restricted while weapons designed for use in Europe might remain largely untouched. In January 1978 Carter had to tell America's allies that he would consult

them before making a final decision. There were monthly brief-
ings to keep NATO informed about progress in SALT, but arguments continued, with the FRG protesting about what it took to be
America's selfishness in attending to its own interests ahead of the
needs of NATO as a whole. In the United States, opinion against
SALT was rising. In Britain, the government noted the American
displeasure when Bonn and Paris agreed to sell nuclear reac-
tors to Brazil and Pakistan. Callaghan shared Carter's concern
about the spread of nuclear facilities. Some of Britain's decisions
caused controversy, though, as when Moscow condemned the projected sale of 'Harrier' jump jets to China. Callaghan pointed out
that China wanted these aircraft for defence purposes only, but
Brezhnev insisted that such deals would wreck SALT II (Peking
subsequently pulled out of the 'Harrier' agreement because of
the cost). In late 1978 it appeared that the SALT II treaty might
soon be ready to sign. Carter implored America's allies to remain
united, for he needed their support if he was going to ask the
US Senate to ratify SALT II. Britain was concerned about its own
deterrent and about European security, and the question arose as
to whether NATO's nuclear forces should be modernized before,
during or after SALT III. London, Paris and Bonn agreed publicly to support the SALT II treaty in order to help Carter domestically, but quarrels raged on behind the scenes. Schmidt was
still maintaining that SALT would make Western Europe unsafe.
This led to a proposal that NATO's conventional forces should be
enlarged. Callaghan objected. Britain was already paying £600
million a year to keep troops in West Germany, had also to fund
its nuclear deterrent and had for years been spending more of
its national wealth on defence than both the FRG and France.
As for SALT III, the British view was that the Soviets should be
asked for a clear statement of what they wished to include. The
French expected them to limit the coverage of SALT III. Carter
wanted to concentrate on getting SALT II ratified. Only then, he
thought, should attention be given to SALT III, but Callaghan
and Schmidt wanted arms control talks and the modernization of
NATO's weaponry to move forward together.[22]

As in the early 1970s, there were lengthy discussions within the
British defence establishment about the implications of SALT for
British security and the Anglo-American nuclear relationship.
In order to reach agreements with the Soviets, it was feared, the

Americans might scale down their cooperation with Britain. The British were soon reassured on this point. The US government proved willing to continue the nuclear link with Britain, and SALT raised the political costs involved in ending it. Carter stressed that there would be no sacrifice of a close ally for the sake of a bargain with Moscow. When Thatcher visited Washington DC for talks in December 1979, one of the results was a joint statement of the importance of the British deterrent and Anglo-American strategic partnership. British leaders were still concerned about other aspects of SALT, though, particularly its effect on America's role as protector of Western Europe. Previously, American promises that nuclear weapons would be used to defend Western Europe had carried more weight, in view of America's superiority over the Soviet Union, but with SALT and the acceptance of parity these undertakings were less convincing. The USSR's offensive capabilities had been enhanced, which meant that the Soviets would pose a greater risk to the United States should the Americans use nuclear weapons in Europe. For Britain, this also meant that US protection was less likely to deter a Soviet attack on the British Isles. Another disconcerting thought was the possibility that the British deterrent would eventually have to be included in a future SALT agreement. This had always been something that Britain's leaders sought to prevent, and they were pleased when the issue was postponed in SALT II. Yet US negotiators assumed that British and French nuclear forces would be part of SALT III.[23]

Britain's political leaders and military experts recognized the importance of arms limitation and of maintaining a stable balance between NATO and the Warsaw Pact. Despite SALT I, doubts crept in, which is one reason why NATO adopted the 'dual track' policy. SALT II promised much, but in the early 1980s the chance for further agreements faded quickly. The former British prime minister, Heath, complained that not enough was done to revive the negotiating process after SALT II. His view was that Britain and Western Europe should coordinate their defence arrangements more closely. This would enable the relevant governments to deal with the Americans on an equal basis, to reshape NATO policy and to gather public support for comprehensive changes in strategy and defence. In the Thatcher years, however, much of this seemed beyond reach. America's failure to ratify SALT II and the belief in Washington DC and elsewhere that the USSR had benefited from a shift in the nuclear balance during the 1970s did not make for a helpful context. Britain had no wish to lose US security commitments, was concerned about new Soviet weapons and did not like the prospect of an arms race. An added complication was that the future of Britain's deterrent had to be settled.[24]

Trident, 'star wars', the INF Treaty and short-range nuclear forces

Although the Callaghan government gave serious attention to Trident as a replacement for Polaris, the issue was not resolved before the Conservative victory at the May 1979 general election. In July 1980 the Thatcher government confirmed that Britain would be purchasing Trident C4 (Trident I) from the United States at a cost of about £5 billion. The deal was good for Britain financially, in that the Americans were going to supply missiles at a rate far below their real cost, but from the outset opinion was divided as to whether Britain should spend so much on its deterrent. Another problem was that Carter did not want to conclude the deal until after SALT II had been ratified. He was concerned about giving the Soviets an excuse to adopt counter-measures and European members of NATO an excuse to hold up the deployment of Cruise and Pershing. There were also figures in Washington DC who insisted that the British should only be given Trident if they expanded their own defence efforts and paid a high proportion of the research and development costs. Then, after Reagan succeeded Carter as president in January 1981, it was announced that Trident would be upgraded. The Reagan administration regarded Trident C4 as a temporary weapon, which would be deployed until an improved version, Trident D5 (Trident II), became available in the late 1980s. The United States offered Trident II to Britain in October 1981. Thatcher and her colleagues were unsure about buying Trident II. Although Trident I would become outdated much earlier than expected and would be difficult to maintain as the United States adapted to a new system, Trident II would cost more and would introduce many new difficulties. It was argued that Britain could not afford it and did not need it, that it would not be possible to exclude it from future arms control arrangements, that it would provoke a Soviet reaction and that British public opinion would not accept it. By January 1982, however, Thatcher had decided that Britain's need for a credible deterrent made Trident II the best option.[25]

The government marshalled arguments for deterrence against its critics and, while denying that there could be any doubt about America's nuclear guarantee to its NATO allies, pointed out (as earlier British governments had done) that it was vital to have a second centre of decision-making in the West, to keep the Soviets guessing. Thatcher insisted that the nuclear programme represented better value for money than an expansion of Britain's conventional forces and that it would help Britain to deal with difficult situations that might arise in the future. She talked less about the need to contribute to NATO than she did about Britain's national interest. The new agreement with the Americans was expected to cost £10 billion. Labour condemned the policy in parliament, and peace campaigners and anti-nuclear protesters did the same in the country. Disputation continued as the running costs of Polaris and the expenditure on Trident swallowed up a growing share of the defence budget and as the government admitted that policy might change as the international situation changed. By the summer of 1987 the United States and Soviet Union were moving towards a bargain for the elimination of land-based intermediate range missiles and a 50 per cent reduction in strategic weapons. How long would it be possible, or wise, to exclude the British deterrent from negotiations for a larger strategic arms treaty?[26]

Trident was a prominent issue in the general election of June 1987, which the government easily won. Having frustrated their domestic opponents, however, ministers now had to face Britain's European allies, who claimed that Trident was interfering with the arms control process and that Thatcher's determination to have Trident was part of a scheme to cut Britain's conventional contribution to NATO. The Europeans kept up their clamour, prompting the British government to announce categorically that Trident was a national force, the minimum that Britain needed, and that it could not be included in a 50 per cent reduction deal. These developments influenced and were influenced by the simultaneous debate on intermediate range nuclear forces. NATO's 'dual track' policy, adopted at the end of 1979, involved the strengthening of western defences while seeking an agreement with the USSR. There was a complication, as Callaghan and Schmidt had been warning, in that American and European security arrangements might diverge as a consequence of talks between the two superpowers. NATO's 'flexible response' strategy was also the subject of ongoing disagreement. In some ways 'dual track' reinvigorated 'flexible response' because NATO's INF capability was enhanced: land-based missiles were to be deployed to fill the gap between short-range weapons and American strategic forces. NATO was making clear its commitment to deterrence and also telling the Soviets that if they reduced their own INF capability, by withdrawing the SS20s, the NATO deployment would become unnecessary.[27]

In the early 1980s the British government was keen to show its commitment to NATO and its willingness to support the United States. Despite considerable domestic opposition the government agreed that Cruise missiles would be stationed in Britain, but British leaders also pressed the Americans on the other side of the 'dual track' policy and insisted that greater efforts should be made to negotiate constructively with the USSR. The Americans put forward the 'zero option': if the Soviets abandoned their INF systems there would be no NATO missile deployments. The general opinion was that this was not a basis on which to proceed, but Thatcher's government supported the 'zero' solution, largely for domestic reasons. The main point for the prime minister was to make sure that Britain's nuclear weapons were not included. At the end of 1983 the first Cruise missiles arrived in Britain. The INF negotiations had faltered but they resumed in 1985 and were helped along by US-Soviet summits at Geneva and Reykjavik. The 'zero' solution was discussed again with respect to intermediate range nuclear forces, and there was also the possibility of a deal on strategic offensive weapons and strategic defences. Moscow's concern for the latter had been dramatically increased by Reagan's announcement, in March 1983, of SDI, the Strategic Defence Initiative, commonly known as 'star wars'. The Soviets wanted all elements to be brought together in a comprehensive treaty, but the Americans wanted to keep them apart, as did the British government. Thatcher insisted that the INF and SDI questions were distinct, and the fact that she had never been comfortable with the 'zero' proposal was made clear by her warnings that an INF treaty should not be allowed to undermine 'flexible response'.[28]

The INF Treaty was signed on 8 December 1987. Soviet leader Mikhail Gorbachev had agreed that neither strategic defence nor the modernization of the British and French deterrents should be discussed in unison with INF. Thatcher was pleased about this but then incurred the wrath of Britain's NATO allies by declaring that the focus on nuclear weapons could not hide the fact that the Soviet Union still enjoyed a vast superiority in conventional and chemical weapons. The rest of NATO condemned Britain for making trouble. Thatcher had to back down. On another matter, though, she gained support from Chancellor Kohl of the FRG. She pointed out that the USSR had many weapons with a range below the INF threshold of 1000 kilometres. This led to the 'double zero' solution: the inclusion of missiles with a range of 500 to 1000 kilometres. As a settlement came closer, Britain's ambivalence was exposed. Thatcher feared the 'decoupling' of American and European defence postures, which seemed inevitable if all intermediate range weapons were removed from Europe. This is why, after the Reykjavik summit of October 1986, she went to the United States to obtain personal assurances on these points from Reagan.[29]

Reykjavik caused a crisis in Anglo-American relations. Reagan had spoken to reporters of a 'non-nuclear world' and a deal with the Soviets for the abandonment of all nuclear weapons. Thatcher became more concerned to monitor America's arms control diplomacy. Not having been at Reykjavik, this was no easy task. There was talk of removing all ballistic missiles within ten years, after which there would be freedom to deploy strategic defence systems. Yet 'double zero' was dropped because of disagreement over SDI (Thatcher supported Reagan in his refusal to abandon the 'star wars' programme). Nothing was settled at Reykjavik, in fact, because the Soviets made conditions that the Americans could not accept, but there was astonishment afterwards when Reagan confirmed that he and Gorbachev had spoken about eliminating all nuclear weapons. The US secretary of state, George Shultz, tried to calm the situation by pointing out that the formal proposals referred only to ballistic missiles. There was consternation in NATO, and the lack of consultation meant that America's allies could not be sure what had or had not been discussed. The British government and chiefs of staff did not want all intermediate range missiles to be removed from Europe and looked for a way to recover what had apparently been conceded at Reykjavik. At the same time, they knew that they would have to accept an INF treaty of some sort, and they did not wish to annoy the Reagan administration in case this jeopardized the Trident deal. Thatcher found that the US government was far from united on nuclear matters when she visited the United States in November 1986. Rather than require Reagan to admit that he had made mistakes at Reykjavik, the prime minister and her advisers used a different method. A draft statement was put together, one that did not specifically renounce anything that Reagan had been prepared to accept at Reykjavik but which rearranged the details and changed the emphasis. Ballistic missiles were not mentioned at all. The statement advocated an INF treaty, a 50 per cent reduction in strategic forces over five years, a ban on chemical weapons, continuing SDI research, the NATO strategy of mixed arsenals, including nuclear, and modernization of Britain's deterrent. Reagan and his colleagues accepted the statement. The administration felt the need for friends at this time: the Republicans had suffered losses in mid-term elections and the 'Irangate' scandal was beginning to cause difficulty as revelations were made about the illegal sale of weapons to Iran, an avowed enemy of the United States, and the use of the proceeds to fund anti-communist insurgents in Nicaragua, despite the limits placed by Congress on the assistance that these insurgents could be offered. Thatcher took advantage. The British statement on nuclear weapons was issued with American approval, and Thatcher also persuaded Reagan that the ban on arms sales to Argentina, imposed during the Falklands crisis, should not be lifted.[30]

The prime minister had reason to be satisfied, for the doctrine of nuclear deterrence had been boosted and the British statement included everything that London regarded as essential. Though Reagan had talked about giving up nuclear weapons, he had no intention of doing so on the USSR's terms. Many of his colleagues and advisers were relieved, and it transpired that they and the British had been working for the same outcome. George Shultz was particularly grateful to Thatcher. The part she played was significant not because she changed the minds of American politicians and experts but because she reinforced the views of those who wanted to confine US-Soviet interaction to what they considered to be correct and advantageous; those who favoured the Reykjavik proposals regretted her intervention. The leaders of Western Europe were thankful for her determination and her ability to gain Reagan's attention so quickly, and the statement issued

by Britain in November 1986 provided the basis for a NATO declaration on nuclear weapons in June 1987.[31]

By this time Reagan and his closest advisers were hoping to conclude an INF agreement with the Soviet Union without further
delay. Embarrassed by 'Irangate', the White House needed a foreign policy success to compensate, and Gorbachev's popularity in
America was rapidly growing on account of his reformist ideas and
his efforts to reduce international tension. Reagan was confident
that the American people would welcome the INF Treaty and that
he could sign it without having to say he had been wrong about
the USSR. The treaty could be presented as the outcome of the
'zero option' first proposed by Washington DC in 1981. Another
reason for making a bargain, as far as Reagan was concerned, was
his belief that America was winning the Cold War.[32]

British leaders greeted the INF Treaty as an important achievement and argued that it proved the importance of bargaining from
a position of strength. Had matters been left to the Labour Party,
the government claimed, the Soviets would have retained most of
their missiles. Concerns that had been developing in recent years,
however, now came to the surface. What would happen to Trident
and where did the removal of American intermediate range missiles leave 'flexible response'? Thatcher decided that disarmament
had gone far enough. She did not want NATO to seek a treaty
on battlefield nuclear weapons and urged Britain's allies not to
undermine 'flexible response' or disconnect European defence
from the US strategic deterrent. The United States and Britain
favoured the updating of short-range nuclear weaponry, but the
FRG wanted a new approach: all of NATO's remaining ground-
based missiles were either situated in or aimed at Germany, and
Kohl was angry about what he took to be inadequate consultation
on the part of the Americans.[33]

The Thatcher government remained very sensitive about the
high cost of defence. Back in June 1981 a thorough review had
arranged for cuts in spending, mostly affecting the Royal Navy. One
of the main reasons for the reallocation of resources was to find
enough money for Trident, and then the Falklands War meant that
some of the economies promised in the review had to be given up.
By the end of the 1980s about 8 per cent of the defence budget was
being spent on Trident. The real cost was even higher, for a careful scrutiny of the defence estimates reveals that the government

excluded some of the costs associated with Trident. Perhaps 20 per cent of the total defence budget was taken up by the Trident programme. There were continuing calls for its cancellation.[34]

Anglo-American defence relations remained close in the Thatcher years. Obviously collaboration was necessary on Trident and INF, but there were other examples of cooperation. In April 1986, in retaliation for acts of terrorism that were allegedly sponsored by Colonel Gaddafi, the Americans bombed Libya using aircraft based in Britain. Thatcher was widely condemned for allowing the US bases to be used in this way. The operation was outside the NATO framework, and several governments in Western Europe had indignantly refused to have anything to do with it. There was more distance between London and Washington DC on the Strategic Defence Initiative, the American attempt to develop a shield against incoming nuclear missiles that would extend beyond the earth's atmosphere and employ advanced laser and particle-beam technology. British experts doubted the feasibility of all this, but the Reagan administration persisted. Thatcher and other senior ministers were worried because SDI represented a shift from deterrence to defence, which was a negation of British strategy, and because there was a possibility that British and American thinking would take separate paths. The project also threatened to make existing offensive weapons obsolete. Even if it did not, massive expenditure would be needed to ensure the continued effectiveness of these weapons, which would be disastrous for Britain and its comparatively small nuclear force. Britain's foreign secretary, Geoffrey Howe, in a speech of March 1985, argued that SDI would cause instability, divide NATO and provoke an arms race. Nobody could be sure that the technology would even work, he added, and in any case deterrence was better than defence. Howe wanted SDI to be included in the US-Soviet negotiations, but Washington DC refused. Though Thatcher agreed with some of Howe's points, she was willing for British companies and experts to participate in 'star wars' because she wanted Britain to have a share in any economic and technological benefits that might result. She told Reagan that she had not given her blessing for Howe's speech, while Howe remained wary of the hawkish elements in Washington DC. In September 1983 he had stressed the need to find 'fresh ways of getting through to the Soviet leadership'. He wanted dialogue, to encourage reforms in the USSR and eastern bloc and to promote westernization, pluralism and openness, and as things turned out he and his fellow sceptics were right to raise questions about SDI. In 1988 the US joint chiefs of staff admitted that SDI would probably allow America to intercept no more than 30 per cent of enemy missiles. By 1990 the programme had cost $16.5 billion. From the late 1980s it was dramatically scaled down, although in later years there were commentators who insisted that it had intimidated Moscow and helped the United States to win the Cold War.[35]

Thatcher's unwillingness to quarrel with the Americans on SDI was related to her fear that 'star wars' might open up a bigger gap between US and European security interests and lead, in particular, to the effective removal of the nuclear deterrence she considered essential for the protection of Britain and Western Europe. She was also aware of the pressure that was building up in Congress for the withdrawal of American forces from Europe. She therefore sought to influence Washington DC by emphasizing her reliability and goodwill. As the prospects for an INF agreement improved, Thatcher again had to combine with the Americans in the hope of influencing them. The Anglo-American 'special relationship' was not greatly damaged in these years, and Britain's cooperation with its European allies on certain issues was not permitted to interfere either. The Western European Union (WEU), originally formed in 1954 following the expansion of the Brussels Treaty Organization of 1948, was revived in 1984, and in 1987 London, Paris and Bonn discussed joint action to replace the US missiles that were going to be withdrawn under the INF Treaty. Thatcher never thought of weakening Britain's bond with America, however, and for the ministry of defence the link with the United States still mattered more than anything else.[36]

On the other hand, Thatcher was not reluctant to side with Britain's EC partners when it suited her purpose. Sometimes the end in view was to gain more leverage in Washington DC. This is one of the reasons why Britain could tolerate the revival of WEU as a defence forum. On matters of special concern the prime minister would present Britain's case directly to the Americans. On some issues Thatcher went along with efforts to find a common European policy, though she normally presented this as a way of strengthening NATO, not as an alternative position. For domestic political reasons she liked to act as if she was struggling against error on the part of European leaders. Her demand for a reform of the EC budget, to Britain's benefit, was divisive, but she was also content to pursue British interests in and through European organizations. While she accepted elements of interdependence, though, she did not want these rigidly formalized or institutionalized in the EC framework, much preferring a pragmatic, intergovernmental approach ('We believe in a free Europe', she declared soon after becoming prime minister, 'not in a standardized Europe. Diminish that variety within the member states, and you impoverish the whole Community'). If Thatcher's wish was to work with the Americans, there were exceptions. On SDI, arms control, sanctions against the USSR and other matters, there was a discrepancy between British and US standpoints. But Britain's independence had been shrinking for years. Economic and military resources were in relative decline and changes in superpower relations made it difficult to pursue specifically *British* interests.[37]

London was not enthusiastic about the revival of the WEU, which was more often a setting for discord rather than harmony. The French sought to use it to put pressure on the United States. Belgium, Italy and Luxembourg pushed for a larger defence component in the moves for further European integration. The FRG pointed out that many proposals, though appealing on paper, would not be easy to implement. Thatcher and Howe opposed any premature abandonment of Cold War policies and perspectives, continued to prioritize NATO and warned that security discussions outside NATO were likely to be unhelpful. There was no end to the quarrelling between the Europeans and the Americans on security issues, and there continued also to be disagreements within Western Europe about nuclear weapons and force reductions. The French insisted that the Soviets were reasonable and ready to bargain. The British and Americans considered the French too willing to compromise with the USSR. Britain's defence secretary from 1986 to 1989, George Younger, maintained that British acceptance of further measures of arms reduction would not be unconditional. The worry was that Britain's allies cared more about making agreements, of any kind, than about the actual terms of those agreements. Thatcher, while pleased that NATO's deployment of Cruise and Pershing had prompted the USSR to agree to withdraw its SS20 missiles, repeated her misgivings about the removal of land-based intermediate range missiles from Western Europe and the 'decoupling' of US and European defence planning. The British position was that submarine-launched Cruise missiles and additional aircraft should be provided for the European theatre, to make up for the withdrawal of weapons specified in the INF Treaty. Britain also wanted the FRG's wish for early talks on the reduction of short-range nuclear forces, or SNF, to be resisted.[38]

The prime minister grew strident on the matter because of several basic assumptions: that SNF were needed to protect British troops stationed in Germany; that nuclear weapons were needed to deter conventional as well as nuclear assault; and that eventually Britain's Trident force would be included in the US-Soviet bargaining process. When Gorbachev met with Thatcher in December 1987, she explained that Britain felt the need to retain its nuclear deterrent because of the USSR's superiority over NATO in conventional forces and chemical weapons. She also suggested that if Moscow showed a willingness to listen to the West's complaints on Afghanistan and human rights, the US Senate would be less likely to block ratification of the INF Treaty. Gorbachev replied that a solution in Afghanistan might be possible if the West stopped arming the insurgents there, and he adhered to the familiar argument that every state should be free to resolve its human rights issues in its own way without outside interference.[39]

Clearly there would continue to be disagreements between the West and the Soviet Union, but a more immediate problem for Thatcher was the changing political environment and its impact on US policy and NATO strategy. The INF Treaty was signed and ratified, progress was made with START (Strategic Arms Reduction Talks), Reagan agreed to visit Moscow and in February 1988, Gorbachev announced that Soviet troops would begin to leave Afghanistan within three months. Still NATO struggled with the SNF question. Bonn was more interested in SNF reduction than SNF modernization. London and Washington DC insisted that talks on SNF reduction should only commence after the Soviets made definite undertakings, including a parity deal on conventional forces and a ban on chemical weapons. Thatcher followed a consistent line in her statements to parliament. She regularly argued that it was the West's resolve that had prompted the Soviets to negotiate and that her cautious stance on disarmament would serve Britain's interests much better than the Labour Party's anti-nuclear predilections could ever do. In nuclear bargaining, the prime minister insisted, the cardinal requirement was to ensure that the West did not give up more than the Soviet Union, and this had to be seen in the context of overall nuclear capability, not just one part of it. Therefore the INF Treaty had to be accompanied by a deal on weapons with a shorter range. In June 1988 the prime minister ridiculed the idea that disarmament could proceed on a missile-for-missile basis. This made no sense, she said, when the USSR had so many more missiles than the West.[40]

In the late 1980s hawkish elements in Washington DC were still influential, which explains the reluctance to give way to Bonn's preferences on SNF. There was confusion as governments and interest groups tried to pursue their own aims and adjust to new circumstances. Thatcher continued to worry about the 'decoupling' of US and European arrangements and about the possibility that Washington DC would go against the wishes of America's allies. Kohl was also worried about this, the more so as controversy grew in the FRG about Soviet intentions and the effects of the INF Treaty on the FRG's security. In France the INF Treaty had a mixed reception. The French had supported NATO's 'dual track' policy, and in Paris it was believed that the treaty marked the success of that policy, yet some French commentators saw in the treaty a damaging tendency towards denuclearization. French concepts of defence did not embrace such a goal.[41]

For years Thatcher had insisted that strong defences and negotiations with the Soviets should go together. She was sure that Gorbachev would continue to bargain with the West and that the improving communication between the Americans and Soviets owed something to British influence. On a personal level she saw that her dealings with Gorbachev had helped both of them to gain more credibility as world leaders. All of this had contributed to the favourable context for the INF Treaty and the progress that was being made in other areas of détente. On arms control Thatcher wanted a step-by-step process. She disliked the idea of an all-encompassing deal and opposed denuclearization, but London's bilateral relationships with Washington DC and Moscow were becoming less significant, and Thatcher was quarrelling with her counterparts in Western Europe over the future shape of the EC. Increasingly out of step with other leaders in the EC and NATO, she was still talking about the Cold War while they were stressing the changes in East-West relations. Thatcher repeatedly told

Kohl that updated SNF were essential for 'flexible response'. She also made this point to Reagan's successor as US president, George Bush. Relations between London and Bonn deteriorated. It was rumoured that Kohl wanted a 'third zero': NATO would not modernize its short-range nuclear forces or require the Soviets to reduce their SNF levels to those of NATO. Kohl promised Thatcher that he would not press for the 'third zero', but he also maintained that it was politically impossible for him to accept that there should be no negotiations to control those categories of weapons that most affected the FRG. Thatcher warned that if he persisted, he would pull NATO apart. He was doing exactly what the USSR wanted, she thought, since the Soviets had strong SNF and wished to delay the improvement of NATO's SNF. The clash with Kohl increased her fear that the FRG was displacing Britain as the United States' main ally. The first head of government to visit Reagan as president had been Thatcher. The first to visit President Bush was Kohl. This was a sign that Washington DC recognized the FRG's political and economic power. Indeed, to get anything done in Europe the Americans had to deal primarily with Bonn.[42]

Thatcher tried to convince Bush that NATO would agree to strengthen its SNF if Britain and the United States stood firm. She realized in May 1989 that Bush was not to be relied upon. Without consulting London, Washington DC decided that SNF negotiations with Moscow should go ahead. Thatcher demanded substantial Soviet SNF reductions towards the NATO level and asserted that no deal should be finalized prior to NATO's deployment of new missiles. She did not carry these points, though she managed to convince NATO that the Soviets should at least be required to cut their conventional forces. NATO's position was shaped more by Bush and Kohl than by Thatcher. She had to accept that the FRG was not going to deploy new short-range weapons even though this refusal would deprive NATO of missiles below the range specified in the INF Treaty. The political situation and the state of public opinion in the FRG were such, Kohl declared, that it was not possible to deploy new missiles (aimed, he stressed, at other Germans). Bush sided with Kohl. NATO and the Warsaw Pact agreed to cut their conventional forces, to an equal level, in order to end the conventional imbalance that had made short-range missiles necessary. The task of replacing NATO's SNF was postponed indefinitely.[43]

Summary

On nuclear matters Britain's influence remained significant, but more frequently the initiative was passing to others, and that there was a limit to what could be accomplished in NATO, and in collective bargaining more generally, is obvious from Thatcher's experiences in the late 1980s. The British had been successful in keeping their deterrent credible and in excluding it from the US-Soviet agreements of the period, but it was not clear that these advantages could be preserved in the longer term. The economic and political rise of the FRG was a related problem, for Bonn wanted more say on a host of issues that affected Britain, including nuclear weapons. An older, simpler, bipolar structure of world power was giving way to an international order that was in many respects multipolar: important questions had to be settled on the basis of wider consultation and broader agreement, and in this context Britain's influence was sometimes enhanced but sometimes more restricted than before, and the usefulness of the 'special relationship' with America could not be taken for granted.

7 The Approach of Victory in the Cold War

The problem of nuclear weapons proliferation outlasted the Cold War, which finally came to an end with the economic and political collapse of the USSR and eastern bloc. The Gorbachev reforms in the Soviet Union from the mid-1980s had a swift impact on the bloc, and the most dramatic change was the fall of the communist regime in the GDR, for there were no more potent or emotive symbols of the Cold War than the Berlin Wall and division of Germany. East Germany had developed as a disciplined one-party state. The GDR's premier, Erich Honecker, disliked Gorbachev's reforms, and his government and others in the eastern bloc became increasingly uncomfortable. Their position ultimately depended on Soviet readiness to intervene if they were challenged by internal opponents, but from 1985 Gorbachev was telling them to change with the times. In 1988 he announced a phased withdrawal of Soviet troops from the bloc. Moscow no longer saw Eastern Europe as a vital buffer, and Gorbachev wanted to persuade the West that there was no need to keep large forces and nuclear weapons directed against the USSR. Honecker defiantly declared that the GDR and Berlin Wall were permanent, yet he could not prevent popular agitation or the exodus from East Germany when Hungary opened its border with Austria in September 1989.[1]

The West and centrifugal pressures in the communist bloc

British observers were fascinated by these events. A demonstration in Leipzig on 23 October 1989, thought to have been attended by 250,000 people, led Conservative MPs to chide the Labour Party and associate it with 'discredited' causes such as economic collectivism and state control. The subsequent change of leadership in the GDR and the opening of its borders prompted Francis Maude, minister of state at the foreign office, to talk of 'a sudden seismic movement in history'. He declared that a point of no return had been passed, called for free elections in the GDR, and encouraged the European Community to extend 'the hand of friendship' to the emerging democracies of Eastern Europe. Demands for reform in Hungary, Poland, Czechoslovakia and especially the GDR arose less from a political awakening, argued the *Observer*, than from communism's failure to deliver higher standards of living. What the people of the bloc wanted most was economic progress, and if established elites wished to retain authority they would have to increase their popular support. They also had to distance themselves from Moscow, for 'popular means national even more than it does democratic'. In the GDR, it was not possible for communists to become 'popular'. The people felt no loyalty towards the regime. After Honecker's fall, the *Economist* expected the new government of the GDR to offer reforms, either to buy time or in a genuine effort to address the country's problems. *The Times* argued that Honecker's opposition to reform and failure to correct the GDR's economic ills had made his 'ignominious departure' inevitable. His successor Egon Krenz, former head of national security, was not trusted by the leaders of the popular movement. They did not believe that he would make concessions. For other bloc leaders the same problem was looming: 'Gorbachev plus popular discontent equals change'. These leaders had to understand that the people were to be pacified with reforms, not with tanks. In a similar vein, US newspapers called upon elites in the eastern bloc to cast off the inflexibility of the past. Further disorder and protest seemed likely unless there was power sharing, open debate and the provision of rights and opportunities for the people.[2]

Britain's official response to these developments was conditioned by the improvement in Anglo-Soviet relations in the mid-1980s, which in turn had a wider impact on defence planning and foreign policy. The Thatcher government approved of Gorbachev's reforms, and the prime minister's aversion to communism was mitigated by the need and the opportunity for a new understanding with the USSR. Even before Honecker's fall and the dismantling of the Berlin Wall, it was thought that the Cold War, Anglo-Soviet relations and the East-West division would never fall back into the pattern they had once had. Thatcher and her colleagues and supporters liked to think that British pressure in the early 1980s and then the shift towards a thaw with Moscow had a significant impact on the course of the Cold War. Cooperation with Reagan and an openly anti-Soviet stance, according to this interpretation, made plain Britain's resilience before Gorbachev's rise to power. Thereafter, a less confrontational approach on Britain's part made possible a new relationship. British thinking was already moving in this direction by June 1984, when the defence secretary, Michael Heseltine, declared that the USSR had legitimate security concerns and that the West, while remaining vigilant, should also be ready to listen to the Soviets. Successive foreign secretaries were in favour of more communication with Moscow. Lord Carrington (1979–82), Francis Pym (1982–83) and Geoffrey Howe (1983–89) all looked to promote a thaw in different ways, and Thatcher welcomed the changes that were evident in the communist bloc, although she added a note of caution, pointing out that nobody could be sure where these changes would lead. Instability might increase, she warned, with border disputes and ethnic conflicts. Through it all, the West would have to be careful. Much to Thatcher's frustration, political change in Europe made the FRG more important to the Americans and she was no longer needed by the latter as an inter-mediary between Washington DC and Moscow, while her resist-ance to closer European integration caused problems domestically as well as in foreign policy.[3]

Events in Germany affected Britain's dealings with both the FRG and GDR. During the 1970s there had been attempts to increase Britain's trade with the GDR. After Thatcher's appointment as prime minister and the Soviet invasion of Afghanistan, Britain began more clearly to differentiate between those regimes in the eastern bloc that were close to Moscow and those that were more independent. The GDR was judged to be a loyal satellite. Some contacts between Britain and the GDR continued despite this, and by opposing German reunification Thatcher in effect argued for the continued existence of the GDR. She tried to separate reform in East Germany from the question of reunification. Chancellor Kohl refused to delay reunification, however, and President Bush backed him, not Thatcher. She also had reason to condemn the French. Instead of standing with Britain they opted for a familiar solution and looked to contain a strong Germany through further European integration, to which Thatcher was averse. The Berlin Wall was breached, Kohl outlined his plan for reunification, and in February 1990 British foreign secretary Douglas Hurd formally announced that Britain would accept it. Germany was finally reunited in October 1990.[4]

Thatcher continued to use Cold War rhetoric. She thought that the international order was changing too much and too quickly. In order to shore up Britain's influence she did what she could to guide and limit what was happening. She had a personal stake in this, because her image as the 'Iron Lady', how she defined herself and what made her appealing to British voters were linked with the Cold War and a positive view of British power. Thatcher and those who thought like her were uneasy about the consequences of change and feared that none of the major powers could control the course of events. Indeed, the ending of the Cold War resulted in part from long-term trends, especially political, military and economic. The disintegration of the eastern bloc had been coming for some time, whatever the plans and policies of the two superpowers and their allies.[5]

Thatcher had first visited the Soviet Union in the late 1960s. While Soviet propaganda painted a picture of social superiority, Thatcher found the USSR characterless and grey. She later recalled the 'empty shops and badly maintained housing blocks'. Cultural achievements originating in pre-communist times were still evident, but conditions were hard for ordinary people. Thatcher's ideological convictions and practical experience made her certain that communism could not survive, primarily because it was not economically viable and 'could never in the end mobilize human talent and energy'. The notion that daily life under communism was almost a fate worse than death was an exaggeration. But even if individuals in the USSR and eastern bloc were not as downtrodden as many in the West assumed, the fact remains that, economically, communist countries were outperformed by the West. Economic growth in the bloc was slow in comparison with the rest of Europe. Historically Eastern Europe had lagged behind, and in the post-1945 era state socialism did not enable it to catch up. This is not to deny that the potential for greater growth existed. The bloc's main problem was the consistent failure to bring real progress into line with potential progress. Gradually some flexibility was allowed, and market forces were tolerated alongside the planning. More consumer goods became available. There were more foreign loans and imports. The eastern bloc's wealth per capita reached 82 per cent of Western Europe's by 1973. By the 1980s over half of the bloc's trade was realized outside Comecon (which had previously prioritized links between its members and orientated their trade away from the West). Although political protest did emerge from time to time, economic modernization probably helped to stabilize the USSR's satellites, and Moscow did accept some variety within the bloc.[6]

The situation became more difficult for Moscow because of the USSR's stagnating economy. Among other things, there had to be cutbacks in arms production at a time when the contest with the United States was growing more intense, and ten years of war in Afghanistan represented a serious drain on top of the Soviet Union's other commitments. Afghanistan was a defeat, moreover, which dented Soviet prestige. Economic failure affected political influence. Under Brezhnev between 15 and 25 per cent of all production had been linked to defence. The needs of the people were neglected. There were mounting social problems: alcoholism, food shortages, the lack of consumer goods, a housing crisis, the black market, a crumbling urban infrastructure, pollution, poor health, and there was also corruption, notably in the USSR's Asian republics. By itself, perhaps, social chaos was not enough to destroy the communist order, but economic exhaustion meant that everything else began to fail too, and the lack of freedom, coupled with the knowledge of the alternative life available in the West, sapped the regime's authority. Brezhnev died in 1982. The party elite elected two ailing men in quick succession, Andropov and Chernenko, both of whom died, and in 1985 Gorbachev became Soviet leader. He arranged the withdrawal from Afghanistan, inaugurated a period of reform and openness (not to end the communist system, but to make it more efficient), suspended the 'Brezhnev Doctrine' and concluded agreements with the Americans. As Thatcher put it, he moved international relations into 'new territory'.[7]

The 'Brezhnev Doctrine' was obsolete before Gorbachev took power. The key development was the crisis in Poland in 1980–81. Civil unrest and demands for reform led the Polish leader, General Wojciech Jaruzelski, to impose martial law. It was the Polish government that intervened, not the Soviets, probably because Moscow wished to avoid a repeat of the 1968 invasion of Czechoslovakia and realized that the 'Brezhnev Doctrine' no longer offered an appropriate framework for relations with the eastern bloc. Détente had altered the context fundamentally and the bloc's leaders had decided that their interests and those of the USSR did not always coincide. The USSR might not have been in a position to do much about Poland in any case. Already engaged militarily in Afghanistan and elsewhere, and with social and economic malaise at home, the Soviet leadership felt more vulnerable than it had for some time. A major concern was the arms race and the inability to keep up with the Americans.[8]

It is possible that the shift in international affairs in the late 1980s had more to do with long-term processes inside the USSR, combined with the Gorbachev reforms, than with the confrontational stance of the United States and the West. Scepticism about the communist system had been growing, and when Gorbachev proved unable to control reform from above, the popular pressure for reorganization became irresistible. This was true of the bloc as well as the Soviet Union. In the West it had been understood that the death of Brezhnev opened the way for change, but there was no consensus on what the results would be. Former US secretary of state Henry Kissinger told journalists that he did not expect a significant reshaping of East-West relations. In Britain the leader of the Labour Party, Michael Foot, said that the new Soviet leader should follow Brezhnev's example and pursue détente and disarmament. Former prime minister and foreign secretary Lord Home considered it unwise to make predictions, while the Moscow correspondent of *The Times* reported that the mood there was one of 'no change abroad, maybe some at home'. In the same issue of *The Times* the USSR was described as 'a country waiting for change, but one so paralysed by political, economic and ideological inertia that any change will be painful and difficult, and threatens to unleash an avalanche of pent-up frustrations'. After nearly two decades in power, Brezhnev's death left 'a vacuum of enormous proportions', remarked the *Guardian*, and the prospects were not altogether comforting, not least because détente had been widely dismissed as a failure.[9]

When Gorbachev rose to power, the *Guardian* referred to a new generation (Gorbachev was about twenty years younger than most members of the Soviet ruling group) and a new approach. The *Economist* looked forward to a 'revolution'. *The Times* urged its readers not to expect too much. Gorbachev wanted to promote economic efficiency at home and favoured détente with the West, but it was not clear that he really stood for thorough change. While he said he wanted to reduce tension he was also following a familiar Soviet line, encouraging Western Europe and Japan to break away from America. There were many in the West who thought that Gorbachev should be offered inducements, to encourage his reformist tendencies, but *The Times* argued that he should pull out of Afghanistan first.[10]

On Afghanistan it took time for Gorbachev to get the West to trust him. In the autumn of 1985 he told Reagan that Soviet forces would not remain in Afghanistan and that he wanted a political settlement, but the Americans did not show much interest in a joint approach to the problem. Gorbachev explained to US secretary of state George Shultz in February 1988 that the Soviet Union needed American help to turn Afghanistan into an independent, neutral and non-aligned state. The Americans became more cooperative, and eventually President Bush agreed that the United States would stop sending weapons into Afghanistan. This facilitated the Soviet withdrawal, after which there were to be free elections under UN supervision. The details were worked out in June 1990.[11]

The fact that the leaders of the West were willing and able to 'do business' with Gorbachev in the later 1980s showed how much the world had changed since the Czech crisis of 1968. In the early 1970s, when Home was Britain's foreign secretary, his outlook was that of an experienced Cold Warrior. He published his autobiography in 1976 and, in it, repeatedly urged that the West could not relax. Even if relations with the USSR improved, 'all communists are dedicated to a single end, victory over every other creed and every other way of life'. For contemporaries who agreed with Home there was no expectation that circumstances would change as dramatically as they did. Although there were others who did not rule out a fundamental change in the international order, they did not think it would happen for some time. During the 1970s, the Labour foreign secretary and prime minister Callaghan predicted that the Soviets would have to come to an understanding with the West because their economy could not support the high defence spending and aggressive momentum of Brezhnev's regime. Lord Carrington visited the Soviet Union in November 1978. He was struck by the 'drab, sad and oppressive' atmosphere and noted that 'Russian inefficiency' was 'general and seemingly endemic'. He later wrote that the USSR was probably weaker than the West supposed.[12]

Even so, there is little indication that the Thatcher government really expected the changes that occurred at the end of the 1980s. While praising Gorbachev's reforms and diplomacy, Thatcher maintained that the Soviets were still dangerous and that the West must be resolute. To the prime minister, the USSR's actions in Asia and Africa showed intent, Soviet military deployments in Europe showed capability, and the threat was real and had to be opposed. Failure to anticipate the end of the Cold War did not mean that there was no awareness of the USSR's problems. Rather, it was assumed that the defects in the Soviet system were not serious enough decisively to reduce Soviet power. Western economists, the intelligence services, government advisers, scholars and other experts all knew that the Soviet Union was suffering economically in the 1980s, but they did not think that a collapse was coming. After the 1980s, as more information became available, it was understood that the Soviet economy was only about a third of the size of America's and that western estimates of per capita income and productivity in the USSR were way off the mark. Another reason why the Soviet Union's problems were not fully appreciated relates to the political contention in the West between hawks and doves. Hardliners favoured confrontation while their opponents wanted a more constructive relationship with Moscow. This produced a serious ideological split, especially in the United States. In addition, there was a growing sense in the West that the USSR could be reformed and that Gorbachev would deal with its economic and other problems. As British foreign secretary between 1979 and 1982 and secretary-general of NATO from 1984 to 1988, Carrington shared Thatcher's view that the Soviets posed a continuing threat. He thought that in dealing with Moscow it was important to bear in mind the long-standing Soviet desire to weaken the West, although he did welcome the agreements between Reagan and Gorbachev.[13]

In due course it became clear that, as some in the West had been saying, the Soviets were indeed experiencing the full effects of over-extension and economic failure. The USSR's power faded quickly in the 1980s. The states of the eastern bloc soon went their own way. As economic performance continued to decline within the USSR and the high level of military spending proved to be unsustainable, the economic situation in the bloc also deteriorated. Pressure for reforms increased. The legitimacy of governments was questioned. Corrupt party elites and their extravagant lifestyles brought discredit upon those who held office, especially in Rumania and the GDR. There were more protests about human rights abuses, and some of Eastern Europe's dissidents became famous in the West. Thatcher insisted on meeting them when she visited the eastern bloc. The Helsinki Accords of 1975 may have been a false dawn, but memories of that time and that mood revived in the 1980s. There was something to build on. In Czechoslovakia the Charter 77 movement inspired a new crop of agitators. In Poland a burgeoning of national pride, the rise of the Solidarity trade union and the election of a Polish pope in 1978 merged together to provide fresh hope. American foreign policy under Carter focused heavily on human rights. The Reagan administration did not regard human rights as a priority, but still included them in its wider anti-communist machinations.[14]

Human rights and East-West relations

Britain often used its contacts with eastern bloc countries in the 1970s and 1980s to bring up humanitarian issues, but the impact was limited. The GDR, for instance, remained close to the USSR, and its government was one of the most repressive regimes in the bloc. Although London pressed the East German leadership to show more respect for human rights, the main effort was in the economic sphere. Trade was seen as a way of influencing the GDR's internal policies. The volume of trade between Britain and the GDR remained small, however, and it did not help the British economy or change the nature of the government in East Germany. On the other hand, the GDR's leaders *were* interested in finding out what could be gained from the European thaw, and this affected their treatment of internal criticism in a limited way. Despite Moscow's lack of sympathy for the human rights aspects of CSCE, they played an important role in British foreign policy during the Callaghan years. Callaghan supported the Helsinki process and repeatedly brought up the plight of Soviet dissidents in his conversations with Gromyko, the USSR's foreign minister. He did not seek to embarrass the Soviet government but gave it opportunities to respond unofficially and in its own time. This calm approach paid off: 'It was my experience that if we did not make huge publicity about certain cases, dissidents and Jews were often quietly allowed to leave'. The main point for Callaghan was, while exercising restraint, to leave the Soviets in no doubt that the West expected progress on humanitarian issues. Howe did the same after his appointment as foreign secretary in 1983. His early exchanges with Gromyko were difficult. Howe complained that the Soviets were not committed to the Helsinki process. He blamed them for the deadlock that prevented agreement at CSCE meetings in Madrid in September 1983 and Stockholm in January 1984. Still, after his visit to Moscow in July 1984 and his tour of several countries in Eastern Europe in the spring of 1985, he was satisfied that he had reaffirmed Britain's commitment to the human rights agenda. Thatcher spoke more about human rights during the later 1980s than she had done previously, because she considered it important to challenge as well as to bargain with the Gorbachev regime. In a speech of March 1987, prior to an official visit to the USSR, the prime minister declared that peace could only exist when there was trust. If Moscow wanted to be trusted, why did it not honour the obligations freely accepted in the Helsinki Final Act? Thatcher later recalled Gorbachev's 'tetchiness' whenever she tried to discuss human rights with him. She noted in her memoirs (which contain many such self-congratulatory passages) that she 'always believed that our western system would ultimately triumph'. It is easy to be wise after the event, but Thatcher did live up to her convictions by consistently bringing up humanitarian issues with the Soviets.[15]

The Thatcher government had elucidated a position on these matters shortly after it was appointed in 1979. By this time it was normal practice for the foreign office to issue reports on the implementation of the Helsinki Final Act every six months, and in June 1979 the new minister of state, Peter Blaker, informed parliament that implementation by the USSR and eastern bloc remained 'slow'. In Czechoslovakia and the Soviet Union, Helsinki monitors, dissidents, critics and religious groups had been persecuted. The leaders of Charter 77 were among those targeted. In the GDR there had been a crackdown on dissidents and journalists from the West were subject to severe restrictions. Western journalists were also being harassed in the Soviet Union. Some had been expelled. In Rumania many reformers and trade unionists had been detained. In Poland teachers and rural dissidents were being arrested. Blaker described the CSCE review conference at

Belgrade as 'disappointing'. If the next meeting (in Madrid) was not better, he thought, the Helsinki process would lose momentum and credibility. Early in 1980 *The Times* pointed to recent crackdowns against dissidents as evidence that Moscow did not care about international opinion and was determined to defy the West's sanctions following the invasion of Afghanistan. The *Observer* reported on long-term political 'offenders' as well as the recent spate of fines, shorter prison sentences, interrogations, house searches and other acts of tyranny, and suggested that the Kremlin was out to quash dissent in the period leading up to the 1980 Olympics in Moscow and the CSCE meeting in Madrid. The *Economist* denied that repression was attributable to the West's response to the invasion of Afghanistan: the 'purge' began before the invasion, at a time when Carter was still trying to persuade the US Senate to ratify the SALT II treaty. American newspapers condemned the crackdown and hailed the dissidents (famous or otherwise) as heroes.[16]

The Gorbachev period did bring a relaxation of internal discipline inside the USSR. Britain's importance also increased in Soviet eyes in the 1980s, owing to the British victory in the Falklands War, Thatcher's strong leadership and evidence of Britain's economic recovery after the difficulties of the 1970s and early 1980s. British leaders welcomed the changes in the Soviet Union but remained wary about bargaining with the USSR, more so than governments in Western Europe, and Moscow still preferred to negotiate with Bonn and Paris rather than London. On humanitarian issues there was a change in the West's tactics. The CSCE meeting in Belgrade in 1977–78 had been a confrontational affair, although the Soviets and their allies did agree to an ongoing review of humanitarian issues. To many of those who saw Belgrade as a failure, the focus on human rights had been a mistake. A balanced perspective had been lost, and, since détente was itself faltering, neither side cared enough about making CSCE work. The follow-up meeting in Madrid opened in November 1980. CSCE was becoming institutionalized as part of a multilateral framework of contact and debate, but the Madrid conference took place at a time when East-West relations were strained by the invasion of Afghanistan, the Polish crisis, crackdowns in the USSR and eastern bloc, the rise of the conservative right in the United States, NATO missile deployments and the suspicion in the West that

Moscow wanted to abandon CSCE altogether. At Madrid the West chose not to concentrate on humanitarian issues. More time was devoted to security matters than had been the case at Belgrade. Eventually a concluding statement was agreed at Madrid, reinforcing the commitments made in the Helsinki Final Act, including those on human rights, and in return the Soviets were promised a conference in Stockholm in 1984 to discuss confidence-building measures and security and disarmament in Europe. The change in tactics therefore brought results. Moscow was still to be pressed on human rights, but less stridently or openly than before. Madrid was also significant because it was the place where the Soviets struck back. They stressed that one concept of human rights was not necessarily less valid than another. Western ideas about the relationship between the individual and the state had reduced the question to a matter of protecting people from government infringements. To the Soviets, this did not apply to socialist states, for the socialist system was itself a guarantee of rights.[17]

The two sides were not speaking the same language. The interpretation of détente endorsed by NATO's political committee was that it was a long-term political and strategic policy, designed to reduce tension, avoid war, strengthen cooperation and enlarge areas of mutual interest. In the USSR and eastern bloc, détente had for years been seen in the context of peaceful coexistence, which entailed competition – not war, unless it was unavoidable, but certainly ongoing ideological, military and economic rivalry. Human rights represented one instrument in this struggle. Arguments at Madrid and afterwards about human rights, trade, disarmament, Afghanistan and other questions often touched on the Helsinki framework, and here too there was a difference in approach. The two sides did not define 'non-intervention' in the same way and disagreed about the extent to which one state could legitimately seek to influence another. Britain's view was that in an interdependent world, it was inevitable and desirable that states should be interested in each other's actions. The purpose of international law was not to prevent them from influencing each other, the British thought, but to ensure that this influence was compatible with the sovereign equality of states and the self-determination of peoples. These ideas were rejected by the Soviets, who saw no justification for interference in the internal affairs of other states. There was a snag, in that Moscow was committed to spreading socialism, and therefore the Soviet concept of 'non-intervention' applied primarily to interstate relations. Non-governmental activity was not covered, since only governments were bound by international law. The West did not accept this distinction. The correct way to deal with humanitarian problems, argued Moscow, was for one government to raise a specific matter with another. It was that simple. Moscow's definition of 'non-intervention' did not apply to apartheid, fascism, colonialism, aggression, racial discrimination or genocide, for these phenomena were obvious violations of human rights and threatened world peace, and, as the UN Charter had established, in such cases no state could be allowed to shelter behind its domestic jurisdiction.[18]

Economic intercourse and its effects

In undermining the Soviet system and hastening the end of the Cold War, the West's persistence and pressure on humanitarian issues played a major part. Probably even more important, however, were the economic problems of the Soviet Union and its allies and the consequences for the communist states of economic interaction with the West.

Positive engagement with the USSR and bloc, with more contacts and the expansion of trade, weakened the foundations of the Soviet system. The Kremlin had long assumed that if western ideas were allowed in they would prove to be popular. More knowledge about the freedom and comforts enjoyed in the West increased the resentment against privation and repression. Meanwhile, despite some economic innovation bloc countries gradually became dependent on western loans. Massive borrowing meant that about $70 billion was owed by 1980. Bankruptcy was looming throughout the bloc, which further highlighted the economic gap between East and West. Many people in the bloc associated prosperity with the capitalism and even the political systems of Western Europe and the United States. This tendency grew stronger as communist reform failed.[19]

The Carter administration made American economic help dependent on human rights improvements, which meant that in the late 1970s some eastern bloc countries began to be viewed more favourably than others. Evidence of change in Poland, for instance, prompted Carter to extend that country's credit.

Czechoslovakia, having borrowed less, was not so amenable. One consequence was that reformers in the two countries fared differently: Charter 77 in Czechoslovakia suffered heavier persecution than that experienced by Polish dissidents and protesters. The eastern bloc's indebtedness made some leaders in the West apprehensive about the imposition of sanctions against Poland and the USSR after martial law was declared in Poland in December 1981. The fear was that American overreaction would cause the Poles to default on their loans. Thatcher warned that this would affect most of Eastern Europe, with potentially disastrous consequences for the banking system in the West. The Siberian gas pipeline also figured in these arguments, the main point being that sanctions would bother the authorities in Poland and the Soviet Union less than they would damage the economies of Western Europe. Thatcher saw at first hand the distress in Poland when she visited the country in November 1988. As was her wont, she drew from this a political lesson: people in the eastern bloc would not take up 'economic responsibility' unless they were granted the personal freedoms enjoyed in the West. Carrington had come to a similar conclusion when he visited Poland in October 1980. Without the relaxation of state communism, he thought, there could be little economic progress.[20]

Britain had actively promoted the opening up of economic links between the West and the USSR and its satellites. As prime minister from 1974 to 1976 this was one of Harold Wilson's chief concerns. Early in 1975 he signed deals on commerce and loans with the USSR that included the provision of generous trade credits. Trade was subsequently promoted by the Anglo-Soviet Round Table, to which a number of influential businessmen belonged, and trade also featured in the Callaghan-Gromyko talks in London in March 1976.[21]

Callaghan's government was eager to increase Britain's trade with the Soviet Union and Eastern Europe, but questions were frequently raised in parliament. In December 1977, trade secretary Edmund Dell was asked about Poland's ability to pay for British exports. Dell argued that 'Polish credit is good'. Many MPs were not convinced. In February 1978 Dell's under-secretary, Michael Meacher, announced that nearly half of the credit allowed under existing Anglo-Soviet agreements had been taken up (worth about £441 million). Meacher was asked if the credit was being used to develop industries in the USSR. The Soviets appeared to be taking credit in order to produce items that they then sold back to the West at fixed prices. Would this not ruin the West's manufacturers? Meacher suggested that this was a matter for businessmen to attend to, not the government. In July 1978 it was claimed that British credit enabled the Soviets to set aside their own resources for the construction of prisons and other facilities, which they used to curb dissent. Dell told MPs that credit arrangements did not really have this effect. Reminded about America's use of economic assets for political ends, Dell insisted that economic pressure was not a means of influence that Britain could successfully employ against the Soviets. The United States sold far more to the USSR than did Britain.[22]

Early in 1980, the *Guardian* suggested that Britain's large deficit in trade with the Soviet Union was unsurprising, since British exporters were given little incentive to try harder to break into Soviet markets, and many items could not be sold to the USSR because of the security implications. Sanctions were likely to be imposed following the invasion of Afghanistan and could provide 'welcome relief for Britain's balance of payments problems', but it was ironic that a disruption of Anglo-Soviet trade would occur when 'the two countries have enjoyed unusually harmonious trading relations of late'. In a speech to the British-Soviet Chamber of Commerce in January 1980, Labour MP and opposition trade spokesman John Smith pointed out that economic relations were always affected by political crises. He hoped that disputes could be resolved and the economic side of détente reinforced. Smith did not think that the obstacles to increased trade with the USSR were insurmountable. *The Times* noted that British companies did not favour sanctions against the USSR. Though trade with the Soviet Union had not lived up to expectations over the whole of the post-1945 era, it was still important, and there was a steady demand for Soviet oil, timber and consumer durables. Unfortunately, however, the trade balance was very much in the USSR's favour. Britain's exports to the USSR were worth £423 million in 1978 and £419 million in 1979, but the value of Soviet exports to Britain in these two years was £688 million and £827 million.[23]

Throughout the 1970s and 1980s, one of the main priorities of the Soviet Union and eastern bloc was to update their own industries. They were keen to import products that were technologically

advanced. Buying them gave the Soviets and their allies the benefit of superior western equipment and techniques. Other motives
behind Soviet economic policy included the wish to enhance
military strength and a desire to minimize hard currency costs.
Western companies saw the USSR and eastern bloc as growing
markets, and there were sound commercial reasons for getting
involved: economies of scale, business potential and diversifica-
tion to reduce risk and adjust to fluctuations in demand. For those
sectors with rapidly changing technologies, communist countries
proved to be good customers for proven products and processes
that were reaching the later stages of their life cycle. But the USSR
and bloc had difficulty in expanding their exports to pay for
imports, and western companies routinely had to purchase a large
quantity of items in order to secure contracts. They also had to
help with credit arrangements.[24]

For Britain the situation changed in the early 1980s. Thatcher's
economic and financial policies and the stronger pound and
higher interest rates compared with earlier years affected export
performance and trade with the USSR and eastern bloc. Political
events also had an impact: as détente lost its way the political context for trade became less favourable. In addition, inflation in the
West made its goods more expensive. The British ambassador in
Moscow from 1978 to 1982, Sir Curtis Keble, thought that Britain's
trade with the USSR was limited for two main reasons: the Soviet
economy was 'limping', and 'in some respects we were less well
placed than our European competitors'. Keble thought at the end
of the 1970s that the Soviets, though still in need of American
grain, had turned completely against the Carter administration.
Meanwhile, France and the FRG were winning contracts in the
Soviet Union, and in them the USSR found agreeable trading partners. This reflected 'a political assessment' on the part of Paris
and Bonn. As one Soviet official told Keble, 'they take us more
seriously'. Though Anglo-Soviet trade was quite stable, Britain's
products did better elsewhere. In 1984 only 1.6 per cent of the
USSR's trade was with Britain. About 2.1 per cent of the USSR's
trade was with Japan in 1984, 2.2 per cent was with the United
States, 3 per cent with France, 3.2 per cent with Italy and 5.4 per
cent with the FRG.[25]

The fact that the British and Soviets could not offer substantial economic incentives to each other had an impact on their

political relationship. Britain and the USSR did not become very important to each other economically. Moscow considered British firms to be less competitive than the big companies in Western Europe, and it was easier for the USSR to trade with the FRG, Italy and France because they imported large quantities of Soviet energy. British firms disliked the bureaucratic obstacles surrounding business in the USSR. British entrepreneurs tended to focus on the short term, whereas the Italians and French and especially the West Germans were willing to put in steady effort over several years.[26]

The Thatcher government made a determined effort to expand Britain's economic links with the Soviet Union and eastern bloc in the mid-1980s, when agreements were concluded on exports, finance and credit. Trade with the USSR and bloc continued to represent a small proportion of Britain's overall trade, however, and, as in the 1970s, there was a concern to make sure that Britain did not make concessions that would damage the British economy, some sectors of which remained fragile. Nevertheless, when he was foreign secretary, Howe believed that the Soviet Union and its satellites needed economic help, that this could be used as a lever and that without aid and trade the West's call for reforms in the USSR and bloc would carry less weight.[27]

What became clear after the end of the Cold War was the extent to which Eastern Europe had been affected by decisions made by the G7. The G7's coordination of policy shaped the international order within which bloc countries underwent economic transformation. Led by the United States, Japan and the FRG, and assisted by such institutions as the IMF, the G7 opened the bloc up to outside influences. Trade and debt relations with the West may have had more impact than earlier measures of military and political containment. From the early 1970s, bloc unity was gradually lost as the USSR and its satellites sought loans, food and energy. Closer links with the West gave domestic reform movements a better chance to grow and altered the relationship between the Soviet Union and Eastern Europe. Eventually Moscow decided that earning hard currency mattered more than preserving the economic unity of the bloc. Leaders in the bloc came to the same conclusion. Eastern Europe wanted things that the Soviet Union could not provide but the West could, and the relaxation of central control within Comecon reversed the previous trend towards integration.[28]

Economic developments alone do not explain the break-up of the eastern bloc. Political and military connections also changed. Gorbachev was reluctant to intervene in Eastern Europe and willing for satellite governments to have more autonomy. Some of them used this relative freedom. Others did not, but the longer Gorbachev remained in power the more the Soviet attitude towards Eastern Europe altered. Stability would be more likely, it was decided, if reform-minded communists were in charge. Moscow underestimated the strength of popular feeling across Eastern Europe and the strength of anti-Soviet sentiment as well. The expression of opinion became easier as political change gathered momentum, and Gorbachev's wish for a thaw with the West prompted the departure of some Soviets troops from the bloc. In improving East-West relations, Gorbachev exposed bloc governments to unprecedented domestic challenges.[29]

The Cold War ended largely as a result of problems in the Soviet Union and eastern bloc. This is not to gainsay the economic difficulties in the West, where an end to the Cold War was seen to have obvious benefits if it meant more trade and less expenditure on the armed forces. Following oil crises in 1973 and 1979, the price of almost everything soared in the West. Output fell and hundreds of thousands of industrial jobs were lost during the 1970s. Growth slowed down even in the FRG. The peak year for the FRG was probably 1970, when almost half of all employment was industrial, but in 1982 West Germany had zero growth. After the end of the Bretton Woods system in 1971, exchange rates were in disarray and the stability of the major currencies was less assured. Greater rivalry in trade, technology and investment developed between Western Europe and the United States. In 1970 the FRG was ahead of the rest of Western Europe in GDP. France was in second place, Britain a close third and Italy not far behind. By the end of the 1970s Italy had overtaken Britain, and throughout the 1980s Britain was in fourth place. Changes in comparative GDP per capita followed a similar pattern.[30]

In 1968, when he was prime minister, Wilson had justified the scaling down of Britain's overseas commitments with the reflection that Britain's role in the world depended on the strength of the economy. Economic difficulties directly affected Britain's international position and added to the ongoing controversy over defence. Money spent on defence could not be spent on social programmes, and vice versa, and there was much debate about the appropriate allocation of resources between nuclear and conventional and within and between the army, navy and air force. Defence industries and their place in the British economy were also discussed at length. Some commentators thought that they should be state-owned or at least receive more government assistance.[31]

The British economy was suffering from structural flaws that successive governments could not correct, whatever they tried, and this problem was exacerbated by the short-term perspective of most ministers and by failed initiatives on such matters as financial management, wage restraint and productivity. Policy-makers were slow to realize that the relatively stable and prosperous conditions of the 1950s and 1960s were unusual rather than the norm. The 1970s were marked by the idea, vocabulary and even acceptance of economic decline. Depending on the choice of criteria, however, it is possible to argue that Britain was not performing far below other industrial nations. Statements about decline were often politically motivated, and the situation might not have been as bad as many assumed or, for their own reasons, claimed. Britain's economic experience was not unique, but 'declinism' became a pervasive force in public debate. Thatcher and the Conservatives used it as a party political weapon.[32]

If Britain sometimes lacked confidence on the international stage in the 1970s, this was partly due to economic weakness. The Heath years saw rapid inflation, an oil shock, a growing trade deficit, industrial strife and emergency measures that went against the government's intentions and principles. In the 1980s, North Sea oil was available to help with the balance of payments. Another change was that the Thatcher government's priority was to control inflation, to the extent that high unemployment was regarded as acceptable, whereas the Heath government had tried to combine anti-inflationary measures with an attempt to reduce unemployment. As for disengaging the state from industry, Heath had envisaged a gradual process. Thatcher opted for quicker privatization. In the early years of her premiership, unemployment increased (and would never return to the pre-Thatcher level) and inflation came close to 20 per cent. Growth rates fell. In fact, all the British governments of the 1970s and 1980s proved unable to tackle the problem of low productivity, which held back economic growth.[33]

Relatively high defence spending was a factor as well. Needing the money for other purposes and concerned about the impact on the British economy of the military burden, Thatcher's government tried to bring down expenditure on defence. This necessitated major adjustments, including state planning and intervention, not least to soften the effect on individual industries and regions, and it was clear that reductions could not be carried too far too quickly, for fear of undermining national security. The need to bring military commitments into line with available resources was no less challenging in the 1980s than it had been in the 1970s. The economic consequences of the war in the Middle East in 1973 had demonstrated Britain's vulnerability, and the Labour governments of 1974–79 tried hard to control the defence budget. At the end of the 1970s, NATO members agreed to increase their military spending in response to the USSR's growing strength. The Thatcher government wanted NATO to be stronger and favoured an expansion of Britain's capabilities, and although an economic recession in 1980–81 prompted a more modest approach, seen in the defence review of 1981, responsibilities continued to exceed resources.[34]

High defence spending was not the main reason for Britain's comparatively poor economic performance between the 1950s and 1980s. As a share of total public expenditure, in fact, defence saw a marked reduction over the long term, while spending on welfare, health and education increased. The abandonment of defence commitments provided funds for other things, but substantial sums were still being spent on defence in the 1970s and 1980s, and the general economic situation was much less helpful than it had been in earlier years. Britain was forced to change its conduct on the international stage – to be more flexible and less ambitious – for it was impossible fully to restore the economic supports of British power. Thatcher's ideological approach, a departure from the pragmatism of Heath, Wilson and Callaghan, possibly made things worse. She believed in market forces at home and in the wider world. Britain's economic position did show signs of improvement, but was this due to Thatcherism? Or were economic growth and a healthy balance of payments the result not of government policy but of North Sea oil? What is clear is that Britain was affected more and more by external events that were largely beyond its control.[35]

Summary

Britain had its problems, but it suffered nothing like the political and economic disintegration of the USSR and eastern bloc. The British had learned how to adapt, retreat, reassess and reorganize. The Soviets did not demonstrate the same abilities. British policy played an important role in influencing the course of the Cold War and in shaping the manner in which it was ended. This was not just a matter of Britain's own diplomatic devices and military strength but also involved relations with allies and the long-standing commitment to trade and human rights, a commitment that was shared with others, although Britain went further than they did in certain respects. The changes in Europe were not all to Britain's liking. In fact, some developments did not suit the British government and there was an urgent need to face up to new difficulties and dangers. Developments outside Europe were no less challenging.

8   Extra-European Affairs

Although Britain's role outside Europe decreased after the 1960s, in some regions and on certain issues of concern it was not unimportant. The general pattern was to reduce overseas responsibilities or to share them with others. With respect to the course of the Cold War, it is significant that while the British were reviewing and drawing back from activities beyond Europe, the Soviets were increasing their role. The USSR's problems were exacerbated by the commitments taken on by the Kremlin outside Europe. For Britain, Commonwealth relations, long-standing political and security interests, trade and finance and arrangements for economic and military aid directly influenced the measures pursued in Africa, Asia and the Middle East. Africa in particular presented British leaders with awkward and complex situations during the 1970s and 1980s, and for the West as a whole there were difficulties in engaging with the developing world and in finding an antidote to Soviet intervention there.

Instability in the developing world

In order to survive, the Soviet system had to be seen as successful and efficient. The USSR had to match the United States' military and economic strength. This became impossible, and the result was something like the 'imperial overstretch' described by Paul Kennedy.[1] The rise of China added to Moscow's security concerns, but 'overstretch' became most obvious during the war in Afghanistan after the Soviet invasion of 1979. Throughout Asia the Soviets had been ceaselessly active, while also maintaining substantial forces in Europe. Activism in Asia may have tied down US forces and contributed to America's humiliation in Vietnam, but the Soviets gained little in Asia despite their heavy involvement. The same was true of Latin America and Africa. The Soviets had an important ally in Cuba, but it was expensive to develop Cuba's economy and armed forces. Though links were established with many left-wing governments and political movements, not all of these could be relied upon to follow Moscow's lead. The Soviets gained no lasting Cold War advantage from their ventures outside Europe.[2]

Soviet involvement in the developing world was extended in the 1970s. According to the Kremlin, it was the USSR's duty to support liberation struggles and spread socialism. Strategic interests dictated that a network of bases was needed for the navy and air force, and economically the Soviet Union wanted markets and raw materials and sought to safeguard trade routes. American policy was such, moreover, that the developing world was a place for competition, and Moscow was eager to prevent developing countries from being used by Washington DC. All these considerations led the Soviets to intervene in Africa, Asia and Latin America, but it was not easy for the Kremlin to reconcile this with détente, and another problem was the negative reaction from some developing countries. Moscow was also restrained by the realization that many such countries were already tied into the international capitalist order, which meant that it would cost too much to turn them into permanent allies of the USSR. In addition, some potential allies had no wish to get drawn into the rivalry between the superpowers. They were reluctant to become dependent on either side.[3]

The Soviets often tried to enlarge buffer zones and spheres of influence because they thought they had no choice. They thought their security was at stake. In southern Asia, for instance, and especially in the approaches to the Middle East, Soviet involvement was stepped up through fear of what might happen if Moscow held back. In Asia and the Pacific, it was Moscow's permanent goal to prevent the establishment of an anti-Soviet coalition involving China, Japan and the United States. In Latin America the USSR's main commitment was to Cuba. Apart from this there were efforts to improve relations with the main regional powers Argentina, Brazil, Mexico and Venezuela. Increasingly Moscow prioritized trade. Political affinity mattered more in Africa. Washington DC was disturbed by the situation in Africa in the mid-1970s. When he was US secretary of state, Kissinger considered Soviet and Cuban involvement in Angola to be 'a blatant threat to international security'. He subsequently wrote that détente, though it was losing support in America, was damaged more by Soviet actions than by quarrels within the United States, and he pointed not only to Angola but also to Ethiopia, South Yemen and Afghanistan, and to Moscow's encouragement to North Vietnam to invade South Vietnam, Laos and Cambodia.[4]

War in Angola

There were three main factions in Angola. They had campaigned for independence from Portugal and were now vying for control of the new state. The factions were known by the acronyms that derived from their Portuguese names. The Marxist MPLA (Popular Movement for the Liberation of Angola) formed the post-independence government, which was opposed by the FNLA (National Liberation Front of Angola) and UNITA (National Union for the Total Independence of Angola).

The Americans aided the FNLA and UNITA. Responding to claims that the United States was interested only in Angola's economic resources and the possibility of securing a naval base, Kissinger declared that the main purpose was to prevent further Soviet infiltration in Africa. He emphasized that the states around Angola had asked for American help and that any hesitation or retreat would affect America's global standing. Weapons were supplied and the employment of mercenaries was promoted, possibly with the connivance of the British and Belgian governments. The United States also welcomed South Africa's military incursion into Angola. This led to other problems because South Africa's blacks gained a boost in their agitation for domestic reform when they saw Cuban and black African forces defeating white troops in Angola. Kissinger was disappointed when the US Congress cut off funding for operations in Angola. The FNLA collapsed. UNITA carried on a guerrilla war but was not strong enough to bring down the Marxist government. As for the Soviets, they intervened to combat what they took to be US assertiveness. American influence was growing in the Middle East. Kissinger had excluded the USSR from the peace process, and Egypt had been turned away from Moscow. The United States had also moved closer to China. In addition, some Soviet leaders were worried that détente was weakening their revolutionary credentials. They were stung by Chinese accusations that the Kremlin was collaborating with the US government at the expense of socialism in the developing world.[5]

The Angolan crisis prompted heated exchanges in the British parliament. In July 1975, Conservative MPs attacked the Labour government for failing to make proper arrangements for the safety of British citizens in Angola and the representation of British interests there following the withdrawal of the British consul. The minister of state at the foreign office, David Ennals, said that although some British property in Angola (worth about £60 million) had been damaged, there had been no British casualties so far. While insisting that the government was not failing to protect British subjects or represent British interests in Angola, Ennals did agree that the situation was likely to get worse. He called on the belligerents 'to call off this very damaging armed struggle so that Angola can have a smooth and peaceful transition to independence'. But he also insisted that Britain would not get involved: 'It is not for us to take sides'.[6]

As revelations were made about the participation of British mercenaries, the Wilson government was not sure how to address the matter. Under British law it was impossible to prevent British citizens from going abroad to fight as mercenaries. Ministers considered introducing new regulations for the future. Wilson announced a public inquiry in February 1976, but many observers regarded the resulting report as vague and unsatisfactory. Its key recommendation, repeal of the Foreign Enlistment Act of 1870, was not acted upon because of Wilson's resignation in April 1976 and because the new government had to focus on other matters. The legislation of 1870 had made it illegal to recruit soldiers for foreign armies. This did not suit the needs of the 1970s with respect to British citizens fighting abroad as mercenaries in a civil war.[7]

For *The Times* the crisis in Angola was notable for the double standards of the United Nations and the cynical scheming of Moscow. The UN had condemned the advance of South African troops into Angola without even mentioning the Cuban presence there, and the Soviets were making a lot of principled comments about non-intervention without living up to the standards they demanded of others. Moscow's concern was to ensure the victory of its friends and clients, and this was true of Africa in general, not just Angola. The *Observer* noted that the Americans were also seeking a bigger role in African affairs. The president of Tanzania, Julius Nyerere, had declared that the Americans must keep out. Tanzania, Mozambique, Botswana and Zambia were working together on regional problems, especially Rhodesia, where, having given up on a negotiated settlement, they had approved an escalation of the guerrilla war. Washington DC warned that if the Cubans intervened in the Rhodesian conflict, American troops would be sent in. Nyerere and his allies replied that this was a matter for Africans to resolve in their own way.[8]

International friction and British interests in Africa and Asia

Seeking more insight into Soviet policy, the *Economist* (usually sceptical about détente) invited a contribution from Nikolai Inozemtsev, director of the Institute of World Economy and World Affairs in Moscow. He wrote that the USSR wished to end confrontation. Some in the West thought that Soviet activity in Africa and Asia, as well as in Europe, proved that Moscow was not serious about détente. In fact, Inozemtsev retorted, Soviet citizens were simply showing solidarity with the working classes in capitalist states and the liberty-seeking peoples of developing countries. Struggles for 'national and social emancipation' were part of the 'normal' condition of the world. Inozemtsev concluded that the West could not expect the Soviets 'tamely to accept capitalist exploitation and national oppression'. In the United States, meanwhile, there were demonstrations against American involvement in Africa, but Kissinger defended his policy and urged the Soviets to stop 'tipping the scales' in local conflicts. Détente could not survive, he told the *Wall Street Journal*, unless Moscow realized that bargaining on one aspect of US-Soviet relations depended on progress in others.[9]

Soviet activism in Asia and Africa worried the British, whose interests in these volatile parts of the world were directly threatened. Home's Cold War experiences made him think that if the West did nothing the USSR would push even harder, which made it essential not only to strengthen NATO but also to stand up to the Soviets outside the NATO area. Commonwealth opinion continued to carry some weight, especially when Callaghan was foreign secretary and prime minister (he had developed an attachment to the Commonwealth in his days as Labour's spokesman on colonial affairs between 1956 and 1961). Anxiety in London about Soviet involvement in the developing world increased because of Soviet rearmament. Callaghan was sure that détente would continue, but he also wanted Britain and NATO to be strong. He decried the Kremlin's aggressive tendencies and tried to convince the Soviet leadership that it was worth negotiating. This became easier once the Gorbachev regime was established, and from 1985 there was a change in the USSR's approach. Britain's foreign secretary at the time, Howe, was pleased to find in the new Soviet foreign minister, Edward Shevardnadze, a willingness to reconsider the USSR's involvement in Asia and Africa.[10]

Although the Soviet Union gained little in the long run from its efforts in Africa, its activity there made life more difficult for the British. When Thatcher took office in May 1979, her government inherited the African problems that had plagued its predecessors, primarily those associated with Rhodesia, Britain's relations with South Africa and division in the Commonwealth. On Rhodesia the prime minister was hoping for a compromise between the illegal regime of Ian Smith and moderate black leaders, and the foreign secretary, Carrington, urged Smith and his colleagues to make the concessions on black rights that would facilitate agreement. US president Jimmy Carter offered his support, as did the prime minister of Australia, Malcolm Fraser. The British government was fearful about appearing to favour Rhodesia's white minority, for this would further alienate African members of the Commonwealth, and the conflict in Rhodesia gave cause for concern as well, for there was a danger that the Soviets and their allies would interfere. In December 1979 a conference in London led to the signing of the Lancaster House Agreement, which provided for the emergence of the independent state of Zimbabwe. It seemed that a settlement had at last been reached and that Britain would emerge from the affair with enhanced prestige, an outcome that in the preceding years had looked very unlikely.[11]

The road to Lancaster House had not been easy. The Wilson and Callaghan governments had kept up the pressure, but Rhodesia's white leaders would not have agreed to negotiate had they been worried only about Britain. They were probably swayed most by the course of the civil war, for the black insurgents were making advances, and by the Marxist regime in Mozambique, which was threatening to impose economic sanctions (Rhodesia's oil came through Mozambique) and offer more help to the insurgents. The Smith regime was influenced also by the Americans, who wanted to impress the developing world by demonstrating leadership on the issue, and by South Africa, where there was concern about the wider destabilizing effects of the civil war. Before Thatcher became prime minister, Smith had agreed in principle to move towards majority rule in Rhodesia. Thereafter, the British knew that the Commonwealth would fall apart if they did not hold Smith to his word. The settlement came as an enormous relief to Carrington, who had tried to be fair to all sides and to be seen as such, only for Britain's impartiality to be repeatedly questioned. Soviet involvement in Africa had been a complication. It had involved support for the black insurgents in Rhodesia. Carrington had also been uneasy about the Conservative right in Britain, in view of its sympathy for the white Rhodesians, and he was pleased when the party conference in Blackpool in October 1979 endorsed the government's policy.[12]

Britain continued to have close links with the region. In 1984 about £87 million was given in aid to Commonwealth states in southern Africa. The relationship continued to be overshadowed, however, by the sanctions campaign against the apartheid regime in Pretoria. Thatcher was reluctant to jeopardize Britain's economic and security links with South Africa, but the strength of international opinion meant she could not avoid taking action of some sort. She condemned apartheid while arguing that sanctions did not provide the best way forward. At home and abroad the government was denounced for this. The question had been causing problems for many years. South Africa left the Commonwealth in 1961. At that time it appeared that South Africa was less important to Britain than the black African members of the Commonwealth. Black Africa surpassed South Africa as a market for British exports during the early 1970s, and Britain's decision to relinquish the Simonstown naval base in 1975 seemed also to indicate that London and Pretoria would no longer have such a close relationship. On the other hand, the two governments still shared certain strategic interests and trade between Britain and South Africa grew quickly. There was no wish to damage the British economy, and it was thought that the pressure for sanctions could probably be resisted, especially while the Americans were also raising objections.[13]

The Rhodesian settlement of 1979 was relevant too. Previously, Britain had been annoyed that South Africa was not doing more to help. Pretoria later pushed for negotiations. This removed a source of tension between Britain and South Africa but not between Britain and the black African members of the Commonwealth. They still resented what they took to be Britain's lack of urgency in bringing down the illegal racist government of Rhodesia, and they found Britain even more culpable with respect to South Africa. They accused Britain of disrespecting Commonwealth opinion and the organization's multiracial character and values. As the struggle over sanctions against South Africa intensified, some British leaders caused offence with their claim that instead of encouraging reform, sanctions would make Pretoria even more recalcitrant and harm South Africa's blacks, the very people who needed help. Critics of British policy looked back on what they took to be a sorry record of empty talk and half-measures. Even the Labour government of the 1960s, which had imposed an arms embargo, had not followed through with hard-hitting economic sanctions or moves against South Africa at the UN. During the 1970s and especially the 1980s, Britain was stigmatized in some quarters as one of the world's leading supporters of the apartheid regime. Britain remained the largest single investor in South Africa. In 1990 the United Kingdom-South Africa Trade Association estimated that Britain accounted for half of all foreign investment in South Africa, to the tune of about £10 billion. South Africa had long been in breach of UN decisions, but Britain often refused to back resolutions against South Africa. Between 1975 and 1984 the British used their veto ten times, of which nine were on matters affecting South Africa. Between 1985 and 1989 the veto was used on nine occasions, of which seven were on matters affecting South Africa. Britain was not alone. For strategic and economic reasons the United States and France usually joined Britain in blocking international action against South Africa.[14]

The American view was that Pretoria should be advised, not isolated. This was Thatcher's preference as well, and she hoped that American leadership would take attention away from Britain's policy. In 1986 the US Congress approved sanctions, despite opposition from the Reagan White House, and Thatcher came under renewed pressure to do more in the fight against apartheid. A serious dispute broke out in the EC. Limited sanctions had already been agreed upon, and Ireland, the Netherlands and Denmark wanted to go further. Britain, France, the FRG and Portugal argued against this, but after much wrangling European sanctions were extended in September 1986. More trouble arose in the Commonwealth. When South Africa's president, P.W. Botha, declared that outsiders would not be allowed to meddle in his country's domestic politics, the Commonwealth resorted to stringent measures. Thatcher protested but the Commonwealth carried on regardless. By this time the foreign secretary, Howe, was at odds with the prime minister and complaining about the mixed signals that she was sending out. He had been trying to build consensus. The prime minister had promised that she would consider tougher measures if the South African government refused to cooperate. Now she was failing to act on this. More countries boycotted the 1986 Commonwealth Games in Edinburgh than participated. Commonwealth conferences in Nassau and London in 1985 and 1986 were marked by disagreements on South Africa. Yet Thatcher persisted with her argument that sanctions, instead of influencing Pretoria, would harm South Africa's black majority. During 1986 there were efforts to draw Botha into talks. Howe had visited South Africa on behalf of the EC. A Commonwealth 'Eminent Persons Group' (EPG) also visited South Africa. Still Thatcher prevaricated. She told the Commons that it would be wrong to rush into drastic action: 'We must not close the door on future negotiations'. Quarrelling continued and the British government tried to lessen the controversy by offering funds for black education in South Africa and by aiding black states in the region, notably Zimbabwe and Mozambique. The prime minister declared that Britain wished for all the countries of the region to be peaceful and prosperous. She wanted apartheid to end but insisted that this required a constructive policy rather than threats and hostility.[15]

Along with difficulties in Africa during this period, there were problems in Asia, the Indian Ocean and the Pacific. Despite the retreat from East of Suez, the Far East continued to be important to Britain because of Commonwealth ties, Britain's residual security role in the region and trade (several Asian countries were by now major participants in the global economy). Yet the 1970s had seen British involvement in the region diminish, especially after the US withdrawal from Vietnam. That the British no longer carried much weight in the region had already been indicated in 1971 when India and Pakistan went to war. One Commonwealth country dismembered another, and Britain had little say in the matter.

Nevertheless, from 1979 the Thatcher government was eager to demonstrate that Britain still had influence in the Far East. The fact that the USSR's SS20 missiles could reach into Asia as well as Europe led Thatcher to bring the matter up during arms control talks. The safety of Japan and of other Asian countries was at stake, and they were pleased when the British spoke up for them and connected European with Asian security.[16]

A major British concern was trade, particularly with China, which had implications for the future of Hong Kong. A small garrison was maintained in Hong Kong because local people wanted it, and London had decided that the departure of British forces would be seen by Peking as an invitation to invade. The softening of China's attitude towards the West and the Heath government's success in opening the door for an improvement in Anglo-Chinese relations facilitated discussion about the future of Hong Kong, which had been a British colony since 1842. The talks were far from straightforward. Thatcher did not like the idea of subjecting Hong Kong's five million inhabitants to communist rule, yet there could be no question of giving them the right to settle in Britain, where immigration was a highly sensitive issue. London encouraged Peking to respect Hong Kong's freedom and prosperity, and the Chinese were willing to offer assurances on these points because they hoped in the future to enter into a similar arrangement with Taiwan. An agreement was reached in December 1984. For a 50-year period after the handover in 1997, China would impose only limited control over Hong Kong. This did not end debate at home, however, and the government was condemned for agreeing to hand over more people to the communists than had ever been given up before. In one cartoon the foreign secretary, Howe, was depicted as a doormat.[17]

For most Asian members of the Commonwealth, the link with Britain was useful. They received aid from Canada, Australia and New Zealand as well as from Britain, and membership of a worldwide organization gave them a status they would otherwise not have had. Britain's continuing association with the Indian subcontinent was assured by the presence in Britain of so many people from India and Pakistan, though relations with these two countries were not close. They were not important trading partners for Britain. India preferred non-alignment to cooperation with the West, and Pakistan succumbed to Islamic fundamentalism and military dictatorship. On the other hand, Pakistan did contribute to the struggle against the Soviets in Afghanistan. The strongest economy in Asia and the Pacific was Japan's, and the Thatcher government gave much attention to the threat posed by Japanese competition and concluded a number of Anglo-Japanese trade agreements.[18]

Change in Africa

There was an abiding concern about the Cold War and its legacy in Africa. The 'developed' world, it was and is claimed, ruined the prospects of 'underdeveloped' nations. Intervention in Africa continued through the 1970s and 1980s, with attendant instability and bloodshed. The war in Angola was not the only catastrophe. In Ethiopia the emperor, Haile Selassie, was overthrown in a Soviet-backed coup in 1974. A brutal totalitarian regime was set up, and there were mass arrests, executions, internal separatist struggles and frontier wars for many years. A violent conflict developed in Zaire during 1977 and 1978. The country was attacked from across the Angolan border. Cuba and the USSR supported the invaders. The French and several African states helped Zaire's government.[19]

The decolonization of Africa was followed by more than thirty wars in about twenty years. A massive refugee problem added to the chronic poverty in much of the continent. Most of the new independent states (except those with oil, Algeria, Libya and Nigeria) turned out to be poorer than they had been under colonial rule.[20]

The Ethiopian revolution of 1974 was marked by what *The Times* described as a 'terrible lapse into savagery'. The *Observer* pointed to Ethiopia's need for international aid and opined that well-wishers would turn their backs on the new regime if it opted for terror and dictatorship. The *Economist* condemned the bloody removal of Ethiopia's previous administrators and political and military leaders. Then Eritrea, in the north of the country, tried to secede. American newspapers claimed that Libya was sending weapons into Eritrea and confessed that the confused situation made it impossible for the West to know how to respond.[21]

The West subsequently became more concerned about Moscow's influence in Ethiopia. The situations in Angola and Zaire also became alarming. By the summer of 1978 it appeared that a stand was going to be made against the Soviets and their allies, with the focus on Zaire. Military and logistical arrangements were made, mainly by the French with US assistance. The West was also offering an aid package, worth $100 million, which the British government had been instrumental in putting together. It was by no means certain that the country of Zaire could be prevented from disintegrating. Order had broken down completely, and the corrupt regime of President Sese Seko Mobutu seemed unlikely to last. Mobutu had benefited from years of western support, but now he was blaming everyone but himself for the prevalent chaos. In June 1978 the *Guardian* asserted that the West should no longer 'prop up African men of straw'. Though it had been assumed that Zaire's size and ethnic diversity made it ungovernable except by the Mobutu dictatorship and that however embarrassing a friend he became, Mobutu had to be supported in order to keep the Soviets out of Africa's 'strategic heartland', his failed policies and the country's political and economic maladies indicated the need for a new approach. The press in the United States speculated as to whether President Carter would act more boldly on African questions. In fact, the prospect of greater involvement in Africa did not appeal to many leaders in the West. French intervention in Zaire was limited and did not represent the commencement of a proactive policy on France's part.[22]

Social, political and economic turmoil across much of the continent was of no small concern to Britain, as a former colonial power that still had economic and strategic interests in Africa. According to Moscow, Africa's problems were attributable to the West and only the USSR could be trusted to work honestly for their solution. Soviet foreign minister Gromyko maintained that the crux of the matter was colonialism, and he condemned the West for seeking to retain economic control after making colonies independent. Cuban and eastern bloc involvement in Africa did not increase purely as a result of Soviet encouragement. The USSR's allies had their own reasons for getting involved. They wanted to expand their trade, to gain diplomatic recognition, to demonstrate the reality of socialist fraternity and actively to support national liberation movements. In seeking to counter these schemes, Washington DC tended to be more impatient and apprehensive than did the governments of Western Europe. There was general cooperation, though, involving economic and cultural initiatives as well as political and military efforts. The Lomé Convention, originally signed by 46 countries in February 1975, was designed to foster cooperation between the EC and the developing world, especially former French, Dutch, Belgian and British colonies. It was renegotiated and renewed three times. Lomé II, III and IV were signed in 1981, 1985 and 1989 respectively. These agreements on aid, investment and trade eventually covered 70 countries. Initially, however, such initiatives did not deter Soviet intervention in Africa, and as this intervention attracted more attention in Britain a call was raised for a more robust British policy. The Callaghan government, for all its friendly concern about Africa's problems, was accused of weakness. In February 1978 the Conservatives issued a direct challenge, moving in the Commons that 'this House regrets the failure of Her Majesty's Government to recognize the threat to world peace posed by Soviet adventurism in Africa'. The motion was defeated by 180 votes to 142.[23]

When the Conservatives returned to office in 1979, they continued to warn that the USSR was dangerous. Even in the Gorbachev era this was a view from which Thatcher did not depart. The existence of a Soviet threat was and is still questioned. To some commentators, the spectres of communism and Soviet military capability were used by British and American leaders to justify heavy defence spending and interference in the developing world, whose resources were craved by the West. Mark Curtis claims that the Soviets focused on Eastern Europe and were disinclined to involve themselves elsewhere.[24] While it is true that Britain and America made self-serving claims about what was going on in the developing world, it would be wrong to assume that they had no legitimate security concerns and wrong to accept that the Soviets were quite as restrained and blameless as Curtis seems to think.

Circumstances in the developing world did change, especially in Africa. The end of the Cold War had a direct impact on South Africa. The African National Congress (ANC), originally established in 1912, had been refounded as a 'Youth League' by Nelson Mandela and his associates in 1944. The South African government resorted to repression and many ANC leaders were imprisoned during the 1960s. Some went into exile. The ANC included communists, and the movement depended heavily on the Soviet bloc for support. There was an attempt to get UN help, and in 1969 the

General Assembly recognized that the people of South Africa were engaged in a legitimate struggle for self-determination and majority rule, but the ANC was frustrated by the lack of international backing for its cause. The situation was transformed after 1989, when F.W. de Klerk became South Africa's president. He realized that Gorbachev's reforms in the USSR and better relations between the USSR and the United States had important implications for South Africa. By this time the Americans and Soviets were working together to stabilize troubled regions. There was a coordinated effort to bring peace to Angola. This in turn deprived the ANC of bases in Angola and meant that Soviet aid was likely to be cut, necessitating a reassessment of the armed struggle against apartheid. At the same time, the easing of security worries meant that de Klerk's government could relax restrictions. Since the Soviet threat was disappearing with the end of the Cold War, de Klerk could negotiate with the ANC without raising the anti-communist fears of his white supporters. South Africa's economy was also suffering. Pretoria found it difficult to borrow the money it needed abroad, which affected business confidence in South Africa and in the country's main trading partners. South Africa began to have a serious balance of payments problem. The value of the currency fell, and the loss of international financial assistance exacerbated the effects of a slowdown in economic growth.[25]

The sanctions issue aroused enormous disputation, in which Britain continued to be centrally involved. Callaghan's government had been firmly committed to sanctions against South Africa, covering sporting and other contacts as well as trade. The Thatcher government's position on sanctions against South Africa was more equivocal, and it tarnished Britain's reputation around the world. Differences between Labour and the Conservatives had been apparent for some time. They were highlighted in a Commons debate of 8 December 1978. The Labour foreign secretary, David Owen, had responded to recent moves at the UN to increase the pressure on South Africa's government by stating that he could not rule out tougher measures. Conservative MPs, led by Malcolm Rifkind, argued against economic sanctions on the grounds that they would be difficult to enforce, could not change South Africa's internal policies or help to secure a Rhodesian settlement, would result in job losses in Britain, and would harm South Africa's blacks and damage the economies of other countries in the region. Labour MPs enjoyed making remarks about apartheid, Rifkind said, but these were irrelevant. P.W. Botha's visit to Britain for talks with Thatcher in 1984 was marked by an upsurge in anti-apartheid agitation, but the prime minister and her supporters maintained that economic sanctions were counterproductive and that it would be best to encourage Botha in a cautious reform agenda. Thatcher persisted in this vein even after the Commonwealth EPG reported in 1986 that Pretoria had no intention of dismantling apartheid. She maintained that the way to influence Pretoria was through dialogue. In 1987 she denounced the ANC as terrorists. The British government did agree to impose limited and voluntary sanctions covering investment and tourism and in due course hoped that de Klerk's flexibility and the release of Nelson Mandela from prison would lower the temperature. Thatcher's wish was to return to 'business as usual' as soon as possible. She had embarked on a tour of black Africa early in 1988, but nothing could silence Commonwealth demands regarding South Africa. Still she refused to budge. She wanted to leave de Klerk unencumbered by any 'ham-fisted outside intervention'. She called upon the ANC to end the armed struggle, abandon its nationalization plans (which, she said, would deter foreign investment and ruin the South African economy) and negotiate with de Klerk for a new constitution.[26]

There was some support for this view in *The Times*, which maintained that if de Klerk was able properly to establish himself in power, he would be willing to talk to black leaders and gradually abandon apartheid. But even when de Klerk was confirmed in office by an election, the *Economist* expected difficulties: 'most of the easily reformable bits of apartheid have now been reformed. The crucial change that remains to be put in place, giving the black majority a say in the running of its own country, is also the hardest to achieve'. Many white South Africans wanted to attach conditions to constitutional changes. The *Guardian* and the *Observer* emphasized the violent unrest in South Africa and the paradox of emergency laws and police brutality alongside de Klerk's promises about reform. In America, the *Washington Post* pointed to the huge gap between the ANC's goal of non-racial universal suffrage and de Klerk's proposals for a power-sharing deal to last for five years. The American press also noted the problems posed for Britain by Thatcher's position on sanctions, not least the split within the Commonwealth.[27]

Early in 1990, when Pretoria confirmed that Mandela would be freed and the ban on the ANC lifted, the British government was quick to praise de Klerk and to claim that his actions, as foreign secretary Douglas Hurd put it, 'vindicate our policy of contact rather than isolation'. The British were criticized by their European partners for ending voluntary sanctions too early and for trying to preserve a special connection with Pretoria, but there were many in the West for whom the Thatcher policy made sense. Though she was often singled out for attack, there were more than a few politicians in the United States and Western Europe who thought as she did. The nature of South Africa's political system mattered less to them than the fact that South Africa was a safe place for trade and investment. The debate about Thatcher's policy went on after her fall from power in November 1990. It was said that she had done nothing to promote a breakthrough and that change in South Africa was attributable to international anti-apartheid agitation, while Thatcher and her supporters maintained that de Klerk had introduced reforms and released Mandela only because he was given time. Coercion had not worked. The key, rather, had been to maintain regular relations with the government in Pretoria in order to assist an orderly transition to a multiracial system. It is not clear, however, that Britain's stance made much of a difference one way or the other. De Klerk did need international backing, but he wanted this from the EC, not just Britain, and within the EC Britain was virtually friendless at this time.[28]

Moscow had loudly condemned apartheid and South Africa's military intervention in neighbouring states. With the improvement in superpower relations in the late 1980s, a regional settlement began to take shape. In December 1988, agreements were made concerning the withdrawal of Cuban troops from Angola and South African troops from Namibia (occupied since the First World War and in defiance of UN instructions since 1966). The independence of Namibia was to be formally acknowledged. Having previously competed in Africa, the United States and Soviet Union began working together there. In 1991, President Bush asked Gorbachev to assist de Klerk's reform policy. Bush thought that some elements in the ANC were blocking democratic change, not promoting it, and he expressed concern about those ANC members who had associated with Libyan dictator Colonel Gaddafi.[29]

Moscow's attitude towards South Africa changed considerably in the 1980s. The region had been important to the USSR for some time. During the 1960s Soviet propaganda, military commitments and policy at the UN all came to be heavily influenced by Moscow's interest in southern Africa. The tension between the USSR and China was significant as well. Peking backed the Pan African Congress, or PAC, and the PAC repeatedly accused the ANC of being Moscow's tool (the PAC was formed in 1959 and rejected the ANC's leftist politics, links with the USSR and efforts to appeal for multiracial support). There was some anti-communist feeling in the ANC, but the ANC also cooperated with the Communist Party of South Africa and had no choice but to seek Soviet aid, given its difficulty in obtaining help elsewhere. In the early 1980s Moscow noted the cooperation between Washington DC and Pretoria and presented the ANC's bid for national liberation both as necessary in itself and as the means to make South Africa act more responsibly on the international stage. When Gorbachev took power he reaffirmed Soviet support for the ANC, but other matters became more important to him, and he participated in the US-led mediation efforts with respect to Angola, Namibia and South Africa.[30]

Afghanistan

The Soviets continued to involve themselves in the affairs of southern Africa, but by far their most important commitment in the developing world in this period was in Afghanistan. The invasion of Afghanistan in December 1979 can be related to Moscow's increased confidence at the end of the 1970s. It appeared to Brezhnev and his colleagues that American power was waning, as evidenced by what had happened in Vietnam and Angola. Meanwhile the Soviets had added to their forces in Cuba, intervened in Africa and encouraged an expansionist policy on the part of Vietnam. The fact that Moscow managed to get away with all this indicated to Brezhnev that détente and the increase in Soviet military capacity had tilted the global balance in the USSR's favour during the 1970s. Brezhnev assumed that invading Afghanistan and installing an amenable regime there would not be problematic. Moscow expected this to have an advantageous effect in south-west Asia and the Middle East and to lessen the threat posed by Islamic fundamentalism.[31]

The Soviets had been worried about their southern neighbour for some years. They wanted a friendly regime in Kabul, for the Soviet Union shared a long border with Afghanistan, and the latter had links with Asian parts of the USSR. Afghanistan became a republic in 1973 and pursued a policy of non-alignment, taking aid from both superpowers. In April 1978 communists seized power. The Soviets recognized the new regime, increased their military assistance and signed a friendship treaty in December 1978, but the regime became more radical and rival leaders vied for control. In March 1979 there was a revolt against the communists in Herat, where Soviet advisers and their families were killed. Moscow decided to install a moderate government that would follow orders. The 'Brezhnev Doctrine' meant that the Soviets could not allow a communist regime to be overthrown, and the mounting instability gave them the chance to consolidate their interests in Afghanistan and make it a full satellite. There was resistance, however, and a guerrilla war broke out. The United States sent guns and money, and the guerrillas were also helped by Muslim states. The conflict cost the USSR about $3 billion a year. The Americans and others gave half a billion dollars a year to the resistance fighters, and the UN spent another half billion a year on relief. The Americans came up with the 'Reagan Doctrine', which essentially rested on non-acceptance of communist coups in the developing world. It countered the application of the 'Brezhnev Doctrine' outside Eastern Europe and accorded with Reagan's confrontational stance towards the USSR, but it offended many people in Western Europe, for they saw little difference between the 'crimes' of the Soviets and those of the United States (which, among other things, had long been sustaining oppressive dictators across the developing world).[32]

The regional situation was complicated by the fall of the Shah of Iran early in 1979. Anxiety about the situation in Iran led the Soviets to express support for one Islamic revolution while trying to prevent another. Moscow had no liking for Islamic extremism but recognized the new regime in Iran in February 1979 for two reasons: to deter the Americans from interfering in Iran and to encourage Iran to accept the existence of a pro-Soviet government in Afghanistan. The US embassy in Tehran was seized in November 1979. The Iranians refused to free the hostages taken in this raid. For strategic and economic reasons Moscow still wished to avoid a quarrel with Iran, and though the Soviets joined in the call at the UN for the hostages to be released, Soviet propaganda continued to make much of the evils of US 'imperialism'. When the Soviets invaded Afghanistan, Iran protested on behalf of its Muslim neighbour. Across the developing world even leaders who were friendly towards the USSR raised objections. Moscow tried to neutralize Iran by taking a stronger anti-American line on the hostage crisis, and early in 1980 the Soviet Union opposed a move at the UN for economic sanctions against Iran. Carter sent a military force into Iran to rescue the hostages in April 1980, but the mission failed, and Moscow claimed that the whole affair was being used by the United States as a pretext for aggression. By such means as this the Soviets thought that they could take attention away from Afghanistan.[33]

Brezhnev maintained that the Afghan government had requested Soviet help to deal with interference from outside and an attempted anti-communist counterrevolution. The evidence for this was thin, however, and the West called upon Moscow to seek a solution through the UN. Talks were opened in Geneva in 1982, sponsored by the UN and attended by representatives from the USSR, Afghanistan, America and Pakistan (acting for the insurgents). Brezhnev's successor, Andropov, was willing to withdraw Soviet forces if he could be certain of the survival of a pro-Soviet regime in Kabul, but the United States and Pakistan refused to accept this precondition.[34]

The official reason for the invasion was self-defence: instability in the region affected Soviet security. Moscow was sure that the Americans would exploit the situation unless something was done, and that there would be domestic repercussions. The Kremlin was nervous about unrest in the central Asian republics of the Soviet Union, where religious fervour was growing and there were demonstrations against rule from Moscow. Gromyko was unapologetic about the invasion and pointed out that the USSR had long had close ties with Afghanistan. The two countries were on good terms and Moscow had been generous with aid. There was no Soviet plan to annex Afghanistan; the Afghans could sort out their own problems. According to Gromyko, the West would not allow them to do this. Western leaders maintained instead that a settlement would be impossible until Soviet troops were withdrawn, but these troops had been sent into Afghanistan as a measure of 'neighbourly assistance between one country and another'. Gorbachev saw things differently. By the time of Brezhnev's death in November 1982 it was clear that this was a 'hopeless military adventure', and when Gorbachev took power in March 1985 one of his priorities was to find a way out of Afghanistan. Initially he thought that the war could be ended if he sent in more troops. This just resulted in more casualties. Gorbachev concluded that a military victory could not be won. By 1987 the financial burden was no longer bearable; Soviet casualties were approaching 30,000 killed or wounded; the USSR was losing prestige; army morale had suffered; Moscow's influence in the developing world, especially among Muslims, was rapidly declining; and the war stood in the way of attempts to improve the Soviet Union's relations with the United States and China. The war was also becoming unpopular within the USSR.[35]

The original Soviet justification for the invasion, that it was a defensive move, could not be accepted in the West. The supposition was that the USSR intended to use Afghanistan as a springboard for further military action in the region. It was claimed that the Soviets were out to capture oilfields to the south, establish themselves on the shores of the Arabian Sea and improve their strategic position in the Middle East and Asia. In Britain, the foreign affairs committee of the House of Commons reported in 1980 that the invasion of Afghanistan did not appear to be part of some Soviet grand strategy, but it was also stated that the Soviets were opportunists and that one act of aggression could easily lead to another.[36]

Carter's response to the invasion was stronger than Moscow had anticipated and covered a range of contacts and activities. The Americans set aside the SALT II treaty, stopped grain sales to the USSR and withdrew Soviet fishing privileges in US waters, suspended high technology exports, stopped cultural exchanges, increased military and economic aid to Pakistan and called for a boycott of the 1980 Olympics in Moscow. As for Western Europe, Moscow knew there would be an outcry but expected it to blow over, and the restrained statements from Bonn and Paris reinforced this opinion. When Reagan won the US presidential election of November 1980, the Soviets hoped that the new administration would give fresh impetus to negotiations on arms control and other issues. Before long the Soviet leadership had to face a different scenario, for Reagan was intent on reviving the Cold War.[37]

Thatcher was one of the most enthusiastic supporters of Carter's firm response to the Soviet invasion of Afghanistan. She agreed that sanctions should be imposed against the USSR and had in mind the denial of credit, restrictions on technology transfer and the cessation of visits and contacts. She understood why the Soviets were in Afghanistan. They regarded the country as strategically important; the Islamic revolution in Iran worried them because it was likely to radicalize Muslims inside the USSR; and another concern was energy, for in any future energy crisis oil supplies in the Persian Gulf would be much in demand and to move into Afghanistan was to move closer to the oil. Understanding why the invasion had happened did not mean acquiescing, and foreign secretary Lord Carrington considered London's breach with Moscow 'an entirely just reaction to an outrageous Soviet act'. In later years, however, Carrington noted that the sense of outrage faded as many people in the West accommodated themselves to the Soviet presence in Afghanistan. Instead of remembering the causes of the rift between East and West, they worried about its consequences. Disturbed by the uncompromising rhetoric of Reagan and Thatcher, they began to think that the West shared some of the blame for what had happened.[38]

Early government statements about the invasion of Afghanistan were entirely negative. Thatcher and her colleagues commended America's retaliatory posture and announced that the Anglo-Soviet credit agreement of 1975, due to expire in February 1980, would not be renewed. In addition, they said, any future economic and financial arrangements with the USSR would have to satisfy a test of mutual advantage. On 24 January 1980 the lord privy seal, Ian Gilmour, told the Commons that the USSR's aggression was 'a breach of all the conventions that have governed East-West relations for the past decade'. On 31 January, when asked if Britain would supply arms to Afghan freedom fighters, the prime minister replied that military assistance was not under consideration. In February 1980 Thatcher complained that despite the international demand for a Soviet withdrawal and statements from the Kremlin that mentioned an end to the occupation, the number of Soviet troops in Afghanistan was rising. By the summer of 1980 the *Economist* considered the Soviets to be 'stuck'. Even if they sent in more troops, resistance would continue, and if they left the pro-Soviet regime in Kabul would fall. The West could help to end the occupation by making Moscow realize that the price of staying would be too high. Arming the insurgents made sense, but it was dangerous, and many of the insurgents would never be friends of the West. Economic sanctions were also in order, but they would probably not be effective. The best policy would be to offer Moscow an escape route, argued the *Economist*, by agreeing to discontinue the flow of weapons or by promising that a new and independent Afghanistan would be neutral. The *Guardian* suggested that if Brezhnev offered to recall Soviet forces from Afghanistan, he would expect a lot in return. He might make the offer, indeed, only to deepen divisions in the West. *The Times* approved of arming the insurgents while admitting that Afghanistan and its neighbours would suffer greatly if the war escalated. *The Times* argued that the West should demonstrate its readiness to share in the sacrifice by cutting back its trade with the USSR.[39]

Thatcher's condemnation of the invasion of Afghanistan was in keeping with the anti-communist rhetoric that characterized her early years in office. At the same time, however, Britain did not want sanctions to be carried as far as the Americans proposed, in part because of the Siberian pipeline project. Britain's position was also shaped by a wish for more coordination in the EC on foreign affairs. This meant that some of Western Europe's doubts about US policy began also to be expressed in Britain. From 1983 Britain's foreign secretary, Howe, worked on the basis that the Soviets should still be challenged but that closer contacts with Moscow had also to be established, in order to promote reforms in the USSR and eastern bloc. The prime minister agreed, but on Afghanistan she continued to be harsh and insistent. In her opinion, the threat to British and western security was growing, outside as well as inside Europe, since the USSR had not given up its expansionist ambitions. This was the context for her approval of NATO's decision to increase defence spending by 3 per cent a year, her belief that preparations should be made in case military action was needed outside the NATO area, and her argument that détente had not made it safe for the Americans to reduce their commitments in Western Europe.[40]

In Eastern Europe there was some disquiet about the Soviet invasion of Afghanistan, though disagreement between the USSR and its satellites was not especially useful to the West, and among eastern bloc leaders only Nicolae Ceausescu of Rumania came out

against Moscow. Ceausescu had for years been pursuing a relatively independent course in foreign affairs, but there was no prospect of him leaving the Soviet camp and in its internal policy his
was one of the most repressive regimes in the bloc.[41]

The invasion and occupation of Afghanistan added to the
resurgent Cold War atmosphere of the late 1970s and early 1980s.
Significantly, Soviet troops entered the country only days after
NATO's 'dual track' plan was adopted, and the American determination to punish the USSR with sanctions also indicated a
renewal of superpower discord. Events in Afghanistan increased
the tension in international affairs, as did the US invasion of
Grenada in 1983, which was designed to remove a Marxist regime
and its Cuban advisers. Mutual criticism intensified between
Washington DC and Moscow, but none of this brought a final rup-
ture between the two. Relations never became so bad that all negotiations ceased. In UN committees, in CSCE, in the arms control
talks in Geneva and in MBFR talks in Vienna, the Americans and
Soviets continued to communicate with each other.[42]

Did the Soviets achieve anything by occupying Afghanistan? In
the short term they used the crisis to exacerbate divisions between
Western Europe and the United States, but this did not mean that
the international order was permanently changed in Moscow's
favour. Thomas Hammond has argued that the USSR gained in
four ways: an improvement in the Soviet Union's geostrategic position, primarily because of the move towards the Persian Gulf and
its oil; combat experience and the testing of weapons; access to
Afghanistan's resources including natural gas; and an increase in
international respect for and fear of the USSR, which was likely to
be important whenever the Americans could be depicted as weak
or indecisive.[43] Yet these gains did not help the Soviet Union in
the long run, bearing in mind how the Cold War developed in the
1980s, and they have also to be balanced against the problems that
involvement in Afghanistan created for the USSR internally and
internationally.

Summary

Britain's refusal to compromise on the Afghan question affected
and was affected by the stance of Washington DC, and the Anglo-
American hard line certainly influenced the thinking of Soviet

leaders, particularly Gorbachev. In Western Europe the attitude towards Soviet policy was usually more forgiving: it was thought that thaw in Europe should not be abandoned because of events outside Europe. The Thatcher government in Britain was determined that the USSR should pay for its aggression in Afghanistan and insisted that the West's relations with Moscow could not fail to be damaged by what the Soviets were doing in Asia, the Middle East and Africa. The occupation of Afghanistan became a principal matter of contention in international affairs during this period, but crises, wars, political upheaval and economic failures across the whole of the developing world, and especially in Africa, also had a major impact. For Britain, the 1970s and 1980s were marked by a number of emergencies and entanglements – Angola, Ethiopia, Rhodesia, South Africa – that tested British resolve, statesmanship, resources and reputation.

9 Dealing with the Middle East

As crises in Africa multiplied during the 1970s and 1980s and were in many cases fomented by the great powers and intensified by their participation, the problems of the Middle East were also exacerbated by intervention from outside. Soviet links with Arab states and US support for Israel made a difficult situation considerably worse. The geographical location of the Middle East and its abiding strategic, economic and political significance in international affairs ensured that developments there had a wide effect. For Britain, with its historic associations with and surviving interests in the region, the task was to try to influence events without alienating others and in accordance with British needs, albeit in the context of limited resources and opportunities. The British remained involved in the Middle East primarily because of its oil, its role in British strategy and global communications, its importance in terms of trade and trade routes, and the political and diplomatic relationships that Britain wished to preserve in the region.

The war of 1973 and its aftermath

One of the main causes of the Six Day War of 1967 was that Egyptian leader Gamal Abdel Nasser, armed by the USSR, felt strong enough to go on the offensive. The Egyptians were beaten, however, and so were Jordan and Syria. Israel took Sinai, the Golan Heights, the West Bank and East Jerusalem. The Soviets continued to supply weapons and equipment, and when Nasser died in 1970 the Egyptian armed forces were twice as strong as they had been in 1967. Nasser's successor as president of Egypt, Anwar Sadat, adopted a different approach. In the long run he wanted to alleviate Arab-Israeli enmity, but in order to bargain from a position of strength he planned an attack on Israel. Sadat forged a new alliance among Arab states and declared in 1971 that there must be either a satisfactory regional settlement or another war. America and Israel thought he was bluffing. The Soviets also underestimated Sadat. After removing opponents from his own government, Sadat expelled Soviet advisers from Egypt in 1972. He was angry because the USSR sent Egypt enough weapons for self-defence but not for another war with Israel. The Soviets feared that providing more would give the Americans an excuse to halt détente. Caring little about Egypt's determination to avenge the defeat of 1967, what Moscow really wanted was a guaranteed role for itself as arbiter in the Middle East. The Kremlin lost faith in Sadat, and he expelled Soviet personnel because he wanted to reposition Egypt in the international order. Since 1967, he thought, the situation in the Middle East had been frozen in Israel's favour. Moscow had done little about this. The Americans had the ability to change things, owing to their influence over Israel, but they had to be pushed into it. Sadat believed that another war would prompt Washington DC to pay more attention to Egypt's interests. On the other hand, Egypt still needed the USSR's help. As a good-will gesture, Sadat extended the facilities that were available to Soviet naval vessels. In February 1973 Moscow agreed to provide him with more weapons.[1]

The Americans and Soviets had been cautiously pursuing détente, and the 'no war, no peace' situation in the Middle East after 1967 suited them, because it offered stability. Although the Soviets armed the Arab states, they never encouraged them to go to war and doubted that Arab armies could overcome Israel. Moscow sought to increase its involvement in the Middle East while simultaneously improving relations with Washington DC. These seemed to be realizable goals: the view in the Kremlin was that internal divisions within NATO, and the disarray in US politics produced by Watergate, made it possible for the USSR to intervene in areas outside Europe without jeopardizing détente. The thaw would go on, the Soviets assumed, because the United States was not strong enough to do without it. The Americans assisted Israel, meanwhile, and agreed that the occupied territories were needed for Israel's security. In the early years of the Nixon presidency, how-ever, the Middle East was not considered a priority and more atten-tion was given to Vietnam, to relations with Moscow and to the future development of NATO. Knowing that peace would reduce their role in the region, the Americans, like the Soviets, were not anxious for a final settlement. Washington DC did not want Israeli security to be compromised but also urged Israel's leaders not to start another war if they wanted to retain US support.[2]

Nixon and Kissinger did not expect the Yom Kippur attack on Israel in October 1973. The Soviets knew in advance but were surprised by Arab successes. When Arab forces had the advantage, the USSR called for a ceasefire and the Americans stalled until Israel could recover. Then, when the Arabs were pushed back and threatened to cut oil supplies, the United States and USSR both pressed for an end to the war. When Sadat asked the Americans and Soviets directly to supervise the disengagement, the Soviets agreed, but the Americans wanted to form a UN peacekeeping force instead. Brezhnev warned that the USSR would act alone if there was no joint operation by the two superpowers, and US forces were put on alert. Kissinger was determined to demonstrate firmness both for domestic purposes and to show the Soviet Union and other countries that Watergate had not weakened the US government. Brezhnev did not order unilateral Soviet action, and Kissinger agreed that a peace settlement would be worked out jointly by America and the USSR.[3]

Moscow had become alarmed about what might happen if the war continued. Although the ideal course would have been for the Arabs to fight on and end the war when they chose, Israeli successes in battle ruled this out. The Soviets did not criticize the Arabs in public and were loath to press them to stop fighting before they were ready, but Moscow was uncomfortable because the situation was beyond its control. There was no easy way to avoid the loss of Arab friendship while maintaining the balance between negotiation and confrontation that, for the Soviets, was the basis for superpower détente. Though some hardliners wanted to prolong the war until Israel, and the United States, had suffered a more significant reverse, the ceasefire came as a relief to Moscow, as did Kissinger's promise of cooperation. Then Kissinger cut the Soviets out of the peace process. A conference in Geneva in December 1973 only lasted a day. The Americans had not intended it to achieve anything. Kissinger's 'shuttle diplomacy' early in 1974 saw him circulating between Tel Aviv, Cairo and Damascus. Israel and Egypt withdrew from each other's positions in Sinai, and in March 1974 the Arab states abandoned their oil embargo and production cutbacks. When the Soviets called for the Geneva conference to be reopened, Kissinger was evasive. UN peacekeepers arrived to separate Arab and Israeli forces, but there was no general settlement. Subsequently a more focused effort began, sponsored by US president Jimmy Carter. Sadat and Israeli prime minister Menachem Begin engaged in talks from 1977. By the Carter-sponsored Camp David Agreement of September 1978, followed by a peace treaty signed in Washington DC on 26 March 1979, the Israelis withdrew from the Sinai peninsula and Egypt recovered sovereignty over land lost in 1967. Again, though, this was not a comprehensive arrangement, for Jordan and Syria did not participate and neither recovered their lost territory. Tension therefore continued in the Middle East. The superpowers had not really improved the situation there. The region had come to have a central role in their contest for international ascendancy.[4]

Nevertheless, the politics of the Middle East were changing, and this had a lot to do with Sadat. He had gambled that a war in 1973 would result in a better set of circumstances for Egypt and open the way for an understanding with Israel and the United States. The Yom Kippur attack was designed not to defeat Israel militarily, even had such a thing been possible, but to prompt the Americans to intervene, since there could be no settlement without their involvement. Kissinger fashioned a mediatory role that was later taken up by Carter. By the late 1970s Egypt was in the American orbit and receiving substantial economic and military aid. This helped Washington DC to shore up its influence in the region after the Iranian revolution of 1979. The fall of the Shah of Iran, one of America's closest allies in the Middle East, led the US government to focus on its friendship with Egypt and Saudi Arabia. Soviet-Egyptian relations deteriorated. Moscow condemned Sadat's economic reforms as a retreat from socialism, and his success in cultivating the Americans meant that Moscow's opinions became less important to him. Egypt had signed a 15-year treaty with the USSR in 1971. Sadat abandoned it in 1976. He no longer needed Soviet weapons because he could buy arms in the West. In 1977 Sadat suspended cotton sales to the USSR and its satellites in Eastern Europe. In order to secure more American aid, Egypt began to take up a policing role in the Red Sea-Horn of Africa region. This helped Sadat to placate his army chiefs. It also impressed the US Congress, which began to value Egypt as an opponent of Soviet and Cuban interference in Africa. The Americans were generous with their economic assistance, hoping that they could ensure Sadat's survival in office and manipulate the peace process. Sadat's move towards the United States was not popular with sections of Egyptian opinion, however, and he was blamed for isolating Egypt from the rest of the Arab world. He was also criticized because the peace process in which he participated did not deliver major concessions from Israel, particularly on the question of Palestinian rights.[5]

The Soviets tried to counteract Sadat's policy and American dominance of the peace process. They strengthened their links with Syria and Iraq and assumed that any big increase in US activity in the Middle East could be matched. This outlook proved over-optimistic. The rift between Egypt and the USSR, greater US involvement in the Middle East and domestic criticism of détente in America all made it easier for Washington DC to exclude Moscow from the peace process. The Soviets soon regretted the decision to allow Kissinger to take the lead in the diplomatic manoeuvring after the 1973 war, and Arab leaders came to see that, although the USSR could help them to fight, only the Americans could facilitate a settlement and secure the return of lost territories. The Arabs also realized that the oil weapon was more useful to them than military aid from the Soviet Union. Moscow claimed that the Americans, instead of seeking peace in the region, were trying to separate the Arabs from the USSR, strengthen Israel and divide the Arab states so that they would be less able to use their oil to combat imperialism.[6]

The Camp David Agreement and peace between Egypt and Israel

After winning the US presidential election of November 1976, Carter expressed a preference for a comprehensive settlement in the Middle East rather than step-by-step bargains, but he accepted that it would not be possible to remove all obstacles in one fail swoop. He was also aware that circumstances had changed since 1973. Though he agreed with the line taken by Nixon and Kissinger that a regional peace was needed in order to check Soviet influence in the Middle East, he saw other reasons to get involved, especially America's energy needs. The Soviets pressed again for the reopening of the Geneva talks, but there was little support for the idea in Congress, and Israel urged Carter not to allow the Soviets to interfere. The Israelis knew that Moscow would expect them to offer something to the Palestinians. As for Sadat, he appeared not to care about the exclusion of the USSR. He had responded to increasing Soviet involvement in Ethiopia with remarks about a plot to encircle Egypt. When Soviet forces entered Afghanistan in 1979, Cairo expelled the Soviet ambassador and all remaining Soviet technical staff. Israel's refusal to participate in a process that would be jointly led by the Americans and Soviets influenced Sadat as well as Carter.[7]

Carter favoured a peace treaty that incorporated the UN resolution of 1967, which had required Israel to return conquered territory. He also held that there could be no lasting stability unless Palestinian interests were taken into account. In return for these concessions by Israel, Carter wanted the Arabs to abandon their hostile posture and to establish diplomatic relations and conclude trade and tourism agreements with Israel. But the Begin government was adamantly opposed to the creation of a Palestinian state and refused to consider withdrawal from Gaza and the West Bank. Despite American and Arab protests, moreover, Israeli colonization of occupied areas increased. Carter and the US secretary of state, Cyrus Vance, were amazed at Israel's willingness to let a peace opportunity slip away. They reminded Begin of the substantial aid that America was giving to Israel and stressed that the United States could not be expected to go on financing a stalemate in the Middle East. Carter found Sadat less dogmatic and more constructive than Begin. The Camp David Agreement of September 1978 was a triumph for Carter but also owed a great deal to Sadat.[8]

Sadat's diplomacy and the promises he made at Camp David alienated Mohammed Ibrahim Kamel, Egypt's foreign minister. Kamel resigned because he thought that Sadat was making too many concessions to Carter, who in turn was giving too much to Begin. Kamel later wrote an insider's account of what happened at Camp David. Carter was desperate for an agreement, mainly for domestic political reasons. Begin was stubborn and demanding. Carter could not persuade Begin to compromise, so he put pressure on Sadat. The resulting accords did nothing for the Palestinians and confirmed Egypt's isolation from the rest of the

Arab world. They did not guarantee a complete Israeli withdrawal from Sinai and failed to link the Sinai question with a solution for Gaza, Jerusalem and the West Bank. Kamel regretted Sadat's policy and vilified the Americans for conveniently forgetting their commitment to human rights and opposition to the seizure of territory by force.[9]

Another insider's account of Camp David has been provided by the American William B. Quandt, who served on the National Security Council from 1977 to 1979 and had special responsibility for Arab-Israeli affairs. He was present at Camp David in September 1978, and he noted that after ten days of deadlock it seemed that the talks would end in failure. Carter saw that a wide-ranging deal was not achievable and decided that a limited agreement would be worth having even if it did not cover Gaza and the West Bank. Though Sadat urged him to reconsider, Carter chose not to confront Begin. Desperate to keep the talks going, Carter focused narrowly on what Sadat and Begin most wanted. For Sadat, this was an Israeli evacuation of Sinai, the price for which would be vagueness on Gaza and the West Bank. Begin indicated that he might give up Sinai if he could protect Israel's claim to future sovereignty over Gaza and the West Bank.[10]

The Camp David Agreement represented a concern with short-term gains rather than long-term consequences. Carter hoped that the framework could be extended to include other Arab states, and that eventually the many difficulties not resolved at Camp David would be properly addressed. Moscow was sceptical. Gromyko gave the established Soviet assessment: Israel should withdraw from Arab territory, the Palestinians had the right to self-determination and all nations in the region should enter into a collective guarantee that they would exist independently and in peace with each other. Gromyko accused Sadat of megalomania and 'political bankruptcy'. The Egyptian leader had given in to American 'blandishments and promises' and had broken up the Arab bloc by negotiating a separate deal with Israel, whereas President Asad of Syria was more principled and understood that there could be no peace until Israel returned the occupied lands and respected Palestinian rights. Asad also knew the importance of Arab-Soviet friendship. Gromyko stressed that the USSR had no objections to the existence of Israel and had long maintained that any settlement must include a statement of respect for Israeli independence

and integrity. Nevertheless, it was up to Israel to make the concessions that were necessary for stability in the Middle East.[11]

Begin did agree to recognize the 'legitimate rights' of the
Palestinians, to consult them about the future of Gaza and the
West Bank and temporarily to halt Israeli settlement in disputed
areas. Israel reserved the right to veto Palestinian participation
in peace talks, however, and ruled out the establishment of a
Palestinian state. Sadat believed that Camp David would build
momentum. He made much of the fact that the Palestinians would
have a say in the future of Gaza and the West Bank. He urged
Jordan to participate. He expected that as Israeli troops pulled
out of Sinai, all interested parties would join in the peace process
and it would become irreversible. Things did not go as planned.
Syria, Jordan, Saudi Arabia, Iraq, Libya and Algeria all rejected
the Camp David Agreement. To make matters worse, in March
1979, shortly before the treaty between Egypt and Israel was due
to be signed, Begin declared that Israel would never return to its
1967 borders and that Jerusalem was its 'eternal capital'. Satisfied
with the agreement with Egypt, Israel clearly had no intention of
dealing with Syria, Jordan and the Palestinians, which meant that
the door Sadat had opened was being closed, and for this Egypt
was punished. Several Arab states broke off diplomatic relations
with Cairo and imposed sanctions. Carter and his national security adviser, Zbigniew Brzezinski, were keen for a speedy resolution
of the Palestinian question. They needed to deliver something substantial for Sadat, in order to keep him involved, and feared that a
change of leadership in Egypt might set the whole process back. Yet
they feared even more the domestic political costs of making more
demands of Israel. Carter therefore had to rely on a Kissinger-style
incremental process, and it proved impossible to move quickly
towards agreements on Gaza, the West Bank, Jerusalem and the
Golan Heights.[12]

When pressed, the Americans were quick to point out that the
treaty signed by Sadat and Begin in March 1979 was not a 'separate'
treaty, since its preamble stated the need for a wider agreement,
and that Egypt and Israel planned to hold more talks on Gaza and
the West Bank. The Soviets dismissed this as nonsense, and the
Arabs blamed America for failing to make Israel negotiate in good
faith. Saudi Arabia was particularly disappointed, which worried
Washington DC, for America needed Saudi oil and valued Saudi

Arabia as a regional ally that was anti-communist and pro-West in sympathies. The Saudis could not accept a partial settlement. They had to distance themselves from US policy and side with other Arab states against Egypt. At the end of the 1970s American power in the region seemed to wane. Iran was gripped by revolutionary fervour. The Soviets, already established in Ethiopia and South Yemen, marched into Afghanistan. Washington DC was further humiliated in Arab eyes by the Tehran hostage crisis.[13]

Britain and the peace process in the 1970s

The British government was not directly involved in many of these transactions, though at times it played an important part. One of the results of Kissinger's diplomacy was that the shrinkage of Britain's role in the Middle East became more obvious. After October 1973 Kissinger's activity was premised upon the exclusion of others, including Britain and the EC. The Heath government argued that the UN resolution of 1967 should be respected and that four-power talks involving Britain, America, France and the USSR should be tried, but Kissinger rejected the multilateral approach. His plan was to persuade Arab governments to deal with Israel under American supervision.[14]

Britain's presence in the region had been scaled down as a result of the East of Suez withdrawal. Having focused their efforts on the Persian Gulf for many years, the British were pulling out, and in response the Americans courted Iran and Saudi Arabia as local powers that could stabilize the area. Britain's commitments in the Persian Gulf had to be given up because of the political and financial problems of the late 1960s. Withdrawal had been agreed upon by the Labour government of the day. Though Heath's government originally intended to amend Labour's policy, it decided to stick to what had been set in motion. Things might have been different. There was no pressure in parliament to bring British forces out of the Persian Gulf, public opinion was not strongly committed either way and most Conservative MPs and supporters probably preferred not to have the withdrawal go ahead. By the beginning of the 1970s, however, the foreign office had decided that Labour's timetable should be retained, not least because the Iranians and Saudis were ready to assume a policing role and would object if British plans were altered. A reversal would be costly financially and politically, and the Heath government was in any case more interested in joining the EC. Washington DC did not welcome London's decision greatly to reduce British commitments East of Suez.[15]

The British knew that their departure might open the door for the Soviets. Increased Soviet involvement was also facilitated by local disputes and particularly the war of 1972 between the left-wing Democratic People's Republic of Yemen and the Yemen Arab Republic. The wider context was not helpful to the West, either, in that some members of NATO were still dealing with the difficulties associated with decolonization, and this provided openings for the USSR in Africa and Asia. NATO's capacity and willingness to act in the Middle East were limited. Britain was drawing back from the region, French forces were not available following France's withdrawal from the alliance's integrated command structure in 1966 and there was rivalry between the two NATO countries that were geographically closest to the Middle East, Greece and Turkey. All this added to Moscow's ability to intervene in the region.[16]

Britain still had friends there, including Jordan. King Hussein of Jordan encouraged British involvement, mainly because he thought Britain would help him in his dealings with Israel.[17] Yet Britain was no longer such an important military power in the region, and Arab leaders realized that the United States had taken over many of Britain's responsibilities. The withdrawal from the Persian Gulf meant that Britain was not able directly to influence the course of events in the Middle East in 1973.

The British viewed US involvement in the Middle East with a mixture of approval and disapproval. There were many disagreements. The Heath government resisted when the Americans wanted to use their bases in Britain to supply Israel during the 1973 war, and London was not consulted in advance before US forces were put on alert, even though Britain would have been targeted in any Soviet response. The Americans were irritated by Britain's attitude, but Heath complained that while his government was trying to contain the Arab-Israeli war, America's pro-Israel policy was likely to extend it. Heath wanted to be seen as neutral and declared that it was ridiculous for the Americans to claim that they wanted a ceasefire when they were helping one side in the conflict more than the other. Kissinger retorted that NATO could not allow the Middle East to fall under Soviet control and that stability would be even more elusive if the region came to be dominated by extremist anti-Israel regimes. Heath's position was not shared by the foreign secretary, Home. The prime minister was pushing for European solidarity. Home wanted this too, but not to the extent that it divided Britain from the United States.[18]

Home's views on the Middle East had been outlined in a speech he made in October 1970. He advocated a settlement that would include the return of lands taken by Israel in 1967 and arrangements for the Palestinians, and he called upon Arab nations to coexist in peace with Israel. Although Home could see that trouble was coming, for the Soviets were arming the Arabs, he still thought that Egypt might be persuaded to recognize Israel. Confident of US help, however, Israel refused to give up occupied territories and would only talk to the Egyptians without preconditions. As Home pressed for a return to the 1967 frontiers, with UN oversight, he found the Arabs receptive and the Israelis hostile. The war of 1973 was a serious blow, but at least it left the Arabs 'purged of their humiliation', and Home imagined that a settlement could now be proposed on the basis of an autonomous area for the Palestinians on the West Bank. He hoped that the Americans would be able both to deter Moscow from further efforts to destabilize the Middle East and to push Israel into a bargain with the Arabs.[19]

Some American newspapers expressed relief late in October 1973 as it was confirmed that Soviet forces would be kept out of the Middle East. Even so, the *Washington Post* regarded the US military alert as a mistake and maintained that goals would have been better accomplished through diplomatic action. The *Los Angeles Times* hoped that Egypt would win general Arab backing for a truce. Among British newspapers, the *Economist* commented that the Yom Kippur War 'has blown away the fog around détente' and that the weapons supplied by the Soviets and Americans to the belligerents were 'a brutal reminder of how little the diplomacy of the past couple of years has really changed the world after all'. In the Middle East the *Economist* wanted security guarantees and demilitarized zones, with international inspection, and a Palestinian statement of Israel's right to exist. The Heath government, worried about oil supplies, appeared to be leaning towards the Arabs. The *Economist* counselled against partiality and exhorted the government to ensure that peace would be made on sure foundations. The *Guardian* wondered if the Arabs could trust Israel, in view of the latter's refusal to abide by previous UN resolutions, and noted the Arab suspicion that America and the Soviet Union would try to impose a settlement that suited their interests rather than those of the people in the region. According to *The Times*, Sadat definitely wanted peace. Did Israel? Having gained the upper hand in the Yom Kippur War, the Israelis were claiming that to return Arab territory would be to reward aggression, yet there could be no settlement unless Israel gave up the occupied areas, since the Arabs would insist on this in return for formally recognizing Israel.[20]

In the Commons on 30 October 1973, Harold Wilson ridiculed the Conservative government's 'misconceived policies' on the Middle East, which he contrasted with the performance of his Labour government in 1967, when Britain had been 'at the top table'. Now, Britain appeared to be playing no part in the framing of a peace accord or in the supervision of ceasefire arrangements. Heath had been content with 'a low profile, allegedly non-interventionist negative unity' with Britain's European allies. In practice this was 'unity only on French terms, which means unity on a pro-Arab posture'. Then there was 'the humiliation of the American alert, which this government did not seem important enough to be consulted about'. The prime minister replied that he regretted the resumption of hostilities in the Middle East, that his government had helped to prevent the war from escalating and had energetically promoted a ceasefire and that much had happened behind the scenes about which Wilson knew nothing. Heath was confident that the ceasefire would hold. He envisaged a permanent settlement that would make Israel safe and return occupied land to the Arabs, and he disparaged Wilson for exaggerating the importance of the US alert – a 'relatively low-level alert, which did not involve the immediate prospect of action'.[21]

Whatever he told parliament, however, Heath harboured a lot of resentment against the Americans for their conduct before, during and after the 1973 war. He blamed the Nixon administration for its failure to consult and for its support for Israel. In his view, America had worked at cross purposes with Britain, France and other states when they tried to end the fighting and resolve the question of oil supplies. Heath and the leaders of Western Europe were disappointed that the Americans seemed not to appreciate the need to maintain good relations with the Arabs. To Washington DC, meanwhile, it was the Europeans who were at fault: they had blinded themselves to the wider strategic ramifications of the Arab-Israeli conflict and selfishly refused to cooperate with US policy when it was clearly in the common interest. Heath was unmoved. He told American journalists in November 1973 that US policy was partly responsible for the troubles of the Middle East.[22]

The friction between London and Washington DC at the end of 1973 attracted a lot of comment in the British press. *The Times* noted that the Americans, expecting Britain to remain their main ally in Europe, were angry that Britain had not lived up to this billing. For years they had wanted Britain to join European organizations so that these could be made more outward looking, more active on global issues and more willing to work with the United States. Britain was meant to 'deliver' the EC, but during the Yom Kippur War this had not happened. American complaints about the attitude of allies in Europe and the suggestion that the United States no longer saw the need for NATO led the *Guardian* to argue that the allies were in fact becoming more important than ever to the United States, because of Soviet strength and assertiveness. The problem was that Western Europe lacked unity and purpose: it 'is not yet even a unit'. The *Observer* regarded the Middle East as a test. It was not clear what the Americans, the British and the Europeans could accomplish in the region while Moscow pushed its own agenda and Arab leaders argued with one another. Divergent concepts of 'peace' meant that a settlement would not be easy to arrange. Israel suspected that the Arabs only wanted to gain time so that they could rearm and start another war at a later date. Therefore the Israeli 'peace' could not involve the surrender of any military advantage. For the Arabs there could be no 'peace' unless the Palestinian problem was solved, but Israel was claiming that a Palestinian state would be economically unviable, ruled by terrorists and friendly towards Moscow. *The Times* considered this excessive and maintained that Israel had to negotiate with whichever representatives the Palestinians decided to select.[23]

Reporting to parliament on 21 January 1974, Home presented Israeli-Egyptian disengagement as a step on the way to a permanent peace. Regarding the post-war difficulties between Israel and Syria, he hoped that Syria would release captured Israelis and not use them to gain leverage on other issues, notably the Golan Heights, and said that the status of occupied territories would have to be settled as part of a general agreement. Home praised

Kissinger's efforts, adding that much had still to be done and that the British government was ready to help. The signs were good. Oil was available again. Home recognized the need to monitor the supply of weapons to Israel and the Arab states, and he suggested that a rationing system might be agreed with the Americans, Soviets and others. In the meantime, Britain would act responsibly and impose a 'strict control' over arms sales so as not to increase the likelihood of another war. On the matter of consultation, Home insisted that Kissinger 'has been assiduous in keeping us informed all the way through, and asking for our comments on the action he was taking'.[24]

In fact Home and Heath both thought that Kissinger was doing too much without reference to Britain and Western Europe. Defence secretary Lord Carrington was more complimentary, referring to Kissinger's 'remarkable achievement' in persuading Arab leaders to place more trust in the United States, but Carrington also agreed with Home and Heath that Britain's stance had to be 'ostentatiously neutral'. The defence secretary came in for some criticism, especially from British Jews, because the decision to withhold spare parts for British-supplied weapons affected Israel more than the Arabs.[25]

Although Kissinger took the lead in working for a settlement in the Middle East, he benefited from the assistance of Callaghan in the mid-1970s while the latter was British foreign secretary. Callaghan had friends in the Israeli parliament but was not as biased towards Israel as Wilson was known to be. Callaghan visited the Middle East early in 1974. He had discussions with Sadat, during which the Egyptian leader made a plea for peace on the basis of Egypt's recognition of Israel and a homeland for the Palestinians. Callaghan passed this on to Israel's government and to Kissinger, whose diplomacy was facilitated by Callaghan's contacts with Israeli politicians, Sadat and King Hussein of Jordan. To the extent that the regional situation was stabilized during 1974 and 1975, this was partly a result of Anglo-American cooperation. Callaghan convinced Kissinger that Sadat was dependable, which made Kissinger more willing to press Israel to negotiate. Wilson also played a supporting role, putting his weight behind an interim agreement on Sinai. One of the main suggestions made by Callaghan to Sadat in 1974 was that there should be direct conversations between Egyptian and Israeli leaders. At that time Sadat said it was 'unrealistic' to expect him personally to go to Israel: 'My people would stone me. The Arab world would condemn me. That kind of peace is impossible'. In November 1977, however, Sadat made his 'historic journey' to Israel and Callaghan paid tribute to his boldness.[26]

When Carter devoted himself to a peace effort, like Kissinger he sought Britain's help. Although Callaghan, who was now Britain's prime minister, was closer to figures on the Israeli left than he was to the right-winger Begin, he hosted Begin for talks in England in December 1977. Callaghan also communicated with Sadat at this time. The possibility of a self-governing Palestinian region on the West Bank was discussed, and in January 1978 Callaghan arrived in Cairo for further conversations. He subsequently advised Carter that Israel should offer something to the Palestinians. He also suggested that Jordan should be consulted, since a link between Jordan and the West Bank would promote stability. Sadat and Begin both contacted Callaghan during the months before and after the Camp David talks, and Carter confided in him, often lamenting Israeli intransigence. Carter considered pulling out of the peace process in the spring of 1978, but Callaghan urged him to persevere.[27]

The British government had trouble with Israel and Egypt in this period. In late 1977 Begin caused embarrassment by announcing that Israel's terms for a peace deal had British support. In fact, Callaghan had only accepted them as a starting point for negotiations. Then, in February 1978 when Sadat and Kamel were in London to meet with Callaghan and British foreign secretary David Owen, a quarrel broke out over Israeli settlements on occupied land. Kamel launched into a heated tirade against Britain's past conduct in the Middle East. He was angry about Owen's idea that some Israeli settlements in Sinai should be allowed to remain. Owen thought that to insist on full removal would complicate arrangements for the West Bank and Gaza. Kamel accused him of racial discrimination and pointed out that none of this land belonged to Israel. In advance of the Camp David meeting a conference was hosted by Britain in July 1978. This took place at Leeds Castle in Kent and was attended by the Egyptian and Israeli foreign ministers and US secretary of state Cyrus Vance.[28]

The Camp David framework did not bring peace much closer, the *Guardian* argued, because Israel was unlikely to live up to its obligations and Egypt would probably not be able to persuade other Arab states to accept Camp David as a model for future agreements. The *Economist* emphasized that the 'Rejectionist Arabs' were divided and their sanctions against Egypt not very stringent, but more alarming were signs that some of them were raising money to buy weapons and undermine Sadat's regime. The *Economist* challenged them to prove that they had something better to offer than the Camp David approach. MPs debated the Middle East on 9 March 1979, when British policy was explained by minister of state at the foreign office Frank Judd. Britain still had a role to play in the Middle East, Judd began, and although the countries in the region were aware of the limits on British power, most of them respected Britain and valued British friendship. Britain in turn wanted to maintain good relations with them, not least because the region was important as a provider of oil, a market for British exports and a place to invest. Peace seemed to be within reach, and Judd hoped that a treaty between Israel and Egypt would quickly merge into a wider settlement on the basis of UN resolutions: Palestinian aspirations would have to be accommodated, Israel should make concessions on the occupied territories, and the Arabs had to accept Israel's need for secure frontiers.[29]

Some British newspapers were not hopeful about the peace process, even if they commended the efforts of the statesmen involved. The *Daily Telegraph* declared in March 1979 that there was no guarantee that the Camp David framework could be extended. A worrying development was the radicalization of the Palestinian leadership, which was probably being encouraged by the revolutionary regime in Iran. The *Observer* praised the treaty between Israel and Egypt but added that Syria, Jordan, Iraq and Saudi Arabia all had demands that were worthy of consideration. The *Observer* also suggested that to exclude the Soviets from the peace process would be to reduce the likelihood of success. The treaty had created an opening, nothing more, and what was required was 'a new political process and a larger number of participants'. The *Economist* agreed, expressing concern about Israeli repression in the West Bank and the Arab half of Jerusalem and about the anti-Sadat front among Arab countries.[30]

As part of the Camp David Agreement, British troops were stationed in Sinai to supervise the Israeli withdrawal. This operation had EC approval and involved forces from several European states, but there was some controversy. Discussions about a common

European defence identity were still in progress, and there were differing opinions about operations outside the NATO area.[31]

British policy in the 1980s

The situation in the Middle East changed quickly. Britain's trade in the region was growing, and the need for oil ensured that the economic and strategic importance of the Middle East was not going to diminish. Britain wanted stability there, but the peace deal between Egypt and Israel split the Arabs and increased tension. A major advantage for the Thatcher government was that by the end of the 1970s North Sea oil was becoming available in large amounts. The sharp rise in oil prices in 1973 had made exploitation of the North Sea deposits an attractive proposition, and when Thatcher became prime minister in 1979 it was predicted that Britain would soon be producing more oil than the country needed, in which case the supply from the Middle East would become less important. As for Britain's military involvement in the region, this continued in a small way. Despite the withdrawal from the Persian Gulf, assistance could still be offered to allies in an emergency, as when the government of Oman was helped to put down a revolt. Nevertheless, the revolution in Iran was a blow to Britain strategically and economically, for it marked the collapse of the Central Treaty Organization, or CENTO, originally founded in 1955, and the loss of Britain's most important export market in the region.[32]

In the Thatcher years, Britain's role in the Middle East was vastly different from what it had been in previous times. The military presence had ended, as had membership of a regional defence pact, responsibility for colonies or mandates, and binding commitments to protected territories and client regimes. Britain's two main goals in the Middle East were to trade and to contain regional disputes. Thatcher's government tried to maintain good relations with Israel and with oil-rich and politically moderate Arab states. Libya, Syria and Iran caused the most trouble for Britain during the 1980s, but other Arab nations also criticized the British because they regarded them as subservient to America and expected them to do more on the Palestinian question.[33]

In Europe there were attempts to build upon those elements of unity that had emerged at the time of the Yom Kippur War of 1973.

Contacts were maintained with the moderate Arab states, and the EC repeatedly called for a settlement in the Middle East. The wish for a distinctive European position, in contrast to America's pro-Israel stance, led to such initiatives as the Venice Declaration of June 1980. This maintained that any peace deal would have to include appropriate arrangements for the Palestinians, which meant a seat at the negotiating table for the Palestinian Liberation Organization (PLO) even though its members were widely regarded as terrorists. The impact of this coordinated European policy in the Middle East was not great, however, and insofar as joint European action was discernible it probably rested most on a temporary overlapping of different national interests.[34]

The EC standpoint was that Jewish settlements in occupied lands were illegal and an obstacle to peace and that the Palestinians should have self-determination. This angered Washington DC, which wanted to retain control of the peace process, and Israel, which was unwilling to return conquered territory or talk to the PLO. The Venice Declaration was bound to cause controversy, therefore, even if EC influence in the Middle East was limited. On the other hand, the EC's position encouraged the Palestinians and the more amenable Arab regimes to think of making an agreement with Israel. Carrington was eager for more EC involvement and regretted the attitude of Washington DC. Carter's interest in the Middle East faded as he focused on his re-election campaign in 1980. The prospects for peace seemed to get worse. Islamic fundamentalism was spreading. The Arabs became more dangerously divided between moderates and extremists. Rising oil prices magnified the West's economic problems and increased Arab leverage. The Venice Declaration signified a wish to get peace efforts moving again, but the Carter administration disliked it, and the Jewish lobby in America claimed that the EC was out to betray Israel and reward terrorism, which Carrington denied. He pointed out that moderate Arab leaders had to be able to show their people that self-restraint paid off. If they could not do this they would either become less moderate or be replaced by extremists. Carrington visited Egypt early in 1981 to meet with Sadat. They spoke of a comprehensive settlement. Sadat wanted Jordan and Saudi Arabia to be brought in but said he was content to wait until Israel was ready. Sadat was assassinated in the autumn of 1981. Carrington reflected that more might have been done previously, to create a better atmosphere, and he began to wonder how significant Camp David really was. He became convinced that everything depended on Arab recognition of the state of Israel and Israeli recognition of Palestinian rights. Arab leaders were indignant about Washington DC's refusal to put more pressure on Israel, and Carrington agreed with them on this point. Although he expected some movement in 1981, when Saudi Arabia agreed to acknowledge Israel's existence and there were international protests about Israeli incursions into Lebanon, the Americans remained reluctant to make demands of Israel. Some Arab leaders were annoyed by EC involvement in the implementation of the Camp David Agreement, which, they argued, did not merit European approval. When Saudi Arabia made proposals that were designed to address all outstanding disputes, Carrington welcomed them and called upon the EC to do the same.[35]

By this time the Americans had turned against Carrington. He kept hoping for a new initiative, while in Washington DC he was reproached for disparaging the Camp David Agreement. Thatcher had to reassure the Americans that this had not been his intention. The prime minister did not share Carrington's wish for greater EC involvement in the peace process. She had reservations about the Venice Declaration, insisting that it was supplemental to the Camp David Agreement and did not supersede it. Carrington took up the peace proposals of Saudi Arabia and was condemned by Israeli politicians and by the US state department. Though he was stigmatized as an enemy of Israel, he said he was ready to go to Israel and meet with Begin face to face. When he did, in March 1982, Begin ruled out negotiations with the PLO and Carrington found him blind to all interests except those of his own country.[36]

While Carrington frequently found fault with US policy, Thatcher's priority was to work with the Americans in the Middle East. An important aspect of this concerned military action outside the NATO area. In 1981 Britain supported a US proposal for a 'rapid deployment force', which was to include a British contingent. Saudi Arabia and states of the Persian Gulf warned London against direct intervention in the region and Thatcher assured them that the 'rapid deployment force' would not act there without their consent.[37]

The Americans were grateful for Thatcher's help, because they were sensitive about unilateral action in trouble spots around the world. They preferred to involve allies so they could claim that they were not serving only their own interests. It was not long before British troops were needed in the Middle East. In 1982 Israel invaded Lebanon to eject the PLO. Talks about an Israeli withdrawal were complicated by Syria's intervention in Lebanon and the civil war that had broken out there. Washington DC saw an opportunity to win friends in the region and suggested that an international force could be sent in to cover the Israeli retreat, separate rival Lebanese militias and prevent further Syrian incursions. Thatcher agreed that Britain would participate, and the peacekeeping force (dominated by the Americans) was deployed in Lebanon in September 1983. It departed in March 1984. If she was committed to cooperation with the United States, Thatcher was less concerned to keep in step with the EC. Having accepted the Venice Declaration of 1980 about the need to bring the PLO into the peace process, she abandoned this position in October 1985 when a joint PLO-Jordanian negotiating team was barred from entering Britain. The EC's policy was to include the PLO, despite its principles and actions, on the grounds that no settlement was possible without the Palestinians. The British government now proclaimed that the PLO should not be consulted while it denied Israel's right to exist.[38]

Friction in the Middle East was again on the increase. Soviet military strength in the region was possibly greater than ever before, owing to the air bases and naval facilities that were available in Ethiopia, Yemen and Afghanistan. This enhanced Moscow's influence, as did ongoing Soviet support for Palestinian rights. Meanwhile there were further calls in the West for a coherent and united policy involving a larger military presence in the Middle East and a genuine attempt to meet the concerns of the governments and peoples there. Without this policy, it was thought, the West would not be able to protect oil supplies or deal with the Soviet threat.[39]

The end of the Cold War brought no end to the instability in the Middle East. Although repeated attempts were made to broker agreements, the deep-seated enmity between the Arabs and Israel and the animosities within and between Arab countries meant that a comprehensive peace could not be constructed. America's willingness to intervene militarily in the region created more problems than it solved and divided world opinion. War broke out in 1980 between Iran and Iraq. There were huge casualties on both sides until a ceasefire was agreed in 1988. The civil war in Lebanon was not ended until 1989. From 1987 the Palestinians staged a popular uprising (the 'intifada'). In 1990 Iraqi forces invaded Kuwait; a US-led coalition was put together to remove them. There were quarrels between the United States and its European allies, however, and the lack of consensus in Western Europe again demonstrated the emptiness of all talk about a common EC foreign policy: there was a split on whether to negotiate with Iraq. Britain was among those EC members that opposed negotiation. During the 1990s, despite contact between Israel and the PLO, an Israeli-Jordanian peace treaty, and the eventual withdrawal of Israeli troops from Lebanon, there was ongoing turmoil. Political disarray meant that negotiations were often suspended and relationships ruined, and terrorism in the region and beyond became a mounting concern.

Summary

During the 1970s Britain supported the American-led Middle East peace efforts. The British also made their own proposals and tried on occasion to take the lead. They still had interests and friendships in the region; they still wanted to play a role there. Middle East politics began to affect Britain even more directly in the 1980s, with assassinations, bombings, embassy seizures and other crimes on British soil, but the Middle East remained important to Britain mainly for economic reasons. The British were fortunate in that North Sea oil made them less reliant on Arab suppliers, and in time Britain combined with others to challenge the dominance in world energy markets of Arab oil producers. In the 1990s it was not easy to increase exports to the region, largely because the oil-producing states were not earning so much for their oil. British arms and engineering exports did grow as oil imports decreased. Britain sold weapons to both sides during the Iran-Iraq war, as did other nations, and this caused some embarrassment later when Iraq invaded Kuwait. Throughout this period Britain was able to maintain cordial relations with some states in the Middle East but not with others, and though there was usually a readiness to cooperate with the Americans, the old idea that the latter did not really understand the region continued to feature in British deliberations.

10 The Falklands Crisis: Causes and Consequences

For Britain the 1970s and 1980s represent a period of adjustment to changed circumstances in which British influence in the world was limited. A continuous effort was required to bring commitments into line with resources. It would be wrong, however, to characterize this period only in terms of retreat. After Britain's victory over Argentina in the Falklands War, Thatcher declared that things had changed and that 'Britain is great again'. She was exaggerating. By dismissing the preceding decades as years of failure and weakness, she was affirming that her own time in office should be seen in a different light. But the Falklands campaign was not a renewed attempt to restore Britain to its former world role. Although Britain went to war over the Falklands and committed itself to the defence of the islands, the usual practice was to limit obligations. Lack of resources had long since brought an end to the 'global system'. The Falklands crisis was an isolated example. Britain generally preferred peaceful withdrawal, as with Rhodesia and Hong Kong.[1] If the Falklands War was not an attempt to revive empire or recreate a world role, what was it? In truth, the war was an accident. It was unintended. Nevertheless, Thatcher had a point when she spoke of British greatness, in that the war was a sign that Britain could still act like a great power, even if this greatness was based on much reduced economic and military foundations. The war rekindled memories of British courage and determination in times of trial and showed that these strengths were still present. Despite the compromises of the 1970s and 1980s, there were things that Britain would not tolerate, fundamental interests that would not be given up and principles on which Britain would make a stand, whatever the costs and drawbacks. The Falklands crisis also reveals something about Britain's relative decline as a world power during the twentieth century. There may have been difficult international and domestic circumstances, but British leaders did well to retard and hide decline. Britain retained status, influence and prestige, and these qualities were enhanced by the Falklands victory. It restored confidence and prolonged an image of strength and competence in international affairs. The importance of perception should not be ignored: power had as much to do with what allies and enemies *thought* Britain could do as with what Britain could actually do.

British territory invaded

The Falkland Islands were first claimed by Britain in 1690, and a British settlement was established there in 1766. Formal British sovereignty over the Falklands could be traced back to 1828, but Argentina contended that the islands had been seized illegally from Spain and that, since they had been part of Spain's Argentine possessions and the independent Argentina was Spain's successor, they rightly belonged to Argentina. The government in Buenos Aires made a formal claim on these grounds at the UN in 1965. Although Britain was willing to negotiate, the inhabitants of the Falkland Islands made clear their opposition to a transfer of sovereignty from Britain to Argentina. Subsequently there was talk of a 'lease back' arrangement: Britain would cede the islands to Argentina and they would be leased back to Britain for a specified period in order for the islanders' interests to be protected. This possibility was also ruled out because of the objections of the Falklanders.[2]

Neither Britain nor Argentina had a watertight case, and it made sense for Britain to seek a settlement that was acceptable to both the Argentines and the Falklanders. Economically, the latter were reliant on the former. London was also conscious that the quarrel could damage Britain's relations with Latin America. The Wilson government of 1964–70 and the Heath government of 1970–74 were not averse to negotiations, but they felt bound to respect the wishes of the 1800 islanders, while Argentina would not yield on the question of sovereignty. When the Wilson government of 1974–76 was in office, a report was received about oil deposits in the region and it was suggested that these could be exploited jointly by Britain and Argentina. The foreign secretary, Callaghan, arranged for talks with the Argentines. Though he insisted that the islanders wished to remain British and that the discussions could have nothing to do with sovereignty, Argentina took the opportunity to repeat its territorial claim and backed this up with threats. Cooperation on energy and environmental matters was possible if Argentina wanted it, Callaghan said, but the Argentines would have to accept that the Falkland Islands were British. In due course HMS *Endurance* was sent to patrol the Falkland waters. Callaghan also ordered an ongoing assessment of Argentine military strength. In December 1975 he consulted Kissinger. Argentina's complaints continued, and at the end of 1976 the Argentines established a small scientific station on an uninhabited island to the south-east of the Falklands. British helicopters and missiles had been sent to the Falklands, but Callaghan decided against the construction of a runway there, capable of accommodating fighter aircraft, in case the military junta that had seized power in Argentina in 1976 cited this as an excuse for retaliation. When he became prime minister, Callaghan resumed the effort to foster joint projects with Argentina while upholding British sovereignty over the Falkland Islands.[3]

At the same time, in senior diplomatic, administrative and military circles the idea had spread that retaining sovereignty would be troublesome. In view of the resolution of the UN General Assembly in December 1965, which called upon Britain and Argentina to negotiate an agreement, the pressure for Britain to make concessions was likely to increase. From this point onwards, indeed, the growing anti-colonial lobby at the UN took a keen interest in the Falklands, and Britain was simultaneously embarrassed by the Rhodesian crisis and by Spain's demand for an end to the dispute over Gibraltar. The British pointed out that the desired 'return' of Gibraltar to Spain was not possible while the people of Gibraltar wished to retain their link with Britain. The same principle applied to the 'return' of the Falklands to Argentina.[4]

Argentina imposed immigration controls on all flights to and from the Falklands. Britain, unwilling to fund regular travel by ship to the islands, had to accept Argentina's action, which in effect made it a condition of travel that islanders were treated as Argentine citizens of the 'Malvinas'. The Labour governments of the 1970s repeated that there could be no transfer of sovereignty unless the Falklanders agreed. Since the islanders' inflexibility was restricting Britain's room for manoeuvre, efforts were made to make them less obstructive. These proved controversial. Reports on the Falklands' economic potential made it clear that a huge amount of investment would be needed. Britain had neither the will nor the means. The foreign office was annoyed because it had expected the islanders to be forced into concessions, so as to facilitate a final settlement. Parliament started to pay more attention, which was awkward, because a body of MPs emerged to argue against any surrender to Buenos Aires.[5]

The Callaghan government remained willing to negotiate on communications, economic development and other Falklands-related issues, but did not waver on sovereignty. Edward Rowlands, minister of state at the foreign office, told MPs in July 1978 that there was no wish for a confrontation with Argentina and that the government's primary concern had to be the islands' prosperity. Clearly, Argentine help was needed if the Falklands were to have a sound economy – 'No one will invest in the area, privately or publicly, while a cloud of political uncertainty hangs over the future of the islands' – but the presence of the scientific station and other irritations, like the harassment of shipping in Falkland waters, were bound to obstruct progress. Britain would continue to combine patience with firmness and to hope that Argentina would adopt a more cordial attitude.[6]

In office from May 1979, Thatcher's government was satisfied that Anglo-Argentine relations would continue much as before, which meant that the Falklands situation was not an urgent priority. Much more important was the struggle to control the defence budget. The prime minister and her closest aides decided that defence secretary Francis Pym was too hesitant about imposing the necessary savings. Pym was replaced. The new defence secretary was John Nott. The defence review of 1981 envisaged wide-ranging cuts, especially in the Royal Navy, and HMS *Endurance* was recalled from the South Atlantic. Callaghan challenged the prime minister about this in the Commons on 9 February 1982. Describing the withdrawal of the *Endurance* as 'an error that could have serious consequences', Callaghan revealed that he had decided against it more than once during his period in office. Thatcher replied that choices had to be made because of many competing claims on the defence budget. She described the 'defence capability' of HMS *Endurance* as 'extremely limited'.[7]

Callaghan later wrote that Thatcher's government did not keep an eye on the situation in the South Atlantic, failed to make clear

Britain's readiness to fight until it was too late for Argentina to back down and sent out misleading signals (principally the withdrawal of the *Endurance*) that led the Argentines to think that there would be no serious response to an invasion. But there are those, including persons close to the events, who deny that the invasion could have been predicted. According to Geoffrey Howe, who was chancellor of the exchequer at the time, 'nothing had ever crossed my desk which made the risk of an Argentine invasion look remotely likely'. Howe approved of the withdrawal of the *Endurance,* and although he saw merit in the proposal for 'leasing' the Falklands he had not been worried when it was dropped owing to opposition from 10 Downing Street and the House of Commons. The invasion of the Falklands took Howe by surprise. The British intelligence services were also surprised. They had evidence of military preparations but assumed that Buenos Aires was bluffing. Thatcher had no inkling of the invasion until the last moment, and, according to her, the Americans knew even less than the British about Argentina's intentions. Buenos Aires had made threats before, and nothing had happened, and the prime minister had no reason to think that things would be any different in the spring of 1982. This, and the Falklanders' wish to remain British, explains why she had put to one side such schemes as 'lease back', for which she had little liking in any case.[8]

The foreign secretary, Carrington, had left for talks in Israel shortly before the Argentines attacked, and he would hardly have done this had he known what was about to happen. The advice he was receiving indicated that the situation was serious but stable. This was the view of the British embassy in Buenos Aires, other contacts in South America, US as well as British intelligence chiefs, and the US state department. Carrington was aware during March 1982 that Argentina's attitude was hardening, and he asked Washington DC to warn Buenos Aires against drastic action, but it was not clear that an invasion was being planned.[9]

The British reaction

If the British were surprised by the invasion, the Argentines were surprised by the strength of Britain's response. In December 1981 General Leopold Galtieri had been appointed president of Argentina, and he and the rest of the military junta that ruled the country decided to invade the Falklands largely because they did not expect Britain to do much about it. Galtieri's regime favoured invasion as a means of enhancing its prestige and taking attention away from Argentina's economic and political problems. The consequences were not those that Galtieri and his associates wanted. Thatcher's government proclaimed an 'exclusion zone' around the Falklands, ordered a task force to the South Atlantic and declared that Britain had right and justice on its side. The Falklands had been continuously occupied for a hundred and fifty years. The islanders wished to remain British. Argentina had violated international law, attacked British territory and subjects and challenged British sovereignty. The Falkland Islands, invaded by Argentine forces at the end of March 1982, were re-conquered by the middle of June. Once the Falklands were retaken, the British military presence there was expanded at great expense to deter further Argentine aggression and to show the world that, though the days of empire were gone, Britain would continue to protect its remaining possessions.[10]

In the first week of April 1982 Thatcher's government was criticized by MPs and others for having failed to deter the Argentines, but the robust response won it much credit, and the government was lucky in that some of the projected cuts in the armed forces could be postponed or cancelled and that a strong task force could be put together. British newspapers called upon the government to show no weakness or hesitation in dealing with the invasion. *The Times* declared that there was absolutely no excuse for Argentina's 'seizure' of the Falklands. The islanders did not want to be ruled by Buenos Aires, and the Falklands had been British for as long as Argentina had been an independent state. *The Times* endorsed the government's appeal to the UN but was dubious about how helpful this would be because the UN's custom was to limit itself to peace-keeping and to stabilize a situation rather than remove an aggressor by force. It was likely, moreover, that any pro-British resolution in the UN Security Council would be vetoed by the Soviets, who wished to maintain good relations with Argentina on account of the USSR's need for grain. Appealing to the UN was appropriate, 'but only as a prelude to taking action and to give Argentina time to realize the foolish mistake she has made'.[11]

Some newspapers considered the government to be at fault. The *Guardian* found it ironic that the Conservative leadership, having promised at election time in 1979 to improve national defence, now had to respond to an invasion of British territory. As Labour MPs and some Conservative backbenchers demanded a full inquiry, the *Observer* suggested that the government ought to have averted the crisis. Nothing could be done about past mistakes, however, and a plan was needed to deal with the present emergency. A military campaign to retake the Falklands would not be easy, because of the distance involved. Sending the task force and imposing a blockade might be enough to prompt the junta in Buenos Aires to back down, but nobody could be sure, for the invasion was proof that Britain, a nuclear power, could not cow Argentina, 'a medium-sized non-nuclear state using conventional forces' (which raised more questions about the expenditure on Trident). The *Observer* did not expect a war and concluded that there would probably be a treaty recognizing Argentine sovereignty over the islands and preserving a special status for the inhabitants. Whatever happened, the Thatcher government had to be held to account for 'the lack of foresight and the level of unpreparedness that makes it possible for such a contingency to be contemplated'.[12]

Like *The Times*, the *Economist* advocated an energetic response to the invasion. It was essential to challenge Argentina, not because of the 'public uproar' in Britain or 'the puff of post-colonial pride' but because democracies had to show that they were no less capable than authoritarian regimes of defending their interests and because 'to shrink' would be 'to encourage bigger losses in future than the Falklands today'. Sending the task force was appropriate, stated the *Economist*. It did not make war inevitable. Rather, it would help to coerce Buenos Aires into a bargain. The time had come to allow a link between Argentina and the Falklands while protecting the rights of the islanders. Thatcher had to be firm. Compromises would make it harder to obtain support from the United States and other allies and harder to make Argentina negotiate.[13]

American newspapers sided with Britain. The *Washington Post* predicted dire consequences for Argentina if the junta did not withdraw its forces and suggested that, despite the United States' wish for Argentina's friendship, Galtieri was in for a rude awakening if he thought that the Reagan administration would accept the seizure of British territory. By committing such aggression, Argentina 'removes itself from consideration as an American partner in other hemispheric matters'. The *Washington Post* also condemned the UN Security Council for its 'shoddy performance'. When a motion calling for an immediate Argentine withdrawal was put to a vote, Panama opposed and the USSR, China, Poland and Spain all abstained. These countries had condemned Israel's occupation of the West Bank but were apparently ready to condone the Argentine invasion of the Falklands. The *Los Angeles Times*, while agreeing that Argentina was in the wrong, wanted a negotiated settlement on the grounds that if there was war, and the United States helped Britain, Washington DC would be denounced across Latin America.[14]

In the British foreign office it was hoped that the sending of the task force would prompt Argentina to evacuate the Falklands without a fight. Diplomatic manoeuvres were tried as well. Britain wanted the EC to impose sanctions, and on 3 April the UN Security Council resolution requiring Argentina's immediate withdrawal gained a two-thirds majority. On 30 April the United States, after repeatedly urging Buenos Aires to negotiate, finally lost patience and imposed economic sanctions. Britain began to benefit from US assistance (particularly fuel, ammunition, missiles and intelligence). Even so, the Falklands campaign was a risky venture. It was hastily planned and, initially, had incomplete intelligence behind it. The British troops that landed on the Falklands were outnumbered. The task force never had air superiority. The expedition cost about £700 million, and another £800 million was needed to make good the losses sustained. Several historians have argued that the Falklands question should have been seriously addressed before the war of 1982. In this interpretation, the idea that the situation was too difficult to change was really an excuse resorted to later on and dangers and possibilities were not properly assessed. There were times when a 'lease back' arrangement gathered support. The two main requirements were for the Argentines to be patient and for the British government to put more pressure on the Falklanders. Carrington thought that 'lease back' had potential. The Argentines lacked the necessary patience, however, and accused the British of stalling, while the islanders rejected 'lease back'. The government might have pushed 'lease back' with more vigour, to show the islanders that it was serious about making a deal with Argentina. By failing to do this, the government committed itself to defending a territory that it was probably ready to give up.[15]

After the war Thatcher dismissed the allegation that Argentine aggression should have been expected and deterred. She also thought that any large military preparations on the islands, as a precaution, would have prompted an invasion, not prevented it. She later maintained that her position was upheld by the official inquiry into the affair, chaired by Lord Franks. Carrington also believed that the government could not have stopped the invasion. Before the Falklands War it made no sense to send substantial forces to protect the islands. Argentina would not have negotiated under such duress, and the costs and distance involved would have eventually led to the withdrawal of these forces, which would have been misinterpreted by Buenos Aires. Carrington thought that the government's policy was correct: like its Labour predecessors it combined a readiness to talk to Argentina with a determination to defend British sovereignty if necessary. The small details might have been handled differently, but the key point is that unlike in earlier years, the Thatcher government was dealing with a regime in Buenos Aires that was intent on aggression.[16]

Argentina's invasion of the Falkland Islands has been linked with broader problems associated with Britain's decline. The intangibles like prestige and perception had long had a bearing on Britain's ability to conclude agreements, exert influence and avoid conflicts. Had Britain's reputation not been so reduced, perhaps, the Argentines would not have attacked. When the House of Commons was called together for an emergency debate on 2 April 1982, there was strong support from all sides for military action against Argentina. There were a few dissenting voices. The suggestion was made that the government should try negotiation, not military action. Some commentators thought that this was the very attitude that was partly to blame for the Falklands crisis, and there had been moments before the invasion when the foreign office in particular was accused of feebleness in its dealings with Argentina. The prime minister did not have a very high opinion of the foreign office, and she was not alone. To Carrington, however, the problem was not any lack of confidence or insight at the foreign office but the nature of the Falklands question: it was impossible to find a settlement that would satisfy everyone. Carrington knew that sovereignty was a sensitive issue, but he also saw, as had many others, that the Falklands were strategically and economically unimportant to Britain and that in the long run it was not feasible to maintain this small colony, close to Argentina and far away from Britain, in the face of intransigent Argentine hostility. He considered 'lease back' the best available option, as did foreign office minister Nicholas Ridley, but Thatcher was hostile and could sense unease among Conservative MPs who already resented the compromises that had been made to arrange a settlement in Rhodesia. Ridley was sent to the Falklands in July 1979 and again in July 1980 for discussions. The islanders were still firmly against a transfer of sovereignty. When the Commons debated the matter, the general view was that no arrangements should be made that weakened Britain's legal title to the Falklands. Carrington complained that this gave the government insufficient discretion.[17]

Foreign office attempts to create the conditions for a settlement with Argentina therefore came to nothing, and the decisions subsequently taken by the government encouraged Galtieri to think that Britain cared little for the Falklands and would not resort to force in response to an invasion. The withdrawal of HMS *Endurance* was important in this regard, whatever might have been said afterwards to minimize its significance. Another noteworthy development concerned immigration policy. The government, seeking to prevent an influx of ethnic Chinese from Hong Kong, clarified the status of British colonial citizens. Entry to Britain was made dependent upon family background: at least one grandparent had to have been born in Britain. It was expected that white people of British descent would qualify without difficulty, but many inhabitants of Gibraltar and the Falklands did not qualify. Controversy arose and the government was pressed to reconsider. Gibraltar was made a special case. The Falklands were not. This increased the suspicion of the islanders and was not without effect in Buenos Aires.[18]

Almost up to the last moment, the prime minister still regarded the Falklands issue as relatively unimportant and peripheral. Thatcher did not send an ultimatum to Argentina in the final days when the likelihood of an invasion increased. Perhaps she did not think it would make any difference. Certainly the junta was in a state of denial: it simply could not believe that the British would go to war. On the other hand, an ultimatum from Britain might have emboldened those elements in Argentina that opposed the invasion, and the junta might have decided to hold back. It is possible that Britain would have needed to send the task force anyway and that an ultimatum would not have stopped the invasion. In this version of events, the task force had to be sent to put pressure on Buenos Aires, in order for a diplomatic solution to be worked out, and war was avoidable notwithstanding the Argentine invasion and the sending of the British task force. What is clear is that there was a lack of understanding between the two governments. They were not communicating with each other and they were both responsible for what was probably an unintentional drift towards war.[19]

Carrington resigned. His analysis of the situation had not been erroneous, but he had been preoccupied with other business. The Falklands did not receive much attention because the Thatcher government had more pressing concerns. Though the prime minister asked Carrington to stay, he insisted that a scapegoat was needed and that his resignation would make it easier for her to unite government, parliament and public and to recover the Falklands quickly. His replacement as foreign secretary was Francis Pym. Thatcher did not like Pym and soon had cause to regret his promotion. Indeed, Pym was still pushing for a non-military solution after she had decided that the Falklands could not be recovered peacefully.[20]

The conduct of the United States and the European Community

Until the Falklands War, Thatcher devoted most of her time to economic policy. Foreign affairs were left to Carrington. The prime minister's role and reputation in foreign affairs were not great, but after the war she began to emerge as an international figure. Cooperation with the United States was one of her constant goals. The Americans assisted Britain during the Falklands War, making the 'special relationship' more visible and meaningful. This reinforced Thatcher's opinion as to its importance. America's help during the Falklands crisis was not unconditional or unlimited, however, and it needs to be seen in the context of Anglo-American disagreement on such issues as arms control, superpower détente and the Siberian gas pipeline. When Argentina invaded the Falklands, several of Reagan's advisers urged that the United States must remain neutral. Some even suggested that support should be expressed for the regime in Buenos Aires, for it was staunchly anti-communist. Reagan was assured that the United States was under no obligation to help a NATO ally in this 'out of area' matter. Business leaders raised concerns about their trade and investments in Latin America. Several US strategists maintained that the priority was to contain communism, which meant cultivating Galtieri. In the end the US secretary of state, Alexander Haig, and defence secretary Caspar Weinberger, who valued the relationship with Britain, agreed on a pro-British policy. Reagan's instinct was to back the British, and after an abortive effort to mediate between Britain and Argentina the US government made its sympathies clear. The Americans enjoyed enormous goodwill from Britain as a result, though some of this was lost in 1983 when Reagan ordered US forces into Grenada after a military coup there. Grenada was a member of the Commonwealth, yet Washington DC did not contact London. The affair did not long interfere with Anglo-American friendship, which was cemented in this period by the Trident deal, agreement on the formation of a NATO 'rapid deployment force', joint action in the Middle East and other collaborative activities.[21]

Thatcher was grateful for US support during the Falklands crisis. She knew that the Reagan administration had been wooing Argentina in an effort to keep together an anti-communist front in Latin America, but she also knew that Washington DC had warned Buenos Aires against a resort to arms in its dispute with London. As the crisis unfolded she watched with satisfaction as the Argentines overestimated their importance to the United States. At the same time, disagreements on the Falklands and Grenada confirmed that British and US interests did not entirely coincide. Obviously Latin America and the Caribbean mattered more to the United States than to the British, whose only defence commitment on the mainland was in Belize. The need to continue this commitment had been questioned in London, and the likelihood was that it would soon be ended. The Falklands were not important to the Americans and would hardly have mattered to Britain either, had it not been for the quarrel with Argentina. The invasion of the Falklands caused trouble for the US government, for it did not wish to choose between two allies, Britain and Argentina, and the initial attempt to remain neutral became unsustainable. London was frustrated by Haig's effort to mediate. His diplomacy seemed to favour Buenos Aires and to be shaped above all by a desire to gratify Latin America. Though the United States subsequently provided equipment and intelligence and even assumed some of the Royal Navy's duties in the North Atlantic in order to free up resources for the British task force, and though the Americans would probably not have done more for anyone else, still there was resentment in London, where it was thought that the United States had been less helpful than it should have been in view of the 'special relationship' and the fact that Argentina was so clearly in the wrong. The US government continued to worry about damaging its reputation in Latin America, and there was some anti-British sentiment in Washington DC. The non-coincidence of interest between London and Washington DC was underlined by the US invasion of Grenada. Though the governor-general of Grenada had requested assistance and several Caribbean states approved of the US action, Thatcher was annoyed that there had been no consultation, and insult was added to injury when it was revealed that the US state department had advised Reagan not to contact Thatcher in advance in case information leaked out.[22]

The aid rendered by the Americans to the British during the Falklands conflict was considerable in extent and in impact. There were quarrels in Washington DC, however, about its advisability and usefulness. Haig continued to think that the crisis had been pointless. He could not accept that the Falklands were worth fighting over. He was not anti-British, but he initially tried to limit the United States to an impartial role despite the concerted British media and diplomatic effort to obtain American help. Haig deemed it expedient that Argentina should gain something and was disappointed by Thatcher's hard line, though he also accepted that aggression should not be rewarded and later expressed admiration for Thatcher's courage. Weinberger had been strongly pro-British from the outset. Indeed, even before it became official policy Weinberger arranged for cooperation between US agencies and their British opposite numbers. US navy secretary John Lehman was to claim that Britain would never have retaken the Falklands without American assistance. Weinberger denied this, describing the support as important but not crucial. Disunity in the US government ensured that when Britain first asked for assistance the response was hesitant and fragmented. The British government was irritated by the divisions in Washington DC, by Haig's mediation efforts, and by the statements of Jeane Kirkpatrick, the US ambassador to the United Nations, who thought that the United

States' relations with Latin America should not be endangered for the sake of Britain and what she viewed as its questionable claim to the Falklands.[23]

Haig's diplomacy was not entirely fruitless. It did not halt the military conflict, which carried on until Argentine forces surrendered, but London was eventually persuaded to accept a detailed peace plan. Haig could not get Buenos Aires to negotiate, however, which is why he had to abandon his effort. The British did not wish to negotiate either, though they did not categorically say so, leaving Argentina to take the blame for the collapse of Haig's initiative. Support for Britain had been growing, meanwhile, in sections of the US government, Congress, media and public opinion. Haig finally admitted to Reagan that US mediation had failed. He advised that the United States should declare itself in Britain's favour. Soon after this the government of Peru issued a peace plan that was similar to the one Haig had proposed, and it was accepted in principle by Britain. It provided for an immediate ceasefire, the withdrawal of British and Argentine forces, the temporary involvement of a third party in administering the Falklands, talks on sovereignty, an acknowledgement that the interests of the islanders would be respected and a settlement to be worked out with the help of a 'contact group' (Peru, Brazil, the FRG and the United States). Thatcher agreed to proceed on this basis, perhaps affected by the losses that had been suffered in the war. On the other hand, it is not likely that she was willing to retreat from her claim that the Falklands would remain British for as long as their inhabitants wished. She probably suspected that Argentina would not accept Peru's plan, in which case it would be useful for Britain to accept it and appear conciliatory. Whatever the motives behind the British decision, the Peruvian plan was rejected by Buenos Aires.[24]

Washington DC's options during the Falklands crisis narrowed quickly, and this made clearer the difficulties the two superpowers were now having when it came to controlling awkward situations in disturbed parts of the world. In the Middle East, US and Soviet efforts to influence events had brought mixed results since the 1960s. The Falklands also presented problems, primarily for the Americans, who found that their ability to manage the crisis was limited. War could not be averted. Britain was helped to recover the Falklands but at some risk to US-Latin American relations. Argentina soon had a democratic government, though, and when it blamed Galtieri and the junta for starting the war the United States was relieved from much of the criticism it received for siding with Britain.[25]

If Washington DC's reaction to the invasion of the Falklands was not all that Britain might have wished for, the European response proved to be even more disappointing. The EC had been slow to react to earlier crises, notably the Soviet invasion of Afghanistan, and in 1981 a new procedure was created. On the request of three member states, a meeting could be held within 48 hours. Britain had strongly advocated this arrangement and used it in April 1982. Although leaders in Western Europe had for years been complaining about Britain's semi-detached attitude towards the Community, Argentina's invasion was condemned and a ban was placed on Argentine imports into the EC. Members of the EC also acted together at the UN to uphold a common position against Argentina. Sanctions were accepted as a necessary economic instrument to back up political action. Yet sanctions on a joint basis only lasted a month. Once Britain resorted to military force the EC's unity collapsed, chiefly because the continentals were worried about their trade and investments in Latin America. Despite pressure from London and Washington DC and despite the fact that a fellow member of the EC was the victim of military aggression, EC leaders chose not to stick to a common policy. Only a minority was prepared to continue sanctions. Later there were quarrels over Britain's refusal to discuss the sovereignty of the Falklands with Argentina's civilian government, appointed in 1984 after the fall of the junta. Even so, the speed of the initial collective response to the Falklands invasion had been impressive. As Britain had asserted, the avoidance of delay in times of crisis could make a big difference. The Americans were also struck by this, and the concept of a European 'defence identity' gained a fillip. Washington DC had not appreciated previous hold-ups when a European response to specific issues had been wanted and expected, particularly when the eventual response was not in line with US policy.[26]

During the Falklands crisis the British focused on winning over the UN and gaining help from the United States, not on working with the EC. The EC's support was welcome but secondary, and Britain did not pay much attention to the EC once it had agreed on sanctions. Thatcher insisted that Argentine forces had to leave the Falklands, and although EC leaders agreed with this they were angered by her reluctance to try out non-military options. They suggested that Britain could do more to end the crisis. They accused Britain of escalation. The EC embargo seemed to be having no effect on Argentina, and Britain was taking EC support for granted. These grumblings were added to existing resentment against Britain's position on agricultural prices and the EC budget. In return for the EC's assistance on the Falklands issue, it was thought, Britain should be more flexible, especially on the budget. The Thatcher government refused to make such a connection. The attitude of the Italian and Irish governments had a lot to do with domestic politics. About a million Argentines were of Italian extraction, and plans were afoot to allow Italians living abroad to vote in elections in Italy, while Dublin was arguing with London about the future of Northern Ireland, and the minority government of Charles Haughey was sensitive about Ireland's neutralism and worried about an upcoming by-election.[27]

The consequences of the war for Britain

In Britain the Falklands crisis brought on a wave of patriotic fervour, sustained by the government and most sections of the media. Some sceptics spoke out against the military response and argued that the affair demonstrated a number of uncomfortable truths about Thatcher's Britain. In particular, it was claimed that a real understanding of Britain's role in the world was being prevented (and had been for years) by a comforting notion of British values and the self-image of Britain as a champion of freedom, democracy and justice. This theme has been taken up by Mark Curtis, who contrasts the claim that Argentina had trampled on the rights of the Falklanders with the British government's indifference towards the rights of other people. There was the case of Diego Garcia, for example. In 1966 Britain had allowed the Americans to establish a base there, but this entailed the forced removal of its inhabitants. After a long dispute Britain agreed to compensate the people of Diego Garcia, just five days, in fact, before Argentina invaded the Falklands. Another case was the Thatcher government's friendship with the Pinochet regime in Chile. Pinochet's usefulness as an ally increased when he backed Britain on the Falklands issue, but his government had one of the worst human rights records in the world. Thatcher did not like to dwell on this and rejected suggestions that Britain should withdraw its ambassador and stop arms sales to Chile. She did not want to jeopardize cooperation on the Falklands or encourage parliament to impose strong measures against Chile.[28]

Britain's actions during the Falklands crisis aroused controversy at home and abroad, but Thatcher described the criticism as 'malicious and misleading nonsense', as when it was asserted that the British government ordered the sinking of the *General Belgrano*, an Argentine cruiser, in order to foil the peace plan proposed by Peru. When pressure mounted at the UN for Britain to abandon its military effort, British representatives emphasized that nothing could be done while the junta refused to talk except on the basis of Argentine sovereignty over the Falklands. As for the idea that the military campaign might be suspended in order for talks to be arranged, Thatcher declared this to be impossible, although she did eventually agree that terms should be put to Argentina by UN secretary-general Javier Perez de Cuellar. The twists and turns in US policy inconvenienced her, but she persuaded Reagan that an Argentine withdrawal was essential, and he agreed that to let the aggressor off the hook would be to put at risk many other territories that were affected by similar disputes.[29]

After the war Argentina continued to claim sovereignty over the Falkland Islands, but as before the inhabitants made plain their wish to remain under British rule. Thatcher's government was prepared to reopen discussions with Buenos Aires on economic cooperation, environmental issues and the exploitation of energy resources but declared that the willingness to negotiate did not indicate any change on sovereignty. There were sections of parliamentary and public opinion in Britain that favoured concessions to Argentina. The issue remained sensitive for obvious reasons. Some argued that the bill for defending the Falklands was too high. Others focused on the sacrifices that had been made and insisted that Britain should never discuss sovereignty. The Falklands question after 1982 showed how difficult it was for Britain to deal with the remnants of empire. There were commitments that the British could not abandon because of political circumstances but which they might otherwise have given up (this applies to the Falklands and probably also to Belize and Gibraltar).[30]

The defence review of 1981 had included cuts in the Royal Navy. The surface fleet was to be reduced to just 50 vessels. The Falklands conflict altered some of these plans, yet the pattern of expenditure was not greatly changed and the navy, army and air force continued to compete for funds. Most of Britain's maritime forces were devoted to NATO duties. Navy chiefs wanted to enhance the capability to act beyond the NATO area, but this was not a government priority. The continental commitment remained Britain's primary concern. It took 16 per cent of the total defence budget (£3.5 billion in 1986). A third of all British frontline forces were in Europe and this continued to represent a heavy financial burden, the annual cost being much higher than that of maintaining the whole navy for a year, which gave the navy lobby a strong argument against the focus on the continental commitment. This commitment did not weaken, however, and the only significant deployments of British forces outside Europe were in Belize, Cyprus, Gibraltar and the Falklands. The Falklands garrison was the largest. By 1986 it was costing Britain £250 million a year, though this did not radically alter the overall picture since most of the available resources were still devoted to NATO-related activities. Victory in the Falklands made the Thatcher government popular and boosted Britain's prestige, but the war cost many millions of pounds, the future defence of the islands proved hugely expensive and the war made it impossible to resolve the sovereignty issue with Argentina. The war also meant that downsizing the Royal Navy became more difficult politically, which complicated the task of controlling defence spending. Victory in the Falklands fostered anew the belief that Britain still mattered in the world, and one result was that the central purpose of the 1981 defence review, to bring Britain's defence roles up to date, in line with real needs and resources, was effectively shelved. In 1981 a beginning had been made and defence requirements had been redefined. The Falklands War changed things. The Falklands garrison became one of the mainstays of Britain's defence planning, along with Trident and the continental commitment. These were the three constants from which there could be no escape.[31]

Announcing the Argentine surrender in the Commons on 15 June 1982, the prime minister promised to provide for the future security of the Falklands. She paid tribute to the armed forces, as did Labour leader Michael Foot. On the future of the islands, Foot urged the prime minister to be flexible and to abide by UN resolutions. He did not think that the possibility of trusteeship should be ruled out, but Thatcher replied that the UN resolutions had specifically mentioned the need for an Argentine withdrawal. The Argentines had not withdrawn and British forces had been obliged to make a hazardous landing: 'I cannot agree...that those men risked their lives in any way to have a United Nations trusteeship. They risked their lives to defend British sovereign territory, the British way of life and the rights of British people to determine their own future'. When pressed, though, Thatcher did agree that there would be an inquiry into the Falklands crisis. She said that this inquiry had to be limited or it would take too long to complete.[32]

While noting that 'Britain's post-Falklands mood is more measured than euphoric', the *Economist* regarded the increase in popular support for the government as truly remarkable. According to opinion polls, 84 per cent were satisfied with the government's handling of the Falklands situation, 76 per cent believed that it had been right to send the task force (despite the 'cost in lives and money'), and 71 per cent were willing to pay more taxes in order for the Falklands to be properly defended. Even so, the *Guardian* insisted that there ought to be an inquiry, and the *Observer* subsequently reported that just two weeks before the invasion, Carrington was overruled when he told the cabinet he wanted to send submarines to the South Atlantic as a precautionary measure. Members of the cabinet, including Thatcher, had been concerned less about the threat to the Falklands than about the defence budget and the need to meet NATO force-level requirements. In the foreign office there was no fear of an inquiry. The key decisions had been made by the prime minister, the defence secretary, Nott, and other members of the cabinet, and Thatcher was on record both for demanding cuts in defence spending and for assuming that a small force would be sufficient to protect the Falklands. The *Observer* hoped that the inquiry would clarify Thatcher's role. Could she explain why she had not confirmed to Buenos Aires that an invasion would be met by force? In July 1982 Galtieri told an Italian journalist that he and his colleagues had been 'amazed' by her response to the invasion. *The Times* wanted to know why Britain had been 'caught napping' and drew attention to some disconcerting features of the Falklands crisis: the failure of deterrence; the apparent indifference, which allowed Buenos Aires to think that Britain would not fight to defend the islands; the bipartisan effort, over many years, 'to negotiate sovereignty away' and give up responsibility for the Falklands; and the withdrawal of HMS *Endurance*.[33]

Thatcher went to Washington DC in June 1982 for talks with Reagan. She also addressed the UN in New York City. The *Chicago Tribune* recognized that she was probably right about the future of the Falkland Islands: Thatcher and Reagan had both said that it would take a long time before a political solution could be worked out and that one of the preconditions was a 'credible' government in Argentina. The *New York Times* highlighted the distance between Reagan's view that the United States had been right to seek a negotiated settlement that would have removed Argentine forces from the Falklands and Haig's belief that the junta in Buenos Aires had been inflexible because it expected such figures as Jeane Kirkpatrick and White House national security adviser William P. Clark to manoeuvre the British into a surrender.[34]

Geoffrey Howe rightly observed that among the most significant results of the Falklands War was the 'transformation' in Margaret Thatcher's standing at home and abroad. For her strong leadership in a difficult situation, Howe thought, the prime minister deserved all the praise she received, but this led to a 'striking change in her perception of herself', and as her confidence in her own judgement increased she became more dismissive of others. She took advantage of her popularity and was regarded in some quarters as little short of a national saviour. In this context her patriotic rhetoric seemed appropriate. As she declared in a speech in Cheltenham on 3 July 1982: 'We have ceased to be a nation in retreat ... Britain found herself again in the South Atlantic and will not look back from the victory she has won'. Thatcher loyalists relied on the 'Falklands factor' for electoral and other party ends. They used victory in war to build support for the Conservatives' domestic programme. Critics, especially on the British left, pointed to what they saw as the damaging consequences of the war, especially the growth of nationalistic prejudice, which, they said, would contaminate British politics and society. In the foreign office there was a desire to demonstrate that Britain should not try to act like a world power but must make itself a strong and economically competitive European power. Many commentators complained that success in the Falklands had inflated the reputation of those whose political future depended on victory, obscured the real causes of the war and exaggerated the importance of the Falkland Islands to Britain. Perhaps there was a wish to cover up Britain's decline. After the war the 'Fortress Falklands' policy was questioned on political, strategic and financial grounds.[35]

As Thatcher's popularity soared, the Labour Party seemed more weak and divided. Labour gained only 28 per cent of votes cast in the general election of June 1983 and lost 60 seats. The Conservatives won 397 seats in 1983, compared with 339 in 1979. During the Falklands crisis Labour found it difficult to challenge the government. Labour pacifists could not support the war, but even the staunchest Labour politicians and voters were willing to express approval for Thatcher's decision to fight for the islands. The precise effect of the 'Falklands factor' at the 1983 general election is not easy to determine. To some historians, the key to the Conservative landslide was not the Falklands but tax cuts and improving economic conditions. For others, public opinion was greatly influenced by the Falklands crisis and there would have been no landslide without it. It should also be noted that the Conservatives' opponents were not strong. The Labour Party was split. Foot thought that Britain had an obligation to the islanders, since they wished to remain British. He accused the Thatcher government of betraying them and declared that it had no option but to recover the islands and make up for its previous mistakes. Foot thereby associated himself with the policy of retaking the Falklands, but a small number of Labour MPs opposed the war, and two members of the Labour front bench were sacked for recommending that the task force should be recalled. Prominent left-winger Tony Benn, who had served in the Wilson and Callaghan governments of the 1960s and 1970s, came out strongly against the war. He wanted a negotiated settlement through the UN. After the Argentine surrender he found the praise expressed for Thatcher in the Commons 'odious and excessive'. Even Foot congratulated her. Benn took a different line, asking her to publish full details about the war. He declared that the war had not been necessary. Nor had it solved anything, since the future of the Falklands had not been settled and negotiations with Argentina would be needed sooner or later. The prime minister replied that she could not publish all the relevant documents, that she would not talk to the Argentines, and that the war had not been unnecessary, 'because the freedom of speech which the Right Honourable Gentleman made such excellent use of had been won for him by people fighting for it'. 'Rubbish', Benn wrote afterwards.[36]

The Falklands victory proved that Britain was just about able to operate effectively outside the NATO area. Yet the time had long since passed when such efforts could be undertaken without much inconvenience, and British leaders knew that another operation on the same scale was best avoided. The 'Fortress Falklands' policy was expensive, and, with no settlement likely, Britain had to shoulder an indefinite defence burden in the South Atlantic. The Franks Report of 1983 highlighted failings on Britain's part in the period before the Argentine invasion, especially with regard to intelligence. Encouraged by this, various commentators continued to suggest that the foreign office should have interpreted the evidence differently and that intelligence chiefs ought to have realized that invasion was coming, particularly in view of the fact that the Galtieri regime in Buenos Aires, which had been losing popularity, was bound to seek a rallying cause to unite the Argentine people. The withdrawal of the *Endurance*, it seemed, had created too much of a temptation. The British people tended not to focus on this, however, and it was Thatcher's determination to resist aggression that lived longest in the public mind.[37]

Summary

The increase in tension between Buenos Aires and London during the 1970s and the obstacles to an agreement on the Falkland Islands created a situation in which mistakes committed by both Argentine and British leaders resulted in invasion and war. Britain emerged victorious, but what did the Falklands War achieve? For all the talk of honour and all the celebrations that marked the end of the war, there were many who, in the words of Max Hastings and Simon Jenkins, 'perceived an underlying absurdity in a struggle so far from home for a leftover of empire'. Most people agreed that the Falklands had to be retaken and that aggressors could not be allowed to win, but there were also regrets, especially over the war casualties. British taxpayers were obliged to cover the much-increased cost of defending the islands, in order to justify a war that had been made necessary, it was widely thought, by political and diplomatic errors. That the victory celebrations were so well attended was possibly an indication of respect for those who had fought in the Falklands War, not so much for the cause itself, and the conflict did not permanently change British society or Britain's place in the world.[38] Appearance and perception are worth bearing in mind, however, for even if Britain's economic performance and military capabilities set a limit to what could be done in international affairs, Britain's status, role and influence were far from negligible, and there *was* something to the Thatcherite mantra of 'Britain is great again'. It affected the thinking of policy-makers. It affected public opinion. It imparted legitimacy to certain principles and activities and had an impact on the Cold War, the 'special relationship', the thaw in Europe, the evolution of the EC, and the involvement of Britain and the West in Africa, Asia and the Middle East. For a time, Britain was a more confident actor on the world stage. This enhancement of British prestige did not last very long, perhaps, but it had considerable short-term effects at home and abroad.

Conclusion

Confidence, prestige, influence and perseverance: British foreign policy during the 1970s and 1980s evinced all these qualities. There were reverses and retreats, but there were also successes. Britain continued to act like a great power and to be treated as such. Through consultation and negotiation and through diplomatic, political, economic and military measures, Britain remained an active participant in international affairs. The British went on pursuing their vital interests, and they could still sway others. Britain was no mere spectator. Although some major events of the 1970s and 1980s happened without British involvement, most did not. While there were significant agreements and relationships that did not depend on Britain's input or approval, on the issues that most affected Britain there could be no progress and no resolution without a British contribution. Britain's decline relative to other great powers of the late twentieth century is not in doubt, but the remarkable thing is not the decline but the ways in which it was hidden, denied, delayed and minimized. The Americans, Soviets and others were aware that Britain carried less weight in the world than it once had, but they also knew that they could not discount British influence.

Britain was a nuclear power, one of only a handful in the world that possessed a formidable destructive capacity and the consequential coercive options. It is true that the British could not compete in the superpower arms race and that the nuclear deterrent could not be maintained without American help. Far from unwanted, however, the close strategic association with America was a matter of established policy. Nevertheless, defence remained problematic. The task of finding the right balance between nuclear and conventional forces, the comparatively high defence spending, and the need to meet commitments to NATO and outside the NATO area were among the main difficulties that had to be addressed. The British were generally in favour of arms control, with two basic

221

provisos: they did not want their nuclear deterrent to be included in the US-Soviet bargaining process, and they insisted that the West's nuclear and conventional strength in Europe should not be reduced too quickly. The situation was complicated by the controversy at home over Trident and by the effects of SALT, the INF Treaty of 1987 and the dispute about SNF.

Britain endorsed, albeit cautiously, the European thaw and superpower détente of the 1970s and played an important role in CSCE, primarily in the human rights strand and in the promotion of East-West trade. The Cold War seemed to change course in this era as the former bipolarity gave way to a more flexible dispensation, largely because of the Nixon-Kissinger effort to arrange the withdrawal of US forces from Vietnam: hence America's overtures to the USSR and China. These were the years of SALT I, the Berlin agreements, 'Ostpolitik' and the Helsinki process. Flexibility was welcomed and exploited by Britain, though it necessitated further adjustments. It did not last, and it did not greatly change the international order. Old rhetoric, practices and principles were revived in the early 1980s when conservative elites enjoyed political ascendancy in Britain and the United States and when the Soviets refused to end their occupation of Afghanistan and other interventions in the developing world, particularly Africa. But even without this revival there would have been a disinclination to compromise for the sake of détente. Domestic opposition to détente had grown in America, and British governments were more wary of thaw than were governments in Western Europe. The British were not surprised and were in some respects relieved when détente faltered.

Though the Soviets frequently complained about the 'linkage' approach of the Americans, Moscow did not invariably treat America's conduct, especially in the developing world, as extraneous to détente. In the early 1970s the war between India and Pakistan, the coup in Chile and the Yom Kippur War all affected US-Soviet negotiations, and later the struggles in Afghanistan and Nicaragua also demonstrated that the Americans and Soviets would go on challenging each other, sometimes through proxies. The British often found fault with US policies in the developing world and saw in Washington DC a propensity to overreact when problems arose, but leaders in Western Europe were even more dissatisfied with the Americans and declared that the thaw in Europe would not be given up on account of events outside Europe.

Britain preserved the relationships appropriate to its rank among the great powers. Despite the military withdrawal from East of Suez, there were still interests and commitments in the Middle East and Far East, and Britain had links with regions all over the world through the Commonwealth. Membership of international organizations – NATO, the EC, UN Security Council, Commonwealth and G7 – brought opportunities, influence and status, though it was not easy to carry these bodies in a chosen direction, and the British had to accept decisions with which they disagreed. Equally frustrating was the extent to which these organizations were prone to schism, although the British could be just as argumentative as anyone else. There were quarrels in NATO over defence posture, Cold War measures, détente, extra-European crises and American leadership. There were quarrels in the EC over the speed and nature of integration, and in the UN over institutional inefficiency, politicization, the anti-West bias of the majority of members, and the self-interested uses to which strong nations could put the UN's procedures and authority. In the Commonwealth there was increasing criticism of Britain's policy on a range of issues, and in the G7 Britain lacked the economic might of the United States, the FRG and Japan and normally had to fit in with what they wanted.

Anglo-Soviet relations were constantly affected by mutual suspicion, but economic and cultural links were expanded during the 1970s and there were hopes for further progress. Circumstances changed and there was more animosity in the early 1980s. Then Anglo-Soviet relations improved again in the Gorbachev period, though the impact of this should not be exaggerated: the benefits to Britain came less from direct contact with the USSR and more from the general relaxation that characterized East-West interaction. Britain developed a new relationship with China from the early 1970s. This led to more trade, broadened the international thaw, increased Britain's foreign policy options and helped the British to manage their interests in Asia, especially with regard to Hong Kong. Nevertheless, Britain and China did not become close.

By far the most important relationship was that with the United States, even if it did appear to be more about convenience than affection or concord. For the most part Britain could not achieve what it wanted in the world without restraining the Americans or gaining their assistance, and both activities became more difficult

during the 1970s and 1980s. Washington DC valued British friendship and cooperation but not as much as the British would have
liked, and the Americans had long since determined not to allow
themselves to be tricked into propping up Britain's international
position except in times and places of the United States' choosing. Anglo-American relations were largely dependent on the level
of mutual respect between leaders. Callaghan and Carter worked
together more effectively than Heath and Nixon, and Thatcher's
suggestions were sought and received by Reagan rather more than
they were by Bush. Even in periods of intimacy, though, there was
a limit to Britain's leverage in Washington DC.

Thatcher was disappointed not to get more US help in her dealings with Europe. Resisting the designs of Paris and Bonn became
one of her chief priorities, but they held the initiative in the EC
and the British managed to alter only some of their schemes.
By the end of the 1980s the effects on the EC and on the wider
international order of changes in the Cold War and the prospect
of German reunification seemed to Thatcher to be potentially
disastrous.

Some other problems, outside Europe, had been overcome,
though they left difficulties in their wake. A settlement had been
agreed for Rhodesia, for example, but it was controversial at home,
and many Commonwealth countries were less than satisfied with
the way Britain had handled the affair. The same was true of the
process of reform in South Africa. In the Middle East circumstances were slow to improve, and they appeared no less ominous
in the early 1990s than they had at the beginning of the 1970s.
Britain's role in the Middle East decreased in this period. There
was still some involvement, but the British could not do much
to stabilize the region and often regretted US as well as Soviet
interference there. Britain played a useful part in offering peace
proposals and especially in supporting American and EC diplomatic efforts, but Arab-Israeli hostility, wrangling about oil, division among the Arab states, the question of Palestinian rights, the
strength of nationalism and Islamic fundamentalism and rising
social and economic inequality meant that conflict in the Middle
East could not be halted.

During the 1970s and 1980s, such was the international context
that a lot was going on over which Britain had little or no control.
Things might have been different had it not been for the resource

gap, but then again, more money and manpower would not have changed every unfavourable situation, and power did not rest only on economic success and the size and quality of the armed forces. They were the tangible underpinnings, however, and they affected opinion at home and abroad with respect to Britain's actual and potential influence. Britain could not afford to sustain a world role, overseas commitments were scaled down and the focus was more on Western Europe as the place where security concerns and economic needs could be met, although the British could and did continue to act beyond Europe. The slow economic growth, low productivity, weakness of sterling, balance of payments embarrassments, loss of manufacturing jobs and failure more quickly to increase exports all took their toll. Britain was not unique. Other leading nations also experienced economic problems in the 1970s and 1980s, but the British economy had been underperforming relative to others since the 1950s, and recovery was harder to bring about in later years.

Economic worries often affected the makers of foreign policy. So did the need to respond to events in a way that did the least damage to British interests. On some matters the British were double-minded. Pragmatic and conservative, they could see both sides to a dispute. There was a degree of equivocation with regard to the 'special relationship'. Heath opposed American policy at the time of the Arab-Israeli war of 1973, for instance, and accused the United States of making a dangerous crisis much worse. Yet he also recognized that the Americans did a lot to mitigate tension in the Middle East, promoting Israel's safety and sponsoring the peace agreement between Israel and Egypt. Looking back on the 1973 war, Heath was willing to accept that despite the way they went about it, the Americans probably meant well. They understood 'that in the long term the Israelis and the Arabs would have to live together on an equal footing'. Thatcher was more committed to the 'special relationship' than Heath had been, but she did not back the Americans on everything. Though she agreed that the West had to respond firmly to the Soviet invasion of Afghanistan and lamented the lack of support from the EC, she also advised Washington DC against carrying sanctions too far. In general, she thought, it was important for Britain to stand with America. Sometimes she found this difficult, and on the Siberian gas pipeline and the US invasion of Grenada she felt betrayed.[1]

The mixed attitude towards détente remained a staple feature of British diplomacy. The governments of the 1970s and 1980s, Labour and Conservative, rarely doubted that a thaw was worth pursuing, but they maintained that this should be done from a position of advantage. Concessions had to be avoided for as long as possible and made only at the right moment. The essential precondition was a stronger, steadfast NATO. London did not trust Moscow. One of the main reasons why the British emphasized human rights in the Helsinki process was their belief that this would subject the Soviets to maximum pressure. At the time of the Helsinki conference in 1975, nobody knew that ten years later a pro-reform leader would emerge in the USSR and help to change the political situation in the Soviet Union, the eastern bloc and beyond. At the end of the 1970s, it appeared that the human rights agenda and the wider détente might collapse. After the Helsinki conference the treatment of dissidents in the USSR and bloc was largely dependent on the course of East-West relations. When Moscow reckoned that more could be gained through contact with the West than by imposing additional controls at home, reform movements in the Soviet Union had relative freedom. When détente stalled, or offered too little to the Soviet government, domestic repression increased. A new crackdown from 1979 was related to the West's response to the invasion of Afghanistan and to earlier indications that the 1970s thaw was already being reversed: Soviet and Cuban involvement in Africa had been resisted, arms limitation talks had reached an impasse, and the USSR's human rights record had been vigorously condemned at the CSCE review meeting in Belgrade in 1977–78.[2]

One of the most significant adjustments the British had to make at this time was that they were no longer able so regularly to play a mediating role between the superpowers. The change was epitomized by SALT and other direct US-Soviet negotiations (in contrast with earlier triumphs such as the 1963 Test Ban Treaty, which owed a lot to British influence). Moreover, the Americans increasingly saw the FRG as their key ally in Europe. The FRG gained strength in NATO and the EC during the 1970s and 1980s. Washington DC could not fail to register the less Atlanticist slant given to British foreign policy by the Heath government's move towards Europe, even if this tendency was only temporary and partial. The Americans had already been disappointed by Britain's refusal to send combat troops to Vietnam, by the clumsy British efforts to make peace there, by Britain's retreat from East of Suez and by Britain's economic and financial weaknesses. It seemed to America that Britain was declining, which made Washington DC less susceptible to London's advice and limited the opportunities Britain had to manipulate the relationship between the United States and Soviet Union.[3]

In the Callaghan years the attempt to influence the Americans, the Soviets and others was kept up, and there were some useful results, not least in the sphere of Anglo-American defence links. Most importantly, Carter provided for the upgrading of the British nuclear deterrent. Polaris eventually went out of service in 1996. Trident was deployed by Britain from 1994. It had been a source of controversy for more than fifteen years. Following the deliberations of the late 1970s and early 1980s, the Thatcher government committed Britain to Trident, but many contemporaries did not believe that Britain needed it. To them, Trident offered a defence capability that was inappropriate and excessive. Still, it kept Britain among the strongest military powers in the world, and it was one of the achievements of the Callaghan government that arrangements were made for the deterrent alongside other demonstrations of Britain's international status and impact. Callaghan contributed to discussions about and measures of détente and disarmament. He helped to resolve disagreements between the United States and Western Europe. He made progress with his main objectives: to keep the talks on arms control going, to promote NATO's 'dual track' in connection with this and to safeguard the future of the British deterrent. Callaghan knew that Britain's influence was limited and that it was impossible quickly to restore the economic and military supports that would have enhanced British power, but he managed to meet the nation's defence needs as they were seen at the time. He also kept his cabinet sufficiently united on these matters and resisted pressure from the Labour left. A fair verdict on these years would be that Britain did as well as could be expected even if foreign policy was 'reactive and not particularly inspired'.[4]

Once the hard-line attitude of the early years of Thatcher's premiership had given way in the mid-1980s to a desire to draw Gorbachev into new agreements, breakthroughs were made, and Britain appeared to be building a more constructive relationship with the USSR. Less was achieved than might have been possible, though, particularly on Anglo-Soviet trade and on British involvement in common EC initiatives relating to East-West relations. One reason was the persistence of the older idea of Britain as a mediator with the capacity to play an independent role in international affairs. Moreover, there were issues on which Thatcher wanted to keep in step with America. She could not go further because she knew that the Americans favoured restraint. When Howe was foreign secretary, he regretted the checks that US policy sometimes imposed on British policy. He went to Washington DC in July 1983 and was disappointed to find a lack of enthusiasm for closer East-West links: 'On the issue that was uppermost in my mind, our attitude towards the Soviet bloc, I left Washington with the impression that my own thinking – in the direction of increased contacts – was ready to be a shade more adventurous than that of the Americans'.[5]

It was and is claimed that Thatcher was too close to the Americans. Some historians have built upon this to suggest that British policy departed from its declared values and goals. Instead of promoting democracy, human rights and justice, the British backed American military action around the world, accepted the United States' collusion with brutal dictators and supported an international order that suited the West's selfish political and economic interests. According to this line of argument, the United States and Britain both became more assertive in the 1980s in order to regain influence that they thought had been lost owing to such developments as decolonization, the rise of the developing nations, the American defeat in Vietnam and the growing power of oil-producing countries. In Britain, the truth was covered up and people were fooled by government propaganda, which was aided by the media and academia. Many policies were justified with reference to the Cold War and the Soviet threat, when in fact the actions of the USSR rarely affected Britain at all. Politicians became so used to accepting this ideological framework that they ended up believing it and thereby deceived themselves as well as everyone else.[6]

Though it is clear that British policy was at times less enlightened and benevolent than the groups responsible for it were ready to admit, exaggerations are unhelpful. There were notable differences between Britain and the United States. Their motives, policies and goals did not always coincide, and there were many quarrels between the two governments. It is important to appreciate the difficulties that faced policy-makers and to ask why some options were taken and others rejected. We cannot simply overlook the possibility that some of the decisions made by British leaders (and by the Americans) were appropriate and justified, whether in response to Cold War developments or other stimuli.

When the invasion of Afghanistan soured US-Soviet relations at the end of the 1970s, France and the FRG led Western Europe's endeavour to protect détente. Thatcher's Britain sided more with the Americans as the Cold War revived. In Reagan the United States had a leader with whom Thatcher could usually cooperate. The rise of Gorbachev made her think that a new thaw was possible, and she was willing to pursue this while trusting also in the British deterrent and a strong NATO. By the late 1980s she was dissatisfied because changes were happening too quickly for her liking. She argued with Britain's allies and resumed a tougher stance on East-West relations. Western leaders, she thought, should be doing more to challenge the USSR on its human rights record and should not be so eager to lavish economic aid on the Soviets and the eastern bloc. Thatcher's thinking on the future of the EC solidified as well. She suspected that reforms in the EC and the continuation of East-West détente would reduce British influence. Paris and Bonn insisted on the need to push ahead with détente and wished to develop the EC in ways that London opposed, and they were encouraged by the realization that with Bush having replaced Reagan in the White House, the British government could no longer expect the same level of US support. Bush wanted to deal with Britain as part of the EC and part of NATO, not as a special ally with a unique importance to the United States. On European matters Washington DC attached most importance to the views of Bonn, not London.[7]

The old military balance between East and West had gone. Soviet troops were leaving the eastern bloc and NATO seemed to be losing its raison d'être. This, along with Eastern Europe's call for economic aid and its desire to merge economically with Western Europe, rapidly increased the importance of the EC. Previously in the West, Atlantic institutions had covered security and European institutions had covered economics, but now this distinction broke down. The British were unsure how to react. They could no longer separate détente and security issues from the EC and European integration: all became mixed together in a debate about Britain's international role. Thatcher sought to convince the Americans that the 'special relationship' should go on. She denied that the EC could deal with matters that were properly the concern of NATO and maintained that it was NATO that should supervise détente. In her celebrated speech of 20 September 1988, delivered at the College of Europe in Bruges, she warned against the creation of 'a European super-state' and argued that individual countries would not fit into 'some sort of identikit European personality'. Thatcher wished to preserve the Europe of independent states and preferred the clarity of NATO's security function to what she saw as illegitimate pan-European concepts. She was marginalized. Britain's demand for a cautious, unhurried approach to security problems and European integration jarred with the wishes of the FRG, France and others for a more ambitious programme. They accused the British of selfishness and obstruction. London could not prevent institutional reorganization, was not regarded by the new leaders of Eastern Europe as a key partner for the future and was unable to control the timing or nature of German reunification. This heightened the quarrels within Britain about the EC, Anglo-American relations and how to respond to reforms in the Soviet Union and Eastern Europe.[8]

Thatcher maintained that the Cold War was transformed and the collapse of the USSR and eastern bloc brought closer by the resilient, explicitly anti-communist position taken by herself and Reagan in the early and mid-1980s. She had long been a critic of détente. Offering concessions to Moscow had not helped to end the Cold War, she thought, but had encouraged the Soviets to make further demands. Thatcher gained added support and respect owing to Britain's victory in the Falklands War. This victory was facilitated by the United States. American secretary of state Alexander Haig thought that even without assistance Britain would have won the Falklands War. Without US help, however, the recovery of the islands would have taken more time and cost more in lives, money and resources, and had the United States opposed Britain's military action the outcome might have been different. Haig considered the war avoidable. In this he was correct. British leaders did not believe that Argentina would invade the Falklands, assuming that there was no intention to act upon the threats that for years had characterized Argentine policy, and nobody in the

Argentine government could believe that the British would go to war over the islands. To these mistakes, failings in intelligence and information certainly contributed. Neither side envisaged a resort to arms by the other. The misunderstanding that prevailed before the war and the amazement that greeted the war probably affected would-be mediators as well. Once the islands had been retaken, none of this mattered much to Thatcher. To her way of thinking, the Falklands War involved a great deal more than the islands and their inhabitants. It concerned 'our honour as a nation' and the fundamental principle 'that aggressors should never succeed'. Victory enhanced Britain's reputation and boosted British self-confidence. Thatcher exploited it, and, understandably, she and her followers did not subsequently depart from the interpretation she had placed upon it.[9]

If the Falklands crisis gave Thatcher her finest hour, Europe was her downfall. At the end of the 1980s several of the prime minister's senior colleagues turned against her because of the quarrels with Britain's European partners. The pace of change in Europe accelerated considerably in the late 1980s. The Single European Act (SEA) was signed in February 1986 and came into effect in July 1987. This was the first fundamental revision of the Treaty of Rome of 1957. It was designed to remove all remaining barriers to free trade between the members of the European Community, and it also codified procedures for a common foreign policy. The ultimate goal was harmonization. The SEA began the legislative changes that were needed to make unity possible and quickened the process by extending the practice of qualified majority voting. Thatcher, who was against the imposition of common arrangements within the EC, especially on financial and social matters, accepted the SEA. She later said that she had been misled as to its real character and purpose. In fact the situation was more complicated than this, because she wanted the single market: it was in line with her commitment to economic liberalism, market forces and deregulation. What she did not want was the political modernization that other EC leaders thought should accompany the economic reforms. Thatcher and her supporters declared that Britain must be ruled not by the EC but by the British government, which was accountable to an elected national parliament. What sense did it make to remove regulations in one sphere (economics) only to increase them in another (governance)?

Another step away from British preferences with regard to European integration was the Maastricht Treaty. Its terms were finalized in December 1991, by which time Thatcher had been replaced as prime minister by John Major. The treaty was signed in February 1992. It established the European Union (EU) on the basis of three core components: the EC and its supra-national institutions; the Common Foreign and Security Policy, which was to be intergovernmental in nature; and Justice and Home Affairs, which was also to be an intergovernmental entity. While making use of pre-existing practices and structures, Maastricht opened a new chapter in the history of European integration. It was made possible by a compromise. It extended the functions of the EC (which itself had grown out of the European Economic Community created in 1957) to cover international relations, defence and judicial and social affairs, but respected the desire of some member states, especially Britain, to keep certain areas outside the remit of supra-national bodies in order for national governments to retain authority. The British negotiated opt-outs from several key provisions in the Maastricht Treaty. Despite this, the European debate raged on in Britain and Euro-scepticism gained ground. The two main political parties, the Conservatives and Labour, were both divided on European issues, and among voters there was increasing support for a partial or even a complete withdrawal from the integrated system. The United Kingdom Independence Party (UKIP) was founded in 1993. In the European elections of 1994 UKIP gained 157,000 votes, but ten years later it gained 2.6 million votes (16 per cent of the total poll).

Britain's international position, it can reasonably be argued, underwent bigger and quicker change in the short period between the end of the 1960s and the beginning of the 1990s than at any other time. Influence was lost in some areas but increased in others. Overall, the difficulties associated with adjustment to new conditions did grow. So did the difficulties associated with projecting the required image abroad, sustaining beneficial relationships, maximizing prestige and power and containing disputes over policy both internally and with allies. Paradoxically, despite more interdependence and homogeneity in the world, societies and nations were breaking up and political instability was on the rise. By the 1990s, moreover, public opinion and the media had a much greater impact than before, and the same was true of legal frameworks, international mobility, multiculturalism, market forces and transnational economic links. The days of formal, traditional policy-making and dealing almost entirely with states and institutions had passed. Britain's leaders had to adapt quickly in order to manage many complex issues that involved a range of public and private interests. Membership of the EU became probably the most important single factor in foreign policy. This was problematic, not only because of the opposing views on Europe in domestic politics but also because of its implications for Britain's international role. New forms of hybrid sovereignty demanded new thinking and behaviour.

Writing in 1992, foreign policy expert Michael Clarke did not think that accommodating new pressures and needs would be easy for the British.[10] Shifts in perspective had not happened quickly in the past, and limited understanding of foreign affairs in parliament did not help (neither did rapid ministerial turnover: from 1960 to 1995 the post of foreign secretary changed hands no less than fifteen times). Influence abroad would also continue to be affected by failure to make the best use of diplomatic assets, incoherent measures (though they were presented as well coordinated), Britain's relative technological weakness, hauteur in high administrative circles, the sway exercised by narrowly focused interest groups, volatility in public attitudes and the lack of bipartisan consensus. Britain's ability to compete in the world politically and economically had been reduced since the Second World War, and the pessimism expressed in some quarters during the 1970s and 1980s was only reinforced as questions were asked about the viability of the 'special relationship' with America and about what the ending of the Cold War would mean in the long term for Britain's role and status. There was also an old and troublesome predicament in the background: how to pursue a foreign policy that would achieve more and cost less. All governments wanted to save money, and defence spending continued to be a contentious issue. Britain's defence posture was the subject of intense speculation in the early 1990s.[11] Policies shaped by the Cold War were no longer thought to be appropriate. Decisions had to be made about the real foundations of Britain's security and the armed forces restructured accordingly. Some experts wanted a withdrawal from collective defence and a narrower definition of security. This entailed defending the British Isles only and was presented as a sensible acknowledgement of Britain's geographical position on the edge of Europe and as a means of transferring funds away from defence. An alternative opinion was that Britain had to spend whatever was necessary and participate in collective security arrangements. Some experts thought that Britain should maintain its military capacity across the range of nuclear and conventional options. Others wanted specialization.

If there was pessimism, though, there was also self-belief. The claim that the British could not act independently of the United States or NATO or the EC during the 1970s and 1980s and after exaggerates Britain's loss of influence. British leaders continued to make decisions based on their understanding of Britain's best interests. If these happened to coincide with the interests of others, this was fortunate and welcome, but opinion in Washington DC, Paris or Bonn was only one element in the broader array of circumstances that British policy-makers had to take into account. Aligning with the Americans on a particular question, therefore, did not necessarily mean that London was submitting to dictation from Washington DC. Rather, it meant that Britain's interests could be served by working with the Americans. This action was decided upon independently – or at least, as independently as it could be in prevalent conditions. When the British cooperated with America, they had their own reasons for doing so. They were not totally dependent on the United States, and there were times when they took their own distinct position. Britain was a loyal supporter of NATO but had commitments outside NATO and acted beyond the NATO area when necessary, as during the Falklands crisis, and this crisis also produced yet another split between Britain and the EC. Britain's wish to evade control by the EC did not diminish during the period covered in this book.

Power is largely a matter of perception. Britain was able to project an image of strength and confidence and usually managed to convince others that they should pay attention to British interests and preferences. They would not have seen the need had they not regarded Britain as an important participant in international affairs. If power is regarded as a relationship, not a possession, its contingent and conditional nature can be better appreciated and it becomes easier to see why, notwithstanding retreats and reverses, Britain remained one of the world's great powers. Britain suffered relative decline, but this did not amount to a complete loss of position, prestige and influence. On the contrary, with some luck, good judgement and strong leadership, and with long experience of adapting to changes in the international order, the British managed the decline and held it back. It did not prevent them from accomplishing many of the things they wanted to do in the world. Thatcher argued that the 1980s saw a national revival after the weaknesses and failures of the 1970s and earlier, but the pre-Thatcher situation was not as bad as she pretended, and the resurgence of the 1980s, symbolized by victory in the Falklands, was not as impressive as it might have seemed. Taken as a whole, the period evinces an ongoing effort to preserve and exercise influence, to protect status and interests, and to act and be treated as a great power. In the years between 1970 and 1991, between the decision to confirm withdrawal from East of Suez and the end of the Cold War, between an acceptance that the world role had to be abandoned and the rush to have more say in European integration, German reunification and other post-Cold War concerns, Britain's international position shifted. But change did not mean a relentless or crippling loss of status and influence. The loss should not be exaggerated. Though Britain's opportunities, resources and ambitions were subject to more pressures and limitations, Britain still mattered and could still impose itself on events, sometimes alone, sometimes in league with others. Never a nonentity, Britain remained and was recognized as one of the world's leading powers.

Notes

Introduction

1. M. Thatcher, *The Downing Street Years* (London, 1993), pp. 173–4.
2. H. Temperley, *Britain and America since Independence* (Basingstoke, 2002), p. 190.
3. C. Hill, 'The Historical Background: Past and Present in British Foreign Policy', in *British Foreign Policy: Tradition, Change and Transformation*, ed. M. Smith, S. Smith and B. White (London, 1988), p. 35.
4. P. Taylor, 'The Commonwealth in the 1980s: Challenges and Opportunities', in *The Commonwealth in the 1980s: Challenges and Opportunities*, ed. A.J.R. Groom and P. Taylor (London, 1984), pp. 311–12; N. Mansergh, *The Commonwealth Experience* (2 vols, London, 1982), vol. 2, pp. 252–3.
5. Thatcher, *Downing Street Years*, pp. 60–1.
6. These phrases appear in the titles of books by Correlli Barnett, Sidney Pollard, Keith Robbins, David Reynolds, F.S. Northedge and Andrew Gambles respectively.

1 Accommodating Change

1. J.W. Young, *Britain and the World in the Twentieth Century* (London, 1997), p. 224; A. Sked and C. Cook, *Post-War Britain: A Political History* (London, 1993), pp. 265–6; C. Hill and C. Lord, 'The Foreign Policy of the Heath Government', in *The Heath Government, 1970–74: A Reappraisal*, ed. S. Ball and A. Seldon (London, 1996), pp. 294–7; D. Judd and P. Slinn, *The Evolution of the Modern Commonwealth, 1902–80* (London, 1982), pp. 112–13, 118–19, 131–3; D.R. Thorpe, *Alec Douglas-Home* (London, 1996), pp. 420–9; Lord Home, *The Way the Wind Blows: An Autobiography* (London, 1976), pp. 251–7, 302–12; Lord Carrington, *Reflect on Things Past* (London, 1988), pp. 268–73; M. Meredith, *The Past Is Another Country: Rhodesia, 1890–1979* (London, 1979), pp. 75–103; D. Judd, *Empire: The British Imperial Experience from 1765 to the Present* (London, 1997), pp. 375, 381–2, 388.
2. J. Campbell, *Edward Heath: A Biography* (London, 1993), pp. 337, 339; E. Heath, *The Course of My Life* (London, 1988), pp. 478–80; Hill, 'The

Historical Background', p. 41; J. Mayall, 'Africa in Anglo-American Relations', in *The 'Special Relationship': Anglo-American Relations since 1945*, ed. W.R. Louis and H. Bull (Oxford, 1986), p. 324.

3. *Economist*, 22 Jan. 1972.

4. *Chicago Tribune*, 29 May 1972; *New York Times*, 8 Dec. 1972; *The Times*, 31 Oct. 1972; *Observer*, 1 Oct. 1972; *Guardian*, 6 Nov. 1972.

5. *The Times*, 31 Oct. 1972.

6. *Hansard*, 5th series, 860 (1973), cols 713–15.

7. Judd, *Empire*, p. 382; W.D. McIntyre, *The Significance of the Commonwealth, 1965–90* (Basingstoke, 1991), pp. 30–2; Judd and Slinn, *Evolution of the Modern Commonwealth*, pp. 112–13, 119; Sked and Cook, *Post-War Britain*, pp. 266, 268–9; M. Curtis, *The Ambiguities of Power: British Foreign Policy since 1945* (London, 1995), p. 125; Hill and Lord, 'Foreign Policy of the Heath Government', pp. 292–4; Carrington, *Reflect on Things Past*, pp. 253–4; Z. Layton-Henry, *The Politics of Immigration* (Oxford, 1992), pp. 79–89, 91, and idem, 'Immigration and the Heath Government', in Ball and Seldon, *The Heath Government*, pp. 215–34; P.B. Rich, *Race and Empire in British Politics* (Cambridge, 1986), pp. 207–8; I.R.G. Spencer, *British Immigration Policy since 1939* (London, 1997), pp. 142–6; Campbell, *Heath*, pp. 299, 337–8, 340, 392–4, 481; Heath, *Course of My Life*, pp. 399, 455–6, 477–8, 481.

8. J. Vogler, 'Britain and North-South Relations', in Smith, Smith and White, *British Foreign Policy*, pp. 194–5.

9. Hill and Lord, 'Foreign Policy of the Heath Government', p. 286; K. Theakston, 'The Heath Government, Whitehall and the Civil Service', in Ball and Seldon, *The Heath Government*, pp. 82–3; McIntyre, *Significance of the Commonwealth*, p. 33; Sked and Cook, *Post-War Britain*, pp. 267–8; Campbell, *Heath*, p. 341.

10. *Guardian*, 12 July 1973; *The Times*, 11 July 1973; *Hansard*, 5th series, 860 (1973), cols 265, 277–8, 280, 284.

11. *Hansard*, 5th series, 858 (1973), cols 91, 329, 400, 1168, 1606; *The Times*, 26 July 1973; *Guardian*, 23 July 1973.

12. Theakston, 'The Heath Government, Whitehall and the Civil Service', p. 83; Hill and Lord, 'Foreign Policy of the Heath Government', pp. 306–7; J.W. Young, 'The Heath Government and British Entry into the European Community', in Ball and Seldon, *The Heath Government*, pp. 272–3.

13. Hill and Lord, 'Foreign Policy of the Heath Government', pp. 289–92; Sked and Cook, *Post-War Britain*, p. 267; Heath, *Course of My Life*, p. 481; Campbell, *Heath*, pp. 340–1; Carrington, *Reflect on Things Past*, pp. 219–20; R. Ovendale, *British Defence Policy since 1945* (Manchester, 1994), pp. 147–8; *Hansard*, 5th series 815 (1971), cols 347–9; *The Times*, 15 May 1971; D. Sanders, *Losing an Empire, Finding a Role: British Foreign Policy since 1945* (Basingstoke, 1990), pp. 122–3, 229–30.

14. Young, *Britain and the World*, p. 179; Sked and Cook, *Post-War Britain*, p. 267; Thorpe, *Douglas-Home*, pp. 431–2; Home, *Way the Wind Blows*, pp. 263–5, 269–71; S.E. Ambrose and D.G. Brinkley, *Rise to Globalism: American Foreign Policy since 1938* (New York, 1997), pp. 232–4; R. MacFarquhar, 'The China Problem in Anglo-American Relations', in Louis and Bull, *Special Relationship*, p. 318.

15. Campbell, *Heath*, pp. 347, 634–5; Heath, *Course of My Life*, pp. 468, 485, 494–5; P. Cradock, *Experiences of China* (London, 1994), pp. 149–50; R. Boardman, *Britain and the People's Republic of China, 1949–74* (London, 1976), pp. 143–62.

16. J.P. Jain, *China in World Politics: A Study of Sino-British Relations, 1949–75* (London, 1977), pp. 109–11, 154–7.

17. Jain, *China in World Politics*, pp. 211–14, 245–8, 340.

18. Hill and Lord, 'Foreign Policy of the Heath Government', p. 309; Sanders, *Losing an Empire*, p. 126.

19. *Hansard*, 5th series, 848 (1972), cols 649–50; *The Times*, 3 Nov. 1972; *Guardian*, 3 Nov. 1972; *Economist*, 4 Nov. 1972; *Washington Post*, 23 Oct. 1971; *Los Angeles Times*, 30 Oct. 1972; Boardman, *Britain and the People's Republic of China*, p. 146.

20. Sked and Cook, *Post-War Britain*, p. 280; Thorpe, *Douglas-Home*, pp. 433–4; T.G. Fraser, *The Arab-Israeli Conflict* (Basingstoke, 1995), p. 102.

21. Heath, *Course of My Life*, pp. 500–1; Ambrose and Brinkley, *Rise to Globalism*, p. 262; W. Laqueur, *Confrontation: The Middle East War and World Politics* (London, 1974), pp. 207, 209–12.

22. Heath, *Course of My Life*, pp. 501–2; *A Survey of Arab-Israeli Relations, 1947–2001*, ed. D. Lea and A. Rowe (London, 2002), pp. 9, 47, 282–3; T.G. Fraser, *The Middle East, 1914–79* (London, 1980), pp. 9, 193–4; M.M. Harrison, *The Reluctant Ally: France and Atlantic Security* (Baltimore, 1981), pp.174–7; V. Israelyan, *Inside the Kremlin during the Yom Kippur War* (University Park, Pennsylvania, 1995), pp. 97–8.

23. Campbell, *Heath*, pp. 557–9, 563, 571–3; Heath, *Course of My Life*, pp. 502–7; C. Farrands, 'State, Society, Culture and British Foreign Policy', in Smith, Smith and White, *British Foreign Policy*, pp. 62–3; Hill and Lord, 'Foreign Policy of the Heath Government', pp. 301–2, 311; J. Smith and G. Edwards, 'British-West German Relations, 1973–89', in *Uneasy Allies: British-German Relations and European Integration since 1945*, ed. K. Larres and E. Meehan (Oxford, 2000), pp. 57–60.

24. Thorpe, *Douglas-Home*, pp. 433–4.

25. *New York Times*, 20, 21 Oct. 1973; *Wall Street Journal*, 22 Oct. 1973.

26. *Economist*, 13 Oct. 1973; *Guardian*, 19 Oct. 1973; *The Times*, 20 Oct. 1973.

27. R. Tooze, 'Security and Order: The Economic Dimension', in Smith, Smith and White, *British Foreign Policy*, pp. 131–2.

28. C. Coker, 'Foreign and Defence Policy', in *Britain since 1945*, ed. J. Hollowell (Oxford, 2003), pp. 12–13; Sanders, *Losing an Empire*, pp. 178–9; C.J. Bartlett, *The 'Special Relationship': A Political History of Anglo-American Relations since 1945* (London, 1992), pp. 142–3; R. Renwick, *Fighting with Allies: America and Britain in Peace and War* (Basingstoke, 1996), pp. 218–19, 221–4; A.P. Dobson, *Anglo-American Relations in the Twentieth Century* (London, 1995), p. 146; Ovendale, *British Defence Policy*, pp. 11–12, 158–61; G. Richey, *Britain's Strategic Role in NATO* (Basingstoke, 1986), pp. 118–20; J. Simpson, *The Independent Nuclear State: The United States, Britain and the Military Atom* (London, 1983), p. 198; E.R. May and G.F. Treverton, 'Defence Relationships: American Perspectives', in Louis and Bull, *Special Relationship*, pp. 174–5; B. Heuser, *NATO, Britain, France and the FRG: Nuclear Strategies and Forces for Europe, 1949–2000* (Basingstoke, 1997), p. 76; J. Callaghan, *Time and Chance* (London, 1987), pp. 553–7; N. Bowles, 'The Defence Policy of the Conservative Government', in *The Conservative Government, 1979–84: An Interim Report*, ed. D.S. Ball (London, 1985), pp. 189–93; J. Haslam, *The Soviet Union and the Politics of Nuclear Weapons in Europe, 1969–87: The Problem of the SS20* (Basingstoke, 1989), pp. 91, 135.

29. J. Steele, *World Power: Soviet Foreign Policy under Brezhnev and Andropov* (London, 1983), p. 206.

30. Young, *Britain and the World*, p. 180; Sanders, *Losing an Empire*, pp. 121, 123, 229, 242; Carrington, *Reflect on Things Past*, pp. 241–6; R.S. Litwak, *Détente and the Nixon Doctrine: American Foreign Policy and the Pursuit of Stability, 1969–76* (Cambridge, 1984), pp. 191–3; Hill and Lord, 'Foreign Policy of the Heath Government', pp. 313–14.

31. Campbell, *Heath*, pp. 349–50; Heath, *Course of My Life*, pp. 500–1; Sanders, *Losing an Empire*, p. 177; Renwick, *Fighting with Allies*, p. 212; D.C. Watt, *Succeeding John Bull: America in Britain's Place, 1900–75* (Cambridge, 1984), pp. 152–3, 156; Dobson, *Anglo-American Relations*, pp. 142, 159; Laqueur, *Confrontation*, pp. 185–6, 215; Coker, 'Foreign and Defence Policy', p. 9; Hill and Lord, 'Foreign Policy of the Heath Government', p. 303; Young, *Britain and the World*, pp. 179, 208; P. Cornish, *Partnership in Crisis: The United States, Europe and the Fall and Rise of NATO* (London, 1997), p. 34; S.F. Wells, 'The United States, Britain and the Defence of Europe', in Louis and Bull, *Special Relationship*, pp. 133–4; Bartlett, *The 'Special Relationship'*, pp. 130–1; W.C. Cromwell, *The United States and the European Pillar: The Strained Alliance* (Basingstoke, 1992), pp. 101–3; Harrison, *Reluctant Ally*, p. 171.

32. Cornish, *Partnership in Crisis*, p. 4; H. Kissinger, *Years of Upheaval* (London, 1982), pp. 1000, 1005; A. Grosser, *The Western Alliance: European-American Relations since 1945* (London, 1980), p. 329;

W. Park, *Defending the West: A History of NATO* (Brighton, 1986), pp. 172, 174, 176.

33. Hill and Lord, 'Foreign Policy of the Heath Government', pp. 307, 313; Thorpe, *Douglas-Home*, p. 431.

34. Young, *Britain and the World*, p. 208; W. Wallace, 'The Management of Foreign Economic Policy in Britain', *International Affairs*, 50 (1974), p. 253; A. Cairncross, 'The Heath Government and the British Economy', in Ball and Seldon, *The Heath Government*, pp. 107–38.

35. Dobson, *Anglo-American Relations*, pp. 144–5.

36. T. McGrew, 'Security and Order: The Military Dimension', in Smith, Smith and White, *British Foreign Policy*, p. 101; Ambrose and Brinkley, *Rise to Globalism*, pp. 321–2.

37. D. Allen, 'Britain and Western Europe', in Smith, Smith and White, *British Foreign Policy*, pp. 170–1; Sanders, *Losing an Empire*, p. 237.

2 Questions of Defence and Détente

1. K. Larres, 'International and Security Relations within Europe', in *Europe since 1945*, ed. M. Fulbrook (Oxford, 2001), p. 220; Young, *Britain and the World*, pp. 208–9; Carrington, *Reflect on Things Past*, pp. 222–3; B. Pimlott, *Harold Wilson* (London, 1992), p. 383; Callaghan, *Time and Chance*, p. 326; K.O. Morgan, *Callaghan: A Life* (Oxford, 1997), p. 605; Ovendale, *British Defence Policy*, pp. 11, 151, 159–60; M. Chalmers, *Paying for Defence: Military Spending and British Decline* (London, 1985), pp. 103–5; P. Nailor, *The Nassau Connection: The Organization and Management of the British Polaris Project* (London, 1988), p. 68; Dobson, *Anglo-American Relations*, p. 146; Simpson, *Independent Nuclear State*, pp. 171–8; Richey, *Britain's Strategic Role in NATO*, ch. 5; Heuser, *NATO, Britain, France and the FRG*, p. 76; Haslam, *Soviet Union and the Politics of Nuclear Weapons*, p. 135; McGrew, 'Security and Order', p. 117; Ambrose and Brinkley, *Rise to Globalism*, pp. 235, 282–3, 286–7, 321; J. Dumbrell, *American Foreign Policy: Carter to Clinton* (Basingstoke, 1997), pp. 3–4, 25; Sanders, *Losing an Empire*, pp. 237–8.

2. W. Stueck, 'Placing Jimmy Carter's Foreign Policy', in *The Carter Presidency*, ed. G.M. Fink and H.D. Graham (Lawrence, Kansas, 1998), pp. 251–2; C. Coker, *The Future of the Atlantic Alliance* (London, 1984), pp. 7–24, 27; J. Baylis, *Anglo-American Defence Relations, 1939–80: The Special Relationship* (London, 1981), pp. 108–9; L. Freedman, *Britain and Nuclear Weapons* (London, 1980), pp. 43–58; M. Dockrill, *British Defence since 1945* (Oxford, 1988), p. 107; H. Wilson, *Final Term: The Labour Government, 1974–76* (London, 1979), p. 26; E. Pearce, *Denis Healey: A Life in Our Times* (London, 2002), pp. 408–27; P. Ziegler,

Wilson: The Authorized Life of Lord Wilson of Rievaulx (London, 1993), pp. 460–1; Carrington, *Reflect on Things Past*, pp. 231–2.

3. Morgan, *Callaghan*, p. 618; Sanders, *Losing an Empire*, pp. 238, 244–5, 249; Dockrill, *British Defence*, pp. 107–9.

4. GNP was used by the United States in its national accounts until 1992, when the more widely used GDP (gross domestic product) was adopted as a measurement of the size of the economy. GNP and GDP both rest on the total value of goods and services produced in a specified period. GDP relates to the place where the value is generated, not who generates it. GNP rests on the value of goods and services produced by the nationals of a country, regardless of where they are located.

5. Morgan, *Callaghan*, pp. 450–1.

6. *Documents on British Policy Overseas*, series III, ed. G. Bennett and K.A. Hamilton (London, 1997), vol. 2, pp. vi–vii; R.W. Stevenson, *The Rise and Fall of Détente: Relaxation of Tension in US-Soviet Relations, 1953–84* (Basingstoke, 1985), pp. 150–1, 167–8.

7. Bennett and Hamilton, *Documents on British Policy Overseas*, vol. 2, p. vii; M. Clarke, 'Britain and European Political Co-operation in the CSCE', in *European Détente: Case Studies in the Politics of East-West Relations*, ed. K. Dyson (London, 1986), pp. 237–53.

8. M. Clarke, 'A British View', in *European Détente: A Reappraisal*, ed. R. Davy (London, 1992), pp. 90–3.

9. Clarke, 'A British View', pp. 93–5.

10. Bennett and Hamilton, *Documents on British Policy Overseas*, vol. 2, pp. vii–ix.

11. C. Bluth, 'Détente and Conventional Arms Control: West German Policy Priorities and the Origins of MBFR', *German Politics*, 8 (1999), pp. 181–206; Harrison, *Reluctant Ally*, p. 187.

12. Bennett and Hamilton, *Documents on British Policy Overseas*, vol. 2, pp. x–xi, 1–15.

13. *Hansard*, 5th series, 848 (1972), cols 645–6, 650, 651–2; Home to Hildyard, 5 Oct. 1973, in Bennett and Hamilton, *Documents on British Policy Overseas*, vol. 2, pp. 191–2.

14. Callaghan to Sir Peter Ramsbotham (British ambassador to the United States), 5 Sept. 1974, in Bennett and Hamilton, *Documents on British Policy Overseas*, vol. 2, pp. 330–2; Morgan, *Callaghan*, pp. 452–3; Callaghan, *Time and Chance*, pp. 365–6; Pimlott, *Harold Wilson*, pp. 669–70; Ziegler, *Wilson*, pp. 461–2; Wilson, *Final Term*, pp. 154–60.

15. Callaghan to Hildyard, 19 June 1975, and Hildyard to Callaghan, 25 July 1975, in Bennett and Hamilton, *Documents on British Policy Overseas*, vol. 2, pp. 419–22, 447–54.

16. Callaghan, *Time and Chance*, pp. 364–6, 368–70; Morgan, *Callaghan*, pp. 453–4.

17. B. White, 'Britain and East-West Relations', in Smith, Smith and White, *British Foreign Policy*, pp. 163–4; H. Kissinger, *The White House Years* (London, 2000), p. 94.

18. Curtis, *Ambiguities of Power*, pp. 116, 140–1.

19. Garvey to Callaghan, 9 Sept. 1975, in Bennett and Hamilton, *Documents on British Policy Overseas*, vol. 2, pp. 474–9.

20. Clarke, 'A British View', pp. 95–7; Ovendale, *British Defence Policy*, pp. 154–6.

21. K. Dyson, 'The Conference on Security and Co-operation in Europe: Europe Before and After the Helsinki Final Act', in Dyson, *European Détente*, pp. 104–6; B. White, *Britain, Détente and Changing East-West Relations* (London, 1992), pp. 21–2, 139–40.

22. White, *Britain, Détente and East-West Relations*, pp. 137–8; D.M. Kendall, 'US-Soviet Trade, Peace and Prosperity', in *Détente or Debacle: Common Sense in US-Soviet Relations*, ed. F.W. Neal (New York, 1979), pp. 39–44; V. Mastny, *The Helsinki Process and the Reintegration of Europe, 1986–91: Analysis and Documentation* (London, 1992), pp. 1–5.

23. Mastny, *The Helsinki Process*, pp. 3–5; Stevenson, *Rise and Fall of Détente*, pp. 172–3, 184.

24. Kendall, 'US-Soviet Trade, Peace and Prosperity', p. 44; D. Reisman, 'The Danger of the Human Rights Campaign', and S. Pisar, 'Let's Put Détente Back on the Rails', both in Neal, *Détente or Debacle*, pp. 10, 56; R. Legvold, 'The Nature of Soviet Power', *Foreign Affairs*, 56 (1977–78), pp. 49–71.

25. Gross Domestic Product is widely used as a method of measuring the size of a country's economy (see n. 4 above). It rests on the total value of all goods and services produced within the country in a specified period, usually one year.

26. Young, *Britain and the World*, pp. 201, 209–10; J. Hollowell, 'From Commonwealth to European Integration', in Hollowell, *Britain since 1945*, p. 92; S. Morewood, 'Divided Europe: The Long Post-War, 1945–89', in *Themes in Modern European History since 1945*, ed. R. Wakeman (London, 2003), p. 28; K. Robbins, *The Eclipse of a Great Power: Modern Britain, 1870–1992* (London, 1997), p. 390; Thatcher, *Downing Street Years*, pp. 65, 68–9, 87–8, 125, 156–8, 160, 452–3, 469–70, 475; G. Howe, *Conflict of Loyalty* (London, 1994), pp. 358–60; D.N. Schwartz, *NATO's Nuclear Dilemmas* (Washington DC, 1983), pp. 197–200; Nailor, *Nassau Connection*, p. 68; Chalmers, *Paying for Defence*, pp. 134–5; Bowles, 'Defence Policy of the Conservative Government', pp. 184–9, 191–6, 198–9; L. Richardson, 'British State Strategies after the Cold War', in *After the Cold War*, ed. R.O. Keohane, J.S. Nye and S. Hoffman (Cambridge, Massachusetts, 1993), pp. 158–64.

27. P. Byrd, 'Defence Policy', in *British Foreign Policy under Thatcher*, ed. P. Byrd (Oxford, 1988), pp. 171–2.

28. Park, *Defending the West*, pp. 189–91; B.S. Klein, 'Hegemony and Strategic Culture: American Power Projection and Alliance Defence Politics', *Review of International Studies*, 14 (1988), pp. 142–3.

29. Howe, *Conflict of Loyalty*, pp. 144–5, 189.

30. McGrew, 'Security and Order', pp. 102–7, 113.

31. Bowles, 'Defence Policy of the Conservative Government', pp. 198–9.

32. T.G. Fraser and D. Murray, *America and the World since 1945* (Basingstoke, 2002), p. 145; W. Bundy, *A Tangled Web: The Making of Foreign Policy in the Nixon Presidency* (London, 1998), pp. 359, 361–2, 364, 371; R. Nixon, *RN: The Memoirs of Richard Nixon* (London, 1978), pp. 748–51, 753–4, 757; S.E. Ambrose, *Nixon* (3 vols, New York, 1987–91), vol. 2, pp. 533–5; W. Isaacson, *Kissinger* (London, 1993), chs 9, 12–13, 20–21; Kissinger, *White House Years*, chs 31–34.

33. Heath, *Course of My Life*, pp. 279, 487, 598; Campbell, *Heath*, pp. 228, 335, 343, 346; Curtis, *Ambiguities of Power*, pp. 147–52; Hill and Lord, 'Foreign Policy of the Heath Government', pp. 292, 303, 307, 312; Thorpe, *Douglas-Home*, p. 431; Sanders, *Losing an Empire*, pp. 147, 149; Fraser and Murray, *America and the World*, pp. 146–7, 160–3; D. Reynolds, *Britannia Overruled: British Policy and World Power in the Twentieth Century* (Harlow, 2000), p. 225; Young, *Britain and the World*, p. 228; Ambrose and Brinkley, *Rise to Globalism*, pp. 228–36, 269; Ambrose, *Nixon*, vol. 2, pp. 440–1.

34. C. Fisher, 'A Requiem for the Cold War: Reviewing the History of International Relations since 1945', in *Rethinking the Cold War*, ed. A. Hunter (Philadelphia, 1998), pp. 94, 108–12.

35. *Hansard*, 5th series, 790 (1969), cols 359, 371–2; *The Times*, 2, 7, 9 Nov. 1972; *Economist*, 4 Nov. 1972; *Guardian*, 3 Nov. 1972; *Observer*, 26 Nov. 1972.

36. Home, *Way the Wind Blows*, pp. 246–7, 264; Young, *Britain and the World*, p. 228; Sanders, *Losing an Empire*, pp. 258, 264–8, 270–2; Curtis, *Ambiguities of Power*, p. 185.

3   The Beginning of a New World Order?

1. Fraser and Murray, *America and the World*, pp. 163–4; Ambrose and Brinkley, *Rise to Globalism*, pp. 229–32; A.B. Ulam, *Dangerous Relations: The Soviet Union in World Politics, 1970–82* (New York, 1983), pp. 46–7, 50–2, 65–6, 68–9; R. Edmonds, *Soviet Foreign Policy, 1962–73: The Paradox of Super Power* (London, 1975), pp. 79–80; Steele, *World Power*, pp. 39–40; J.L. Nogee and R.H. Donaldson, *Soviet Foreign Policy since World War Two* (New York, 1988), pp. 279–80.

2. A.B. Ulam, *Expansion and Coexistence: Soviet Foreign Policy, 1917–73* (New York, 1974), pp. 768, 773; Edmonds, *Soviet Foreign Policy*, pp. 80, 109.

3. *The Times*, 17, 21 Apr. 1970; *Observer*, 19 Apr. 1970; *Chicago Tribune*, 21 Apr. 1970; *Washington Post*, 24 Apr. 1970.

4. T.W. Wolfe, *The SALT Experience* (Cambridge, Massachusetts, 1979), pp. 8–13; Schwartz, *NATO's Nuclear Dilemmas*, pp. 201–4; Litwak, *Détente and the Nixon Doctrine*, pp. 93–5, 110, 112; M. Sheehan, *The Arms Race* (Oxford, 1983), pp. 54–5; P.H. Nitze, *From Hiroshima to Glasnost: At the Centre of Decision* (New York, 1989), pp. 293–5, 303–5; P.J. Murphy, *Brezhnev: Soviet Politician* (Jefferson, North Carolina, 1981), pp. 272–3, 275–6.

5. Nixon, *Memoirs*, pp. 524–31, 609–21; Kissinger, *White House Years*, pp. 819–21, 823–918, 1202–57; Bundy, *Tangled Web*, pp. 248–50, 309–12, 322–7, 344–7; Fraser and Murray, *America and the World*, pp. 163–7; Young, *Britain and the World*, p. 178.

6. Ambrose and Brinkley, *Rise to Globalism*, p. 235; *Hansard*, 5th series, 812 (1971), cols 28–9, 822 (1971), col. 348; *The Times*, 4 Sept. 1971; *Observer*, 4 Sept. 1971; *Economist*, 11 Sept. 1971; *Los Angeles Times*, 3, 4 Sept. 1971; *New York Times*, 3 Sept. 1971.

7. Murphy, *Brezhnev*, p. 274; Fraser and Murray, *America and the World*, pp. 166–7; Sheehan, *Arms Race*, pp. 55–7; Schwartz, *NATO's Nuclear Dilemmas*, pp. 201–3; Litwak, *Détente and the Nixon Doctrine*, pp. 108–16; Nixon, *Memoirs*, pp. 609–21; Kissinger, *White House Years*, pp. 833–41, 1202–57; Wolfe, *SALT Experience*, pp. 12–22; N.K. Calvo-Goller and M.A. Calvo, *The SALT Agreements: Content, Application, Verification* (Dordrecht, 1987), pp. 11–39, 343–61; Nogee and Donaldson, *Soviet Foreign Policy since World War Two*, pp. 280–1; Edmonds, *Soviet Foreign Policy*, pp. 114–16; Steele, *World Power*, pp. 39–40; Ulam, *Expansion and Coexistence*, pp. 768–70, 772–4.

8. Murphy, *Brezhnev*, p. 275; Haslam, *Soviet Union and the Politics of Nuclear Weapons*, pp. 33–4; R.L. Garthoff, *Détente and Confrontation: American-Soviet Relations from Nixon to Reagan* (Washington DC, 1994), pp. 335–7.

9. *Hansard*, 5th series, 838 (1972), cols 135, 191, 839 (1972), col. 158.

10. *Guardian*, 29 May 1972; *Economist*, 3 June 1972; *The Times*, 27 May 1972.

11. Heath, *Course of My Life*, p. 617.

12. Campbell, *Heath*, p. 344; Heath, *Course of My Life*, pp. 485–6; Kissinger, *White House Years*, pp. 852–3, 856, 891, 899; Thorpe, *Douglas-Home*, pp. 430–1; *New York Times*, 17 Dec. 1971; *Chicago Tribune*, 17 Dec. 1971.

13. *Observer*, 19 Dec. 1971; *The Times*, 17, 20 Dec. 1971; *Hansard*, 5th series, 828 (1971), col. 1302, 829 (1972), cols 215–21.

14. P. Spear, *The Oxford History of India* (Delhi, 1994), pp. 875–6; S. Wolpert, *A New History of India* (New York, 1997), pp. 386–90; G.W. Choudhury, *The Last Days of United Pakistan* (London, 1974), pp. 195, 198; D.K. Palit, *The Lightning Campaign: The Indo-Pakistan War of 1971*

(Salisbury, 1972), pp. 117–19; Ulam, *Expansion and Coexistence*, pp. 764–6; Nogee and Donaldson, *Soviet Foreign Policy since World War Two*, pp. 184–7; Steele, *World Power*, pp. 157–8; Edmonds, *Soviet Foreign Policy*, pp. 110–11.

15. Litwak, *Détente and the Nixon Doctrine*, pp. 102–5; Bundy, *Tangled Web*, pp. 269–92; Garthoff, *Détente and Confrontation*, pp. 318–22.
16. Bundy, *Tangled Web*, p. 327; Kissinger, *White House Years*, pp. 526–7; Isaacson, *Kissinger*, ch. 15; Ambrose, *Nixon*, vol. 2, pp. 441–3, 524, 612; K. Dyson, 'European Détente in Historical Perspective: Ambiguities and Paradoxes', and A. Carter, 'Détente and East-West Relations: American, Soviet and European Perspectives', both in Dyson, *European Détente*, pp. 43–4, 63; P. Malone, *The British Nuclear Deterrent* (London, 1984), p. 183.
17. Dyson, 'European Détente in Historical Perspective', p. 44; White, *Britain, Détente and East-West Relations*, pp. 126–7.
18. Wilson, *Final Term*, pp. 186–7.
19. White, *Britain, Détente and East-West Relations*, pp. 131, 137; D. Reynolds, 'A "Special Relationship"? America, Britain and the International Order since the Second World War', *International Affairs*, 62 (1986), pp. 14–15.
20. Clarke, 'A British View', pp. 96–8; Baylis, *Anglo-American Defence Relations*, p. 109; Thorpe, *Douglas-Home*, p. 431; Dockrill, *British Defence*, p. 97; Freedman, *Britain and Nuclear Weapons*, pp. 96–7.
21. Hill and Lord, 'Foreign Policy of the Heath Government', pp. 303–8.
22. Ambrose and Brinkley, *Rise to Globalism*, pp. 230–2, 290; E.R. Kantowicz, *Coming Apart, Coming Together* (Grand Rapids, Michigan, 2000), pp. 337–40; Bundy, *Tangled Web*, pp. 198–203, 421–3; Litwak, *Détente and the Nixon Doctrine*, pp. 101–2; Kissinger, *Years of Upheaval*, p. 374; *Chile and Allende*, ed. L.A. Sobel (New York, 1974), pp. 174–6; P.E. Sigmund, *The Overthrow of Allende and the Politics of Chile, 1964–76* (Pittsburgh, 1977), chs 6–11; A. Valenzuela, 'Party Politics and the Crisis of Presidentialism in Chile', in *The Failure of Presidential Democracy*, ed. J. Linz and A. Valenzuela (2 vols, Baltimore, 1994), vol. 2, pp. 91–150; C. Blasier, *The Giant's Rival: The USSR and Latin America* (Pittsburgh, 1987), p. 181, and idem, *The Hovering Giant: US Responses to Revolutionary Change in Latin America, 1910–85* (Pittsburgh, 1985), pp. 259–60.
23. Sanders, *Losing an Empire*, p. 177; Curtis, *Ambiguities of Power*, pp. 129–36; *Hansard*, 5th series, 865 (1973), cols 462–538; *The Times*, 28 Sept. 1973; *Guardian*, 25, 27 Sept. 1973; *Economist*, 29 Sept. 1973.
24. A. Gromyko, *Memories* (London, 1989), pp. 229–30, 282; Steele, *World Power*, pp. 169, 217–19; Blasier, *The Giant's Rival*, pp. 5, 8, 38, 99–100, 159.
25. Litwak, *Détente and the Nixon Doctrine*, pp. 156–67; Fraser and Murray, *America and the World*, pp. 174–7; Bundy, *Tangled Web*,

pp. 434–44; Fraser, *Arab-Israeli Conflict*, pp. 98–103; T.G. Paterson and J.G. Clifford, *America Ascendant: US Foreign Policy since 1939* (Lexington, Massachusetts, 1995), pp. 197–9; C. Smith, 'The Arab-Israeli Conflict', in *International Relations of the Middle East*, ed. L. Fawcett (Oxford, 2005), pp. 226–8; Israelyan, *Inside the Kremlin*, pp. 115–75; Ambrose, *Nixon*, vol. 3, pp. 255–6; Ambrose and Brinkley, *Rise to Globalism*, pp. 259–65; A. Bregman, *Israel's Wars: A History since 1947* (London, 2002), pp. 102–41; P. Mansfield, *A History of the Middle East* (London, 1991), pp. 292–6; Fraser, *Middle East*, pp. 126–34; Laqueur, *Confrontation*, pp. 38–75, 129–58.

26. Lea and Rowe, *Arab-Israeli Relations*, pp. 9–10, 43–52; Kissinger, *Years of Upheaval*, pp. 549–52, 712–13, 1033; Harrison, *Reluctant Ally*, pp. 178–80; Fraser and Murray, *America and the World*, pp. 178–9; Bundy, *Tangled Web*, pp. 444–52; Ambrose and Brinkley, *Rise to Globalism*, pp. 265–7; Paterson and Clifford, *America Ascendant*, pp. 199–200; Fraser, *Middle East*, pp. 131–47, and idem, *Arab-Israeli Conflict*, pp. 105–8; Smith, 'Arab-Israeli Conflict', pp. 228–9; Mansfield, *History of the Middle East*, pp. 295–8; Isaacson, *Kissinger*, pp. 546–72, 630–5; Ambrose, *Nixon*, vol. 3, pp. 250–1, 253–6.

27. Laqueur, *Confrontation*, pp. 187–95, 222–31; Israelyan, *Inside the Kremlin*, pp. 216–18.

28. Thorpe, *Douglas-Home*, p. 434.

29. Ambrose, *Nixon*, vol. 3, pp. 293–4, 347–8, 354–61, 369–74; Fraser and Murray, *America and the World*, pp. 179–80; Bundy, *Tangled Web*, pp. 462–9; R. Crockatt, *The Fifty Years War: The United States and Soviet Union in World Politics, 1941–91* (London, 1995), pp. 229–30, 260–1; R.A. Melanson, *Reconstructing Consensus: American Foreign Policy since the Second World War* (New York, 1991), pp. 70–1; Schwartz, *NATO's Nuclear Dilemmas*, pp. 202–7; Sheehan, *Arms Race*, pp. 57–8; Kissinger, *Years of Upheaval*, pp. 1010, 1123–50, 1153, 1160–76; Nixon, *Memoirs*, pp. 1023–4; Wolfe, *SALT Experience*, pp. 85–6, 94–5; Litwak, *Détente and the Nixon Doctrine*, pp. 164, 166–7; Carter, 'Détente and East-West Relations', pp. 64–5; Garthoff, *Détente and Confrontation*, pp. 460, 469–79; Nitze, *From Hiroshima to Glasnost*, pp. 340–1.

30. Callaghan, *Time and Chance*, pp. 335, 480; *Hansard*, 5th series, 872 (1974), col. 1132, 877 (1974), cols 419, 421–3.

31. *The Times*, 4 July 1974; *Guardian*, 4 July 1974; *Observer*, 7 July 1974; *Economist*, 6 July 1974.

32. Carter, 'Détente and East-West Relations', p. 65; Dyson, 'The Conference on Security and Co-operation in Europe', pp. 105–6; P. Williams, 'Britain, Détente and the Conference on Security and Co-operation in Europe', in Dyson, *European Détente*, p. 228; Clarke, 'A British View', p. 96.

33. Malone, *British Nuclear Deterrent*, pp. 68, 78; A.J.R. Groom, *British Thinking about Nuclear Weapons* (London, 1974), pp. 593–5, 598–9.

4 Quarrelling with Allies

1. Heath, *Course of My Life*, p. 493; Campbell, *Heath*, pp. 342–3, 346; Fraser and Murray, *America and the World*, pp. 180–2; Paterson and Clifford, *America Ascendant*, p. 193; Sheehan, *Arms Race*, pp. 57–8; Litwak, *Détente and the Nixon Doctrine*, pp. 167–72; Schwartz, *NATO's Nuclear Dilemmas*, pp. 203–4, 210; Crockatt, *Fifty Years War*, pp. 261–4; Haslam, *Soviet Union and the Politics of Nuclear Weapons*, pp. 56–7, 65–6; Ulam, *Dangerous Relations*, pp. 124–5.
2. Kissinger, *Years of Upheaval*, pp. 272–3; Edmonds, *Soviet Foreign Policy*, p. 175; Nogee and Donaldson, *Soviet Foreign Policy since World War Two*, p. 275; Steele, *World Power*, p. 40; Isaacson, *Kissinger*, pp. 621–9; Garthoff, *Détente and Confrontation*, pp. 494–505; Melanson, *Reconstructing Consensus*, p. 71; A.J. Reichley, *Conservatives in an Age of Change: The Nixon and Ford Administrations* (Washington DC, 1981), pp. 353–4; S. Talbott, *Endgame: The Inside Story of SALT II* (New York, 1979), pp. 31–7.
3. White, *Britain, Détente and East-West Relations*, p. 18; Clarke, 'A British View', pp. 98–9; *Guardian*, 26 Nov. 1974; *The Times*, 25 Nov. 1974; *Economist*, 30 Nov. 1974.
4. Calvo-Goller and Calvo, *The SALT Agreements*, pp. 43–6, 370; Wolfe, *SALT Experience*, pp. 173–97; W.K.H. Panofsky, *Arms Control and SALT II* (Seattle, 1979), p. 66; Kissinger, *Years of Upheaval*, pp. 1028–9, 1172–3; Ambrose and Brinkley, *Rise to Globalism*, pp. 231, 282; Gromyko, *Memories*, p. 284; Murphy, *Brezhnev*, pp. 280, 282.
5. Pimlott, *Harold Wilson*, p. 669.
6. Freedman, *Britain and Nuclear Weapons*, pp. 97–100.
7. Sanders, *Losing an Empire*, pp. 238, 241–2; Kantowicz, *Coming Apart, Coming Together*, pp. 353, 355; Morewood, 'Divided Europe', p. 27; Curtis, *Ambiguities of Power*, p. 47; Stevenson, *Rise and Fall of Détente*, p. 173; Bundy, *Tangled Web*, p. 483; Litwak, *Détente and the Nixon Doctrine*, pp. 89–90; D.H. Allin, *Cold War Illusions: America, Europe and Soviet Power, 1969–89* (New York, 1994), pp. 55–6; Kissinger, *Years of Upheaval*, pp. 702, 710, 1164–5; Isaacson, *Kissinger*, pp. 660–3.
8. Isaacson, *Kissinger*, pp. 663–5; Garthoff, *Détente and Confrontation*, pp. 529–33, 549–50, 554; R. Pearson, *The Rise and Fall of the Soviet Empire* (Basingstoke, 2002), p. 95; R. Davy, 'Perceptions and Performance: An Evaluation', in Davy, *European Détente: A Reappraisal*, p. 245; Nogee and Donaldson, *Soviet Foreign Policy since World War Two*, pp. 262–4; Steele, *World Power*, pp. 74, 104, 109.

9. Williams, 'Britain, Détente and the Conference on Security and Co-operation in Europe', pp. 234–6.
10. White, *Britain, Détente and East-West Relations*, pp. 130–3.
11. Wolfe, *SALT Experience*, ch. 10; Calvo-Goller and Calvo, *The SALT Agreements*, pp. 46–83, 374–413; Panofsky, *Arms Control and SALT II*, pp. 49–53, 67–75; Morgan, *Callaghan*, p. 451.
12. Sanders, *Losing an Empire*, pp. 177, 193; Curtis, *Ambiguities of Power*, pp. 120, 180–1.
13. Morewood, 'Divided Europe', pp. 21–3; Larres, 'International and Security Relations', p. 225; Stevenson, *Rise and Fall of Détente*, pp. 204–5; Allin, *Cold War Illusions*, pp. xii, xiv, 37–41, 59–77, 90–101, 197; Dobson, *Anglo-American Relations*, pp. 147, 150–1, 158; W.F. Hanrieder, *Germany, America, Europe: Forty Years of German Foreign Policy* (New Haven, 1989), pp. 363–7; L.T. Caldwell and A. Dallin, 'US Policy toward the Soviet Union', in *Eagle Entangled: US Foreign Policy in a Complex World*, ed. K.A. Oye, D. Rothchild and R.J. Lieber (New York, 1979), pp. 199–227; Ambrose and Brinkley, *Rise to Globalism*, pp. 272–3, 276–7, 286–9, 320–1, 344–6; Dumbrell, *American Foreign Policy*, pp. 24, 40–5, 48–9, 56–8, 77, 112–13; Melanson, *Reconstructing Consensus*, pp. 105, 109, 118, 123, 142–3, 189, 227–8; Crockatt, *Fifty Years War*, pp. 257, 259, 261, 267, 288, 290, 307–8, 356–62; Garthoff, *Détente and Confrontation*, pp. 1076–86; Paterson and Clifford, *America Ascendant*, pp. 237, 252–3, 261–6; K.E. Morris, *Jimmy Carter: American Moralist* (Athens, Georgia, 1996), pp. 273–4; Stueck, 'Carter's Foreign Policy', pp. 257–8; C. Bell, *The Reagan Paradox: US Foreign Policy in the 1980s* (New Brunswick, New Jersey, 1989), pp. 74–7; S.K. Smith and D.A. Wertman, *US-West European Relations during the Reagan Years* (Basingstoke, 1992), ch. 3; Haslam, *Soviet Union and the Politics of Nuclear Weapons*, ch. 7.
14. White, *Britain, Détente and East-West Relations*, pp. 27, 136–7; Carter, 'Détente and East-West Relations', pp. 64–5; R. Davy, 'Up the Learning Curve: An Overview', and F. Bozo, 'A French View', both in Davy, *European Détente: A Reappraisal*, pp. 19–20, 71.
15. Sanders, *Losing an Empire*, p. 193.
16. Allen, 'Britain and Western Europe', pp. 179–80.
17. Sanders, *Losing an Empire*, pp. 238–9, 248; G. Smith, *Reagan and Thatcher* (London, 1990), p. 121; Sheehan, *Arms Race*, pp. 129–37; J. Sperling and E. Kirchner, *Recasting the European Order* (Manchester, 1997), pp. 64–5; Heuser, *NATO, Britain, France and the FRG*, pp. 90–1.
18. Haslam, *Soviet Union and the Politics of Nuclear Weapons*, pp. 153–64; M. Donhoff, *Foe into Friend: The Makers of the New Germany from Konrad Adenauer to Helmut Schmidt* (London, 1982), pp. 131–44; H. Simonian, *The Privileged Partnership: Franco-German Relations in the European Community* (Oxford, 1995), pp. 85–6, 96, 115–16,

181–4, 186–8, 277–86, 367–70; A. Daltrop, *Politics and the European Community* (London, 1986), pp. 168–9; Smith and Edwards, 'British-West German Relations', pp. 51–2, 56–7; K. Larres, 'Uneasy Allies or Genuine Partners? Britain, Germany and European Integration', in Larres and Meehan, *Uneasy Allies*, pp. 1–24; Reynolds, *Britannia Overruled*, pp. 225–6; Wilson, *Final Term*, pp. 94–5, 203; Morgan, *Callaghan*, pp. 614–15, 617, 622; J. Carr, *Helmut Schmidt: Helmsman of Germany* (London, 1985), pp. 90–2, 140–6; D. Hanley, A. Kerr and N. Waites, *Contemporary France: Politics and Society since 1945* (London, 1991), p. 52; Callaghan, *Time and Chance*, pp. 301, 305, 322, 329, 492–3.

19. Larres, 'International and Security Relations', pp. 209–10, 217–19, 232–3; T.G. Ash, *In Europe's Name: Germany and the Divided Continent* (London, 1993), pp. 53–8, 67–83; W. Brandt, *My Life in Politics* (London, 1992), pp. 170–218; A. Stent, *From Embargo to Ostpolitik: The Political Economy of West German-Soviet Relations, 1955–80* (Cambridge, 1981), pp. 127–8, 180–95; W.E. Griffith, *The Ostpolitik of the Federal Republic of Germany* (Cambridge, Massachusetts, 1978), pp. 135, 137, 177–223; Morewood, 'Divided Europe', pp. 20–1; Donhoff, *Foe into Friend*, pp. 131–44; Simonian, *Privileged Partnership*, pp. 180–4; Hanrieder, *Germany, America, Europe*, pp. 196–209; Young, 'The Heath Government and British Entry into the European Community', p. 265; Hill and Lord, 'Foreign Policy of the Heath Government', p. 309. For early assessments of 'Ostpolitik' see *The Ostpolitik and Political Change in Germany*, ed. R. Tilford (Farnborough, 1975), especially G. Roberts, 'The Ostpolitik and Relations between the Two Germanies', pp. 77–93, and R. Morgan, 'The Ostpolitik and West Germany's External Relations', pp. 95–108. On the long-term impact of the thaw in central Europe see A. Hyde-Price, *The International Politics of East Central Europe* (Manchester, 1996), pp. 142–6.

20. Sanders, *Losing an Empire*, p. 142; *Guardian*, 21 Feb. 1973; *The Times*, 20 Oct. 1973; Bennett and Hamilton, *Documents on British Policy Overseas*, vol. 2, pp. v–vi.

21. A. Deighton, 'British-West German Relations, 1945–72', and K. Larres, 'Britain and the GDR: Political and Economic Relations, 1949–89', both in Larres and Meehan, *Uneasy Allies*, pp. 41–3, 64–5, 88–9; Heath, *Course of My Life*, pp. 361, 486–7; Campbell, *Heath*, p. 346; Home, *Way the Wind Blows*, pp. 249–50; Morgan, *Callaghan*, pp. 399, 403; Callaghan, *Time and Chance*, pp. 295–6.

22. Larres, 'International and Security Relations', pp. 219–20; Pearson, *Rise and Fall of the Soviet Empire*, pp. 94–5; Mastny, *The Helsinki Process*, pp. 4–7; White, 'Britain and East-West Relations', pp. 163–4; P. Kennedy, *The Realities Behind Diplomacy: Background Influences on British External Policy, 1865–1980* (London, 1981), pp. 382–3; Ambrose

and Brinkley, *Rise to Globalism*, pp. 235, 282–4; Dumbrell, *American Foreign Policy*, pp. 17–21; Reisman, 'The Danger of the Human Rights Campaign', pp. 51–7; Callaghan, *Time and Chance*, pp. 363–4, 366, 369–70; Wilson, *Final Term*, pp. 174–5; Bennett and Hamilton, *Documents on British Policy Overseas*, vol. 2, pp. xxxiv–xxxv.

23. *Los Angeles Times*, 1 Aug. 1975; *Washington Post*, 1 Aug. 1975; *The Times*, 2 Aug. 1975; *Guardian*, 2 Aug. 1975; *Observer*, 3 Aug. 1975; *Economist*, 2 Aug. 1975.

24. A. Heraclides, *Security and Co-operation in Europe: The Human Dimension, 1972–92* (London, 1993), pp. 32–40.

25. *Hansard*, 5th series, 897 (1975), cols 230–42.

26. J.M. Hanhimaki, 'Ironies and Turning Points: Détente in Perspective', in *Reviewing the Cold War: Approaches, Interpretations, Theory*, ed. O.A. Westad (London, 2000), pp. 326–7, 334–6; Morgan, *Callaghan*, pp. 452–4, 602–3; Larres, 'International and Security Relations', pp. 222, 232–4; Morewood, 'Divided Europe', p. 23; D. Armstrong and E. Goldstein, 'Interaction with the Non-European World', in Fulbrook, *Europe since 1945*, p. 242; Young, *Britain and the World*, p. 178; Grosser, *Western Alliance*, pp. 295–321; Hanrieder, *Germany, America, Europe*, pp. 310–16; Thatcher, *Downing Street Years*, pp. 768, 783–4, 789, 794–6; Simonian, *Privileged Partnership*, pp. 292, 333–4, 359–60; D.W. Urwin, *The Community of Europe: A History of European Integration since 1945* (London, 1991), pp. 221, 225, 227–8, 237–41, 245; D. Dinan, *Ever Closer Union: An Introduction to European Integration* (Basingstoke, 1994), pp. 81, 88–93, 95, 105, 108, 110, 114–15, 120, 122, 129–39; K. Dyson, 'Chancellor Kohl as Strategic Leader: The Case of Economic and Monetary Union', and A. Cole, 'Political Leadership in Western Europe: Helmut Kohl in Comparative Perspective', both in *The Kohl Chancellorship*, ed. C. Clemens and W.E. Paterson (London, 1998), pp. 38, 59–60, 134–5; T. Cutler, C. Haslam, J. Williams and K. Williams, *1992: The Struggle for Europe* (New York, 1989), pp. 7, 141–6, 149, 163; A. Gamble, 'The European Issue in British Politics', in *Britain For and Against Europe*, ed. D. Baker and D. Seawright (Oxford, 1998), pp. 20–3; Smith and Edwards, 'British-West German Relations', pp. 48, 51–2, 54–61; Richardson, 'British State Strategies', pp. 150–1; P. Sharp, *Thatcher's Diplomacy: The Revival of British Foreign Policy* (Basingstoke, 1997), pp. 160–2, 168–70, 209–10.

27. Curtis, *Ambiguities of Power*, pp. 156, 162, 180; Sanders, *Losing an Empire*, pp. 177, 192.

28. Reynolds, *Britannia Overruled*, p. 22, and idem, 'Britain and the World since 1945', in *The British Isles since 1945*, ed. K. Burk (Oxford, 2003), pp. 174–5; Dinan, *Ever Closer Union*, p. 132; Young, *Britain and the World*, p. 211; L. Kettenacker, 'Britain and German Reunification, 1989–90', in Larres and Meehan, *Uneasy Allies*, pp. 119–22; Howe,

Conflict of Loyalty, pp. 583, 632–3; Carrington, *Reflect on Things Past*, pp. 319, 323–5; N. Ridley, *'My Style of Government': The Thatcher Years* (London, 1991), pp. 136–7, 140, 155–6; 223–5; *The Times*, 16 July 1990; *Economist*, 14 July 1990; *Guardian*, 18 July 1990; A. El-Agraa, 'Mrs Thatcher's European Community Policy', in Bell, *The Conservative Government*, pp. 180–2.

29. Thatcher, *Downing Street Years*, pp. 789–96; Simonian, *Privileged Partnership*, pp. 2–6, 32–45; Allin, *Cold War Illusions*, p. 183.

30. Morewood, 'Divided Europe', pp. 23–5; Bartlett, *The 'Special Relationship'*, p. 153; Cromwell, *The United States and the European Pillar*, pp. 118–22; Allin, *Cold War Illusions*, pp. 144–54; M. Smith, 'Britain and the United States: Beyond the Special Relationship?' in Byrd, *British Foreign Policy under Thatcher*, pp. 15–16; Smith and Edwards, 'British-West German Relations', p. 58; Allen, 'Britain and Western Europe', p. 176; Ambrose and Brinkley, *Rise to Globalism*, pp. 324–5; Dumbrell, *American Foreign Policy*, pp. 75–6.

31. *Hansard*, 6th series, 26 (1982), col. 1041, 28 (1982), cols 7–9, 240; *Los Angeles Times*, 23 June 1982; *Washington Post*, 24 June 1982; *The Times*, 30 June 1982; *Economist*, 26 June 1982; *Guardian*, 30 June, 1 July 1982; *Observer*, 4 July 1982.

32. Thatcher, *Downing Street Years*, pp. 253–6; Smith, *Reagan and Thatcher*, pp. 53, 72–5, 96, 99–102; Sharp, *Thatcher's Diplomacy*, pp. 112–16.

33. A.J. Blinken, *Ally versus Ally: America, Europe and the Siberian Pipeline Crisis* (New York, 1987), pp. 104–6, 151–3.

34. Steele, *World Power*, pp. 66–8; P. Savigear, *Cold War or Détente in the 1980s: The International Politics of American-Soviet Relations* (Brighton, 1987), pp. 125–6.

35. T.L. Ilgen, *Autonomy and Independence: US-Western European Monetary and Trade Relations, 1958–84* (Totowa, New Jersey, 1985), pp. 105–36; Morgan, *Callaghan*, pp. 602–6, 617–21; Bartlett, *The 'Special Relationship'*, pp. 140–1.

36. Larres, 'International and Security Relations', pp. 222–3; Farrands, 'State, Society, Culture and British Foreign Policy', pp. 155, 165; J.B. Poole, *Independence and Interdependence: A Reader on British Nuclear Weapons Policy* (London, 1990), pp. 112–13, 118–20; Allen, 'Britain and Western Europe', p. 189; Ambrose and Brinkley, *Rise to Globalism*, pp. 282–7, 321–2; Dumbrell, *American Foreign Policy*, pp. 25–7, 44–5, 47–50, 54–9; Paterson and Clifford, *America Ascendant*, pp. 252–3, 262–3; Richey, *Britain's Strategic Role in NATO*, pp. 55–6; Freedman, *Britain and Nuclear Weapons*, pp. 117–26; Heuser, *NATO, Britain, France and the FRG*, p. 82; Ovendale, *British Defence Policy*, pp. 131, 165–6; Baylis, *Anglo-American Defence Relations*, pp. 113, 127; Dockrill, *British Defence*, pp. 112–13; Sanders, *Losing an Empire*, pp. 177–8, 238; Callaghan, *Time and Chance*, pp. 542–4; S. Duke, *The Elusive Quest for European*

Security (Basingstoke, 2000), p. 66; Allin, *Cold War Illusions*, pp. 85–98, 117–34; Grosser, *Western Alliance*, pp. 315–17; Park, *Defending the West*, pp. 109–17; Renwick, *Fighting with Allies*, pp. 240–2. On peace movements and anti-nuclear protests in Britain and Europe see P. Byrne, *The Campaign for Nuclear Disarmament* (London, 1988), pp. 32–4, 37–9, 118–22, 137, 146–55, 161–2, 228–9; J. Mattausch, *A Commitment to Campaign* (Manchester, 1989), pp. 139–48; P. Calvocoressi, *A Time for Peace: Pacifism, Internationalism and Protest Forces in the Reduction of War* (London, 1987), pp. 105–8, 164–5; T.R. Rochon, *Mobilizing for Peace: The Anti-Nuclear Movements in Western Europe* (Princeton, 1988), chs 1, 4.

37. M. Thatcher, *The Path to Power* (London, 1995), pp. 360–2, 364–6.
38. Cornish, *Partnership in Crisis*, p. 12; Cromwell, *The United States and the European Pillar*, pp. 110, 115.

5   Confronting the Soviets

1. A. White, *Symbols of War: Pershing II and Cruise Missiles in Europe* (London, 1983), pp. 28–30.
2. Schwartz, *NATO's Nuclear Dilemmas*, pp. 237–8; Smith and Edwards, 'British-West German Relations', p. 58; Haslam, *Soviet Union and the Politics of Nuclear Weapons*, pp. 101–5.
3. Carrington, *Reflect on Things Past*, pp. 385–6.
4. *The Times*, 26 Nov. 1979; *Economist*, 10 Nov. 1979; *Observer*, 25 Nov. 1979; *Guardian*, 26 Nov. 1979; *New York Times*, 26 Nov. 1979; *Chicago Tribune*, 1 Dec. 1979.
5. Schwartz, *NATO's Nuclear Dilemmas*, p. 246.
6. Sheehan, *Arms Race*, pp. 199–201.
7. Thatcher, *Downing Street Years*, pp. 240–4, 771.
8. E. Regelsberger, 'EPC in the 1980s: Reaching another Plateau?' in *European Political Co-operation in the 1980s: A Common Foreign Policy for Western Europe?* ed. A. Pijpers, E. Regelsberger and W. Wessels (Dordrecht, Netherlands, 1988), pp. 3, 7–8, 18–19, 22, 27.
9. Ambrose and Brinkley, *Rise to Globalism*, pp. 284, 321, 323; Paterson and Clifford, *America Ascendant*, pp. 252–3; Dumbrell, *American Foreign Policy*, pp. 25–7, 75; Sanders, *Losing an Empire*, pp. 248, 254, 284; Morewood, 'Divided Europe', p. 21; Larres, 'International and Security Relations', pp. 223–4; Crockatt, *Fifty Years War*, pp. 324–30; Bell, *The Reagan Paradox*, pp. 121–30; Smith and Wertman, *US-West European Relations*, pp. 10–11, 93–103; Allin, *Cold War Illusions*, pp. 132–9, 146, 154–9; J. Spanier, *American Foreign Policy since World War Two* (New York, 1983), pp. 209–13; Hanley, Kerr and Waites, *Contemporary France*, p. 52; Carrington, *Reflect on Things Past*, pp. 318, 325–6; Smith and Edwards, 'British-West German Relations', p. 58.

10. *The Times*, 7, 9 Feb., 19, 20, 21 May 1980; *Guardian*, 20 May 1980; *Washington Post*, 20, 25 May 1980; *Los Angeles Times*, 21 May 1980.

11. Sharp, *Thatcher's Diplomacy*, pp. 43, 185; A. Hyman, *Afghanistan under Soviet Domination, 1964–91* (Basingstoke, 1992), pp. 161–2; Thatcher, *Downing Street Years*, pp. 87–8, 91; Smith, *Reagan and Thatcher*, pp. 72, 130; Garthoff, *Détente and Confrontation*, pp. 1087–9.

12. Davy, 'Up the Learning Curve', pp. 23–4; Clarke, 'A British View', p. 104; Garthoff, *Détente and Confrontation*, pp. 812–13, 1081–3, 1089; Dyson, 'European Détente in Historical Perspective', pp. 46–7, 51.

13. T.T. Hammond, *Red Flag over Afghanistan* (Boulder, Colorado, 1984), pp. 105–24; H. Jordan, *Crisis: The Last Year of the Carter Presidency* (New York, 1982), pp. 99–101.

14. Garthoff, *Détente and Confrontation*, p. 1103; P. Johnson, *A History of the Modern World* (London, 1984), pp. 677, 680, 682–3; D. Sassoon, 'Politics', in Fulbrook, *Europe since 1945*, p. 38; Ambrose and Brinkley, *Rise to Globalism*, pp. 282–4; Dumbrell, *American Foreign Policy*, pp. 17–21; Murphy, *Brezhnev*, pp. 260–2, 273.

15. Bennett and Hamilton, *Documents on British Policy Overseas*, vol. 2, pp. 476, 486–8.

16. T. Beamish and G. Hadley, *The Kremlin's Dilemma: The Struggle for Human Rights in Eastern Europe* (London, 1979), pp. 34–41; Nogee and Donaldson, *Soviet Foreign Policy since World War Two*, pp. 300–2; Steele, *World Power*, pp. 63–4, 74.

17. R.C. Tucker, 'Swollen State, Spent Society: Stalin's Legacy to Brezhnev's Russia', *Foreign Affairs*, 60 (1981–82), pp. 430–5; A. Solzhenitsyn, 'Misconceptions about Russia Are a Threat to America', *Foreign Affairs*, 58 (1979–80), pp. 797–834; J. Keep, *Last of the Empires: A History of the Soviet Union, 1945–91* (Oxford, 1995), pp. 200–2, 281–3; M.S. Shatz, *Soviet Dissent in Historical Perspective* (Cambridge, 1980), p. 134; Z.A.B. Zeman, *The Making and Breaking of Communist Europe* (Oxford, 1991), pp. 288–9; R. Medvedev, *On Soviet Dissent* (London, 1980), p. 113; Thatcher, *Path to Power*, pp. 363–4, 371, 388.

18. *The Times*, 4 June, 5 Oct. 1977; *Observer*, 5 June 1977; *Los Angeles Times*, 12 June 1977; *Chicago Tribune*, 11 Oct. 1977; *New York Times*, 10 June 1977.

19. Johnson, *Modern World*, pp. 539, 684–5; Armstrong and Goldstein, 'Interaction with the Non-European World', p. 246; Ambrose and Brinkley, *Rise to Globalism*, pp. 276–7, 290, 316–17; Dumbrell, *American Foreign Policy*, pp. 23–5, 37–40; Sanders, *Losing an Empire*, pp. 177, 193, 241–2; C. Legum, 'Communal Conflict and International Intervention in Africa', in C. Legum, I.W. Zartman, S. Langdon and L.K. Mytelka, *Africa in the 1980s: A Continent in Crisis* (New York, 1979), pp. 40, 46, 49–51, 53–7, 60–4; W. Freund, *The Making of Contemporary Africa* (Basingstoke, 1998), pp. 237–9; Steele, *World Power*, pp. 32–6,

159–60, 201–2, 220, 222–3, 226–44; P. Shearman, *The Soviet Union and Cuba* (London, 1987), pp. 67–75.

20. Ulam, *Dangerous Relations*, pp. 175–6; S.G. Gorshkov, *The Sea Power of the State* (Oxford, 1979), pp. 178–89; Nogee and Donaldson, *Soviet Foreign Policy since World War Two*, pp. 166–8, 199–200, 202–4, 288–91; Steele, *World Power*, pp. 219–20; M. Perez-Stable, *The Cuban Revolution* (New York, 1993), pp. 148–9; R.E. Quirk, *Fidel Castro* (New York, 1993), ch. 28.

21. Curtis, *Ambiguities of Power*, pp. 157–65; Blasier, *Hovering Giant*, pp. 288–9, 291–2.

22. *Daily Telegraph*, 18 July, 4, 9 Aug. 1979.

23. Blasier, *The Giant's Rival*, pp. 4–6, 144–51.

24. W.D. Rogers, 'The "Unspecial Relationship" in Latin America', in Louis and Bull, *Special Relationship*, pp. 345–9; Thatcher, *Path to Power*, p. 371; Johnson, *Modern World*, p. 685.

25. T. Taylor, 'Conventional Arms: The Drives to Export', in *The Defence Trade: Demand, Supply and Control*, ed. T. Taylor and R. Imai (London, 1994), p. 117; H. Tuomi and R. Vayrynen, *Transnational Corporations, Armaments and Development* (Aldershot, 1982), p. 122.

26. D.C. Gompert and A.R. Vershbow, 'Controlling Arms Trade', in *Controlling Future Arms Trade*, ed. A.R. Vershbow (New York, 1977), pp. 1–4, 7–8; R.E. Harkavy, *The Arms Trade and International Systems* (Cambridge, Massachusetts, 1975), pp. 101–3; Grosser, *Western Alliance*, p. 292.

27. Morgan, *Callaghan*, p. 456.

28. Morgan, *Callaghan*, pp. 441, 451–2, 595–6, 619; Thatcher, *Downing Street Years*, pp. 87, 158, 329; Johnson, *Modern World*, pp. 713–16; A. Sampson, *The Money Lenders* (London, 1981), pp. 262–7.

29. D. Morgan, *Merchants of Grain* (New York, 1979), pp. 242, 255–7, 259–61, 263, 268–71, 273, 275–9.

30. *Economist*, 11 Oct. 1975; *Guardian*, 13 Oct. 1975; *The Times*, 22 Oct. 1975; E. Rothschild, 'Food Politics', *Foreign Affairs*, 54 (1975–76), pp. 285–307; R.F. Hopkins, 'How to Make Food Work', *Foreign Policy*, 27 (1977), pp. 89–107.

31. Ambrose and Brinkley, *Rise to Globalism*, pp. 236, 245, 268, 284–5, 288–9, 324–5; Dumbrell, *American Foreign Policy*, pp. 48, 73–4.

32. Bennett and Hamilton, *Documents on British Policy Overseas*, vol. 2, pp. 457, 461–4.

33. M. Clarke, 'The Soviet Union and Eastern Europe', in Byrd, *British Foreign Policy under Thatcher*, pp. 59–64.

34. Clarke, 'Soviet Union and Eastern Europe', pp. 64–7.

35. Howe, *Conflict of Loyalty*, pp. 309–12; Clarke, 'Soviet Union and Eastern Europe', pp. 68–74; M. Gorbachev, *Memoirs* (London, 1996), pp. 160–1; A. Brown, *The Gorbachev Factor* (Oxford, 1996), pp. 75–8; Gromyko, *Memories*, p. 163.

36. *Guardian*, 7, 8, 9 Dec. 1987; *The Times*, 7 Dec. 1987.

37. Gromyko, *Memories*, pp. 308–9, 343; Brown, *Gorbachev Factor*, pp. 236–7; Gorbachev, *Memoirs*, pp. 435–6, 443.

38. White, 'Britain and East-West Relations', pp. 164–6.

39. White, 'Britain and East West Relations', pp. 166–7.

6 Multipolarity and Nuclear Weapons

1. Fraser and Murray, *America and the World*, p. 162; Reynolds, *Britannia Overruled*, p. 225; Young, *Britain and the World*, p. 207.

2. Cradock, *Experiences of China*, pp. 142–3; Nixon, *Memoirs*, pp. 522–3, 525, 545; Ambrose, *Nixon*, vol. 2, pp. 451–3; J.K. Fairbank, *The United States and China* (Cambridge, Massachusetts, 1979), pp. 457–62; R. Medvedev, *China and the Superpowers* (Oxford, 1986), pp. 98–105; R.S. Ross, 'US Policy toward China: The Strategic Context and the Policy-Making Process', in *China, the United States and the Soviet Union: Tri-Polarity and Policy Making in the Cold War*, ed. R.S. Ross (New York, 1993), pp. 149–77; M. Schaller, *The United States and China: Into the Twenty-First Century* (New York, 2002), ch. 9.

3. *The Times*, 21 Aug. 1972; *Guardian*, 30 Aug. 1972; *Economist*, 26 Aug. 1972.

4. Kissinger, *White House Years*, p. 1049; H.R. Haldeman, *The Haldeman Diaries: Inside the Nixon White House* (New York, 1994), pp. 315, 319, 421–4; Bundy, *Tangled Web*, pp. 304–5; Ambrose and Brinkley, *Rise to Globalism*, pp. 230, 232, 234, 270; Dumbrell, *American Foreign Policy*, pp. 45–6.

5. McGrew, 'Security and Order', p. 103.

6. McGrew, 'Security and Order', p. 103; White, 'Britain and East-West Relations', pp. 163–4; Heath, *Course of My Life*, p. 468; Hill and Lord, 'Foreign Policy of the Heath Government', pp. 313–14; Campbell, *Heath*, pp. 350–1.

7. Callaghan, *Time and Chance*, pp. 478–81, 483–6, 488–90, 495–7; Armstrong and Goldstein, 'Interaction with the Non-European World', p. 265.

8. W.H. Lash, 'The International Trade Policies of President Reagan', in *President Reagan and the World*, ed. E.J. Schmertz, N. Datlof and A. Ugrinsky (Westport, Connecticut, 1997), pp. 353–64; R.D. Puttnam and N. Bayne, *Hanging Together: The Seven-Power Summits* (London, 1984), pp. 113–14, 153, 190–1; Dumbrell, *American Foreign Policy*, pp. 115–20.

9. Armstrong and Goldstein, 'Interaction with the Non-European World', pp. 265–6; Ambrose and Brinkley, *Rise to Globalism*, pp. 425–6; Dumbrell, *American Foreign Policy*, p. 58; J.W. Holmes, *The Changing United Nations: Options for the United States* (New York, 1977), p. 35.

10. Curtis, *Ambiguities of Power*, p. 183.

11. Sperling and Kirchner, *Recasting the European Order*, pp. 88–92; S. Zamora, 'Economic Relations and Development', in *United Nations Legal Order*, ed. O. Schachter and C. Joyner (2 vols, Cambridge, 1995), vol. 1, pp. 537, 573.

12. Morgan, *Callaghan*, pp. 430, 572–3, 600–1; C.F. Bergsten and C.R. Henning, *Global Economic Leadership and the Group of Seven* (Washington DC, 1996), pp. 58, 76; Sanders, *Losing an Empire*, pp. 188, 214–15, 294; Thatcher, *Downing Street Years*, pp. 299–300, 498, 587.

13. Vogler, 'Britain and North-South Relations', pp. 196–9, 208; *The United Nations in 1985: A Report on the Proceedings* (London, 1986), pp. 21–5; J. Chopra, 'United Nations Peace-Maintenance', in *The United Nations at Work*, ed. M.I. Glassner (Westport, Connecticut, 1998), p. 312; Johnson, *Modern World*, p. 686; Dockrill, *British Defence*, p. 128; D. Fischer, *Stopping the Spread of Nuclear Weapons* (London, 1992), pp. 232–5. On the spread of nuclear weapons outside the West, see also part 3 of *Western Europe and the Future of the Nuclear Non-Proliferation Treaty*, ed. P. Lomas and H. Muller (Brussels, 1989).

14. G. Kemp, *Nuclear Forces for Medium Powers: Strategic Requirements and Options* (London, 1974), pp. 20–1; Haslam, *Soviet Union and the Politics of Nuclear Weapons*, pp. 32, 40, 135–6; Ambrose and Brinkley, *Rise to Globalism*, p. 323; Dumbrell, *American Foreign Policy*, pp. 27–8, 78; M.J. Wilmshurst, 'The Development of Current Non-Proliferation Policies', in *The International Nuclear Non-Proliferation System: Challenges and Choices*, ed. J. Simpson and A.G. McGrew (London, 1984), pp. 35–7.

15. Ovendale, *British Defence Policy*, pp. 11–12, 131, 151, 158–61, 165–6, 169–79, 180–3.

16. Morgan, *Callaghan*, pp. 616–19.

17. Morgan, *Callaghan*, pp. 619–20; Callaghan, *Time and Chance*, pp. 553–7.

18. Armstrong and Goldstein, 'Interaction with the Non-European World', p. 247; Johnson, *Modern World*, pp. 686–7; Crockatt, *Fifty Years War*, p. 363; Ambrose and Brinkley, *Rise to Globalism*, pp. 229–32, 269, 284, 286–8, 303, 322, 334–5, 345–7, 400–2, 418–19; Dumbrell, *American Foreign Policy*, pp. 101, 148, 171, 184, 188; Lomas and Muller, *Western Europe and the Future of the Non-Proliferation Treaty*, part 3; Fischer, *Stopping the Spread of Nuclear Weapons*, ch. 10; R.K. Betts, 'Paranoids, Pygmies, Pariahs and Non-Proliferation Revisited', in *The Proliferation Puzzle: Why Nuclear Weapons Spread and What Results*, ed. Z.S. Davis and B. Frankel (London, 1993), pp. 100–24; W.C. Potter, *Nuclear Power and Non-Proliferation* (Cambridge, Massachusetts, 1982), ch. 5. See also a publication of the Stockholm International Peace Research Institute, *Arms Control: A Survey and Appraisal of Multilateral Agreements* (London, 1978), pp. 7–35.

19. Nogee and Donaldson, *Soviet Foreign Policy since World War Two*, p. 279; Stockholm International Peace Research Institute, *Postures for Non-Proliferation* (London, 1979), ch. 4; A. Kelle and H. Muller, 'Western Europe and the Geopolitics of Nuclear Proliferation', in Lomas and Muller, *Western Europe and the Future of the Non-Proliferation Treaty*, pp. 93–101; Fischer, *Stopping the Spread of Nuclear Weapons*, pp. 193–4.

20. Freedman, *Britain and Nuclear Weapons*, pp. 88–96; Grosser, *Western Alliance*, p. 294; Harrison, *Reluctant Ally*, p. 186; A.G. McGrew, 'Nuclear Non-Proliferation at the Crossroads', in Simpson and McGrew, *International Nuclear Non-Proliferation System*, pp. 9–10.

21. D. Keohane, 'British Nuclear Non-Proliferation Policy and the Trident Purchase', in Simpson and McGrew, *International Nuclear Non-Proliferation System*, pp. 120–2.

22. Stevenson, *Rise and Fall of Détente*, pp. 134, 157–8, 201, 204–5; Talbott, *Endgame*, pp. 141–2 (and 279–310 for a copy of the SALT II treaty); Callaghan, *Time and Chance*, pp. 483–4, 529–30, 542–4, 546–52; Carrington, *Reflect on Things Past*, p. 278.

23. Malone, *British Nuclear Deterrent*, pp. 78, 96, 183–4.

24. Heath, *Course of My Life*, pp. 616–17; Smith, 'Britain and the United States', p. 16.

25. Dobson, *Anglo-American Relations*, pp. 146, 152; Callaghan, *Time and Chance*, pp. 553–7; Baylis, *Anglo-American Defence Relations*, pp. 126–9; Freedman, *Britain and Nuclear Weapons*, pp. 66–8; Thatcher, *Downing Street Years*, pp. 244–8; Renwick, *Fighting with Allies*, pp. 218–19, 221–4; Dockrill, *British Defence*, pp. 113–14; Byrd, 'Defence Policy', pp. 159–60.

26. Byrd, 'Defence Policy', pp. 160–3. See also the debate between Ken Booth and John Baylis in their *Britain, NATO and Nuclear Weapons: Alternative Defence versus Alliance Reform* (Basingstoke, 1989).

27. Byrd, 'Defence Policy', pp. 163–5.

28. Smith, 'Britain and the United States', pp. 16–17; Byrd, 'Defence Policy', pp. 165–7.

29. Byrd, 'Defence Policy', p. 167; Smith, 'Britain and the United States', p. 17.

30. Smith, *Reagan and Thatcher*, pp. 214–24.

31. Smith, *Reagan and Thatcher*, pp. 224–6.

32. B. Glad and J.A. Garrison, 'Ronald Reagan and the Intermediate Nuclear Forces Treaty: Whatever Happened to the "Evil Empire"?' in Schmertz, Datlof and Ugrinsky, *Reagan and the World*, pp. 91–107. For a denial of the pro-Reagan understanding of the Cold War, see in the same volume J.E. Ullmann, 'Ronald Reagan and the Illusion of Victory in the Cold War', pp. 109–21.

33. Byrd, 'Defence Policy', p. 168; Duke, *Elusive Quest*, pp. 65–6.

34. Chalmers, *Paying for Defence*, pp. 146, 148, 152–3; Sheehan, *Arms Race*, pp. 42–4.

35. Byrd, 'Defence Policy', pp. 168–70; Smith, 'Britain and the United States', p. 18; Howe, *Conflict of Loyalty*, pp. 316–18, 321–2, 356–7, 388–93, 542–3; Schmertz, Datlof and Ugrinsky, *Reagan and the World*, pp. 125–7, 138.

36. Dobson, *Anglo-American Relations*, pp. 158–9; Byrd, 'Defence Policy', p. 170; White, 'Britain and East-West Relations', p. 166; Allen, 'Britain and Western Europe', pp. 176, 188; Farrands, 'State, Society, Culture and British Foreign Policy', p. 63.

37. Smith, 'Britain and the United States', pp. 15, 19, 32; Thatcher, *Downing Street Years*, p. 60; D. Allen, 'British Foreign Policy and West European Co-operation', in Byrd, *British Foreign Policy under Thatcher*, pp. 35–6, 49, 52.

38. W. van Eekelen, *Debating European Security, 1948–98* (The Hague, 1998), pp. 10–11, 14–19; *Choices: Nuclear and Non-Nuclear Defence Options*, ed. O. Ramsbotham (London, 1987), p. 455; Thatcher, *Downing Street Years*, pp. 771–2.

39. Thatcher, *Downing Street Years*, pp. 772–3.

40. Thatcher, *Downing Street Years*, pp. 774–6; *Hansard*, 6th series, 111 (1987), cols 723–6, 135 (1988), col. 166.

41. Allin, *Cold War Illusions*, pp. 104, 138–9; C. Bluth, 'A West German View', in Davy, *European Détente: A Reappraisal*, pp. 47–8; Bozo, 'A French View', pp. 77–8. On the FRG and France see also M. Sturmer, 'Deutschlandpolitik, Ostpolitik and the Western Alliance', and P. Cerny and J. Howorth, 'National Independence and Atlanticism: The Dialectic of French Politics', both in Dyson, *European Détente*, pp. 134–54, 198–220.

42. White, *Britain, Détente and East-West Relations*, pp. 142–3, 147–9, 153; Thatcher, *Downing Street Years*, pp. 784–7; Smith, *Reagan and Thatcher*, pp. 56–8, 182, 244, 254, 267–8.

43. Thatcher, *Downing Street Years*, pp. 787–9; Smith, *Reagan and Thatcher*, p. 254.

7 The Approach of Victory in the Cold War

1. Brown, *Gorbachev Factor*, pp. 247–51; Gorbachev, *Memoirs*, pp. 522–7; M. Galeotti, *Gorbachev and His Revolution* (Basingstoke, 1997), pp. 100–1; Larres, 'International and Security Relations', pp. 225–6; Sassoon, 'Politics', p. 47; Kantowicz, *Coming Apart, Coming Together*, pp. 392–3; G. Swain and N. Swain, *Eastern Europe since 1945* (Basingstoke, 1998), pp. 173–4, 183–5; I.T. Berend, *Central and Eastern Europe, 1944–93* (Cambridge, 1996), pp. 281–3, 287–8, and idem, 'The Central and

East European Revolution', in Wakeman, *Modern European History*, p. 198; H. Adomeit, *Imperial Overstretch: Germany in Soviet Policy from Stalin to Gorbachev* (Baden-Baden, 1998), pp. 215–41; Morewood, 'Divided Europe', pp. 29–30; Pearson, *Rise and Fall of the Soviet Empire*, pp. 131–9; G. Schopflin, *Politics in Eastern Europe* (Oxford, 1993), pp. 220–2, 235, 239–40; B. Fowkes, *The Rise and Fall of Communism in Eastern Europe* (Basingstoke, 1995), pp. 184–6; Zeman, *Making and Breaking of Communist Europe*, pp. 312, 324–6; Allin, *Cold War Illusions*, ch. 7; Keep, *Last of the Empires*, ch. 17; D.S. Mason, *Revolution in East-Central Europe: The Rise and Fall of Communism and the Cold War* (Boulder, Colorado, 1992), pp. 49–52, 58–60; M. Fulbrook, *Interpretations of the Two Germanies, 1945–90* (Basingstoke, 2000), pp. 80–1. See also Fulbrook's *Germany, 1918–90: The Divided Nation* (London, 1991), pp. 321–32, and idem, *Anatomy of a Dictatorship: Inside the GDR, 1949–89* (Oxford, 1995), pp. 236–46.

2. *Hansard*, 6th series, 158 (1989), col. 663, 160 (1989), col. 381; *Observer*, 15 Oct. 1989; *Economist*, 21 Oct. 1989; *The Times*, 19 Oct. 1989; *New York Times*, 14 Oct. 1989; *Washington Post*, 19 Oct. 1989.

3. Clarke, 'Soviet Union and Eastern Europe', pp. 74–5; White, 'Britain and East-West Relations', pp. 150–2; Thatcher, *Downing Street Years*, pp. 789–90; Bartlett, *The 'Special Relationship'*, p. 171.

4. Larres, 'Britain and the GDR', pp. 96–7; Kettenacker, 'Britain and German Reunification', pp. 106–22.

5. White, *Britain, Détente and East-West Relations*, pp. 149–54; R. Wakeman, 'The Golden Age of Prosperity, 1953–73', D. Kalb, 'Social Class and Social Change in Post-War Europe', and M. Hanagan, 'Changing Margins in Post-War European Politics', all in Wakeman, *Modern European History*, pp. 63, 68–9, 96, 124–6; Sassoon, 'Politics', p. 45; Larres, 'International and Security Relations', p. 188; Schopflin, *Politics in Eastern Europe*, ch. 6; B. Eichengreen, 'Economy', in Fulbrook, *Europe since 1945*, pp. 117–18, 139.

6. Thatcher, *Path to Power*, pp. 155–6, 355, 600; A. Kahan, 'Some Problems of the Soviet Industrial Worker', and A. Pravda, 'Spontaneous Workers' Activities in the Soviet Union', both in *Industrial Labour in the USSR*, ed. A. Kahan and B.A. Ruble (Elmsford, New York, 1979), pp. 302–3, 333–66; D. Good and T. Ma, 'The Economic Growth of Central and Eastern Europe in Comparative Perspective, 1870–1989', *European Review of Economic History*, 2 (1999), pp. 122, 124–5, 127; Eichengreen, 'Economy', pp. 117, 139; Berend, 'Central and East European Revolution', p. 192; Wakeman, 'Golden Age of Prosperity', p. 69; Sassoon, 'Politics', p. 15; Kalb, 'Social Class and Social Change', p. 93; Hanagan, 'Changing Margins', p. 129; Fowkes, *Rise and Fall of Communism*, pp. 142–4; A. Koves, *Central and East European Economies*

in Transition (Boulder, Colorado, 1992), pp. 2–5; D. Lane, *The Rise and Fall of State Socialism: Industrial Society and the Socialist State* (Cambridge, 1996), pp. 98–9, 152–5; D.H. Aldcroft and S. Morewood, *Economic Change in Eastern Europe since 1918* (Aldershot, 1995), chs 6–8; Schopflin, *Politics in Eastern Europe*, ch. 7.

7. Swain, *Eastern Europe since 1945*, pp. 146–74; Berend, *Central and Eastern Europe*, ch. 6, and idem, 'Central and East European Revolution', p. 195; Armstrong and Goldstein, 'Interaction with the Non-European World', p. 269; Kantowicz, *Coming Apart, Coming Together*, pp. 382–4; Morewood, 'Divided Europe', pp. 25–7; A. Korner, 'Culture', in Fulbrook, *Europe since 1945*, p. 158; Larres, 'International and Security Relations', p. 226; Ambrose and Brinkley, *Rise to Globalism*, pp. 190, 321, 333, 340, 346, 348–9, 362–4, 370–4; Dumbrell, *American Foreign Policy*, pp. 108–20; Keep, *Last of the Empires*, chs 11–13 and pp. 335–62; Zeman, *Making and Breaking of Communist Europe*, pp. 312–32; C. Keble, *Britain and the Soviet Union, 1917–89* (Basingstoke, 1990), p. 283 and ch. 11; Nogee and Donaldson, *Soviet Foreign Policy since World War Two*, p. 352; Steele, *World Power*, pp. 105, 250–1; Koves, *Central and East European Economies*, pp. 6–9; Aldcroft and Morewood, *Economic Change*, pp. 134–7, 175, 177–8, 183–5; Lane, *Rise and Fall of State Socialism*, pp. 99–103, 106–9, 152–5; R.V. Daniels, *The End of the Communist Revolution* (London, 1993), pp. 124–31, 136–40; M. Mazower, *Dark Continent: Europe's Twentieth Century* (London, 1999), pp. 384–6; Galeotti, *Gorbachev and His Revolution*, pp. 65–66, 77–8; Thatcher, *Downing Street Years*, p. 774.

8. W. Loth, 'Moscow, Prague and Warsaw: Overcoming the Brezhnev Doctrine', *Cold War History*, 1 (2001), pp. 103–18; A.L. Friedberg, 'The United States and the Cold War Arms Race', in Westad, *Reviewing the Cold War*, pp. 221–2.

9. V.M. Zubok, 'Why Did the Cold War End in 1989? Explanations of "The Turn" ', in Westad, *Reviewing the Cold War*, pp. 360–1; *The Times*, 12 Nov. 1982; *Guardian*, 12 Nov. 1982.

10. *Guardian*, 12 Mar. 1985; *Economist*, 16 Mar. 1985; *The Times*, 12 Mar. 1985.

11. Brown, *Gorbachev Factor*, pp. 233–5, 239–40, 250; Gorbachev, *Memoirs*, pp. 406, 450–2, 458, 541–2.

12. Home, *Way the Wind Blows*, pp. 245, 250–1; Morgan, *Callaghan*, pp. 451, 617–18, 621; Carrington, *Reflect on Things Past*, p. 278.

13. Sanders, *Losing an Empire*, pp. 186, 239, 242; Thatcher, *Downing Street Years*, pp. 87, 158, 329, 801; Steele, *World Power*, p. 105; M. Cox, 'The End of the Cold War and Why We Failed to Predict It', in Hunter, *Rethinking the Cold War*, pp. 157–74; Carrington, *Reflect on Things Past*, pp. 387–9.

14. Wakeman, 'Golden Age of Prosperity', pp. 77–8; Sassoon, 'Politics', pp. 45–6; Eichengreen, 'Economy', p. 139; Armstrong and Goldstein, 'Interaction with the Non-European World', p. 244; Morewood, 'Divided Europe', pp. 26–8; Berend, *Central and Eastern Europe*, pp. 238–60, and idem, 'Central and East European Revolution', p. 198; Swain, *Eastern Europe since 1945*, pp. 157–8, 167–70; Korner, 'Culture', p. 158; Larres, 'International and Security Relations', p. 220; Kantowicz, *Coming Apart, Coming Together*, p. 384; Zeman, *Making and Breaking of Communist Europe*, pp. 283–8; Beamish and Hadley, *Kremlin's Dilemma*, pp. 73, 84–93; Daniels, *End of the Communist Revolution*, pp. 69–74, 128–9; A. Judt, 'The Dilemmas of Dissidence: The Politics of Opposition in East-Central Europe', in *Crisis and Reform in Eastern Europe*, ed. F. Feher and A. Arato (New Brunswick, New Jersey, 1991), pp. 253–301; Lane, *Rise and Fall of State Socialism*, pp. 65–8, 120–1; Aldcroft and Morewood, *Economic Change*, pp. 152–3, 189–90; Fowkes, *Rise and Fall of Communism*, pp. 157–66, 175–80, 186; Ambrose and Brinkley, *Rise to Globalism*, pp. 283–4, 304, 363–4; Dumbrell, *American Foreign Policy*, pp. 17–21, 57, 74, 81, 85; Thatcher, *Path to Power*, pp. 351–5, 364–5, 371–2, 508–9, 591. On the general context, see E. Hobsbawm, *The Age of Extremes* (London, 1995), pp. 398–400. For more on Czechoslovakia see J. Krejci and P. Machonin, *Czechoslovakia, 1918–92: A Laboratory for Social Change* (Basingstoke, 1996), ch. 16, and appendices 3–5 in *Czechoslovakia, 1918–88: Seventy Years from Independence*, ed. H.G. Skilling (Basingstoke, 1991), pp. 217–22; and on Poland see J. Staniszkis, *Poland's Self-Limiting Revolution* (Princeton, 1984), chs 2–3, and T.G. Ash, *The Polish Revolution: Solidarity* (London, 1991), pp. 21–37.

15. Larres, 'Britain and the GDR', pp. 93–7; D. Bathrick, *The Powers of Speech: The Politics of Culture in the GDR* (Lincoln, Nebraska, 1995), pp. 82–3; A.J. McAdams, *East Germany and Détente* (Cambridge, 1985), p. 182; Keble, *Britain and the Soviet Union*, pp. 282–3; Callaghan, *Time and Chance*, pp. 366, 369–70; Morgan, *Callaghan*, pp. 452–3; Howe, *Conflict of Loyalty*, pp. 314–15, 351–2, 433–5; Thatcher, *Downing Street Years*, pp. 452, 460, 477–8; 773–4.

16. *Hansard*, 5th series, 969 (1979), cols 75–83; *The Times*, 24 Jan. 1980; *Observer*, 27 Jan. 1980; *Economist*, 26 Jan. 1980; *Los Angeles Times*, 15 Jan. 1980; *Chicago Tribune*, 16 Jan. 1980; *Washington Post*, 14, 23 Jan. 1980.

17. A. Pravda and P. Duncan, 'Soviet-British Relations under Perestroika', in *Soviet-British Relations since the 1970s*, ed. A. Pravda and P. Duncan (Cambridge, 1990), pp. 232–55; Heraclides, *Security and Co-operation in Europe*, pp. 51–9, 61, 67; A. Bloed and F. van Hoof, 'Some Aspects of the Socialist View of Human Rights', and A. Bloed and P. van Dijk,

'Human Rights and Non-intervention', both in *Essays on Human Rights in the Helsinki Process*, ed. A. Bloed and P. van Dijk (Dordrecht, Netherlands, 1985), pp. 31, 34, 65, 77.

18. A. Bloed, 'Détente and the Concluding Document of Madrid', in Bloed and van Dijk, *Essays on Human Rights*, pp. 1–3; Bloed and van Dijk, 'Human Rights and Non-intervention', pp. 61–6.

19. Morewood, 'Divided Europe', pp. 27–8, 32; Sassoon, 'Politics', p. 17; Larres, 'International and Security Relations', p. 200; Berend, *Central and Eastern Europe*, pp. 222–38, and idem, 'Central and Eastern European Revolution', pp. 191–2, 195; Wakeman, 'Golden Age of Prosperity', pp. 77–8; Swain, *Eastern Europe since 1945*, pp. 162–8, 175, 179; Schopflin, *Politics in Eastern Europe*, ch. 7; T. Bauer, 'Reforming or Perfecting the Economic Mechanism', in Feher and Arato, *Crisis and Reform*, pp. 99–120; Hobsbawm, *Age of Extremes*, pp. 399–400; Lane, *Rise and Fall of State Socialism*, pp. 65–9, 152–5; Koves, *Central and East European Economies*, pp. 3–6; Aldcroft and Morewood, *Economic Change*, pp. 156–76; Fowkes, *Rise and Fall of Communism*, pp. 142–56; Steele, *World Power*, pp. 5, 20–1, 250–1; Savigear, *Cold War or Détente*, pp. 63, 121; Nogee and Donaldson, *Soviet Foreign Policy since World War Two*, pp. 323, 335–6; Zeman, *Making and Breaking of Communist Europe*, pp. 289–91; S. Haggard and A. Moravcsik, 'The Political Economy of Financial Assistance to Eastern Europe, 1989–91', in Keohane, Nye and Hoffman, *After the Cold War*, pp. 246–85; R. Vinen, *A History in Fragments: Europe in the Twentieth Century* (London, 2002), p. 516.

20. Davy, 'Perceptions and Performance', p. 256; Bartlett, *The 'Special Relationship'*, p. 153; Thatcher, *Downing Street Years*, pp. 777–8; Carrington, *Reflect on Things Past*, p. 330.

21. Morgan, *Callaghan*, pp. 451–3; Callaghan, *Time and Chance*, pp. 295–6, 365–7, 369.

22. *Hansard*, 5th series, 941 (1978), cols 8–9, 943 (1978), col. 994, 954 (1978), cols 1135–6.

23. *Guardian*, 4 Jan. 1980; *The Times*, 18, 24 Jan., 18 Mar. 1980.

24. M.R. Hill, *East-West Trade, Industrial Co-operation and Technology Transfer: The British Experience* (Aldershot, 1983), pp. 4–5, ch. 3.

25. Hill, *East-West Trade*, pp. 190–1; Keble, *Britain and the Soviet Union*, pp. 281, 290; M. Kaser, 'Trade Relations: Patterns and Prospects', in Pravda and Duncan, *Soviet-British Relations*, pp. 193, 204.

26. A. Pravda, 'Pre-Perestroika Patterns', in Pravda and Duncan, *Soviet-British Relations*, pp. 7–8.

27. Clarke, 'Soviet Union and Eastern Europe', pp. 68, 72, 74; Howe, *Conflict of Loyalty*, pp. 429, 433.

28. Sperling and Kirchner, *Recasting the European Order*, pp. 88–90; H. Friedmann, 'Warsaw Pact Socialism, Détente and the Disintegration

of the Soviet Bloc', in Hunter, *Rethinking the Cold War*, pp. 213–31; C. Gati, *The Bloc That Failed: Soviet-East European Relations in Transition* (Bloomington, Indiana, 1990), pp. 132–5.

29. Gati, *Bloc That Failed*, pp. 99–103, 155–7.
30. Wakeman, 'Golden Age of Prosperity', p. 78; Eichengreen, 'Economy', p. 121; Kalb, 'Social Class and Social Change', p. 91; Armstrong and Goldstein, 'Interaction with the Non-European World', pp. 264–5; A. Boltho, 'Growth', in *The European Economy: Growth and Crisis*, ed. A. Boltho (Oxford, 1982), pp. 9–37, and on the FRG and Britain specifically see in the same volume, K.H. Hennings, 'West Germany', pp. 492–8, and M. Surrey, 'United Kingdom', pp. 547–52; H. James, *International Monetary Co-operation since Bretton Woods* (New York, 1996), chs 11–12; Ilgen, *Autonomy and Independence*, ch. 5; L. Neal, 'Impact of Europe', in *The Cambridge Economic History of Modern Britain*, ed. R. Floud and P. Johnson (3 vols, Cambridge, 2004), vol. 3, p. 278.
31. Ovendale, *British Defence Policy*, pp. 144–5; K. Hartley, 'The Defence Economy', in *Britain in the 1970s: The Troubled Economy*, ed. R. Coopey and N. Woodward (London, 1996), pp. 212–35.
32. R. Coopey and N. Woodward, 'The British Economy in the 1970s: An Overview', in Coopey and Woodward, *Britain in the 1970s*, pp. 1–33; J. Tomlinson, *The Politics of Decline: Understanding Post-War Britain* (Harlow, 2001), pp. 84–94, 96.
33. Cairncross, 'The Heath Government and the British Economy', pp. 107–38; Neal, 'Impact of Europe', p. 294; N. Crafts, 'Economic Growth', in *The British Economy since 1945*, ed. N. Crafts and N. Woodward (Oxford, 1991), pp. 261–90. On the economic problems of the 1970s and 1980s see also R. Middleton, *The British Economy since 1945: Engaging with the Debate* (Basingstoke, 2000), pp. 57–66, and pp. 132–5 on the extent to which government policies could or did make a difference.
34. P. Dunne and R. Smith, 'Thatcherism and the UK Defence Industry', in *The Economic Legacy, 1979–92*, ed. J. Michie (London, 1992), pp. 91–111; McGrew, 'Security and Order', p. 109; Tooze, 'Security and Order: The Economic Dimension', pp. 124–45.
35. T. Clark and A. Dilnot, 'British Fiscal Policy since 1939', in Floud and Johnson, *Cambridge Economic History*, vol. 3, pp. 377–8; Sanders, *Losing an Empire*, pp. 210–24.

8 Extra-European Affairs

1. P. Kennedy, *The Rise and Fall of the Great Powers: Economic Change and Military Conflict from 1500 to 2000* (New York, 1987). But see also W. Rostow, 'Beware of Historians Bearing False Analogies', *Foreign Affairs*,

66 (1988), pp. 863–8; H. Nau, 'Why *The Rise and Fall of the Great Powers* was Wrong', *Review of International Studies*, 27 (2001), pp. 579–92.

2. Armstrong and Goldstein, 'Interaction with the Non-European World', pp. 246–7.

3. Nogee and Donaldson, *Soviet Foreign Policy since World War Two*, pp. 205, 207; Steele, *World Power*, pp. 176–8; Ulam, *Dangerous Relations*, pp. 55–6, 132–40, 160–1, 175–6, 195–6.

4. M. McCain, 'Thinking South: Soviet Strategic Interests in Iran, Afghanistan and Pakistan', in *Soviet-American Relations with Pakistan, Iran and Afghanistan*, ed. H. Malik (New York, 1987), pp. 39–53; Y.R. Kim, 'The Soviet Union's Shifting Policy towards East Asia: Its Major Determinants and Future Prospects', in *The Soviet Union and East Asia in the 1980s*, ed. J.K. Park and J.M. Ha (Seoul, 1983), pp. 136–59; N. Xiaoquan, 'Gorbachev's Policy toward the Asia-Pacific Region', in *The Soviet Union and the Asia-Pacific Region*, ed. P. Thambipillai and D.C. Matuszewski (New York, 1989), pp. 13–22; N. Miller, *Soviet Relations with Latin America, 1959–87* (Cambridge, 1989), ch. 6; Z. Laidi, *The Superpowers and Africa: The Constraints of a Rivalry, 1960–90* (Chicago, 1990), chs 4–5; W.P. Limberg, 'Soviet Military Support for Third World Marxist Regimes', in *The USSR and Marxist Revolutions in the Third World*, ed. M.N. Katz (Cambridge, 1990), pp. 80–93; A.J. Klinghoffer, 'The Soviet Union and Angola', R.B. Remnek, 'Soviet Policy in the Horn of Africa', D.E. Albright, 'Gauging Soviet Success in Africa and the Middle East: A Comment', and J.L. Nogee, 'The Soviet Union in the Third World: Successes and Failures', all in *The Soviet Union in the Third World: Successes and Failures*, ed. R.H. Donaldson (Boulder, Colorado, 1981), pp. 97–124, 125–49, 214, 438–51; Kissinger, *Years of Upheaval*, pp. 252, 1030.

5. Isaacson, *Kissinger*, pp. 681–3; Garthoff, *Détente and Confrontation*, pp. 556, 575, 579, 586–7, 590, 592; P. Gleijeses, *Conflicting Missions: Havana, Washington and Africa, 1959–76* (Chapel Hill, North Carolina, 2002), chs 12, 15–16; Laidi, *Superpowers and Africa*, pp. 64–72; Murphy, *Brezhnev*, pp. 283, 285–6, 293.

6. *Hansard*, 5th series 896 (1975), cols 1291–5.

7. Wilson, *Final Term*, pp. 220–1; S.V. Percy, 'Mercenaries: Strong Norm, Weak Law', *International Organization*, 61 (2007), pp. 367–97.

8. *The Times*, 2 Apr. 1976; *Observer*, 18 Apr. 1976.

9. *Economist*, 24 Apr. 1976; *Los Angeles Times*, 1 Jan. 1976; *New York Times*, 18 Jan. 1976; *Wall Street Journal*, 1 Oct. 1976.

10. Home, *Way the Wind Blows*, pp. 250–1, 283–4; Morgan, *Callaghan*, pp. 451, 455–6, 595–6, 617–18, 621; Howe, *Conflict of Loyalty*, pp. 439, 525.

11. J. Barber, 'Southern Africa', in Byrd, *British Foreign Policy under Thatcher*, pp. 96–8.

12. Judd, *Empire*, pp. 399–400; McIntyre, *Significance of the Commonwealth*, pp. 35–6, 111–15; Mayall, 'Africa in Anglo-American Relations', pp. 324–5; Carrington, *Reflect on Things Past*, pp. 272, 287–307.

13. Barber, 'Southern Africa', pp. 100–1, 106–7; Hill, 'The Historical Background', pp. 36–7, 49.

14. Sanders, *Losing an Empire*, pp. 124, 149, 182–3; Curtis, *Ambiguities of Power*, pp. 120–2; Crockatt, *Fifty Years War*, p. 366.

15. Barber, 'Southern Africa', pp. 107–16; M. Holland, *The European Community and South Africa: European Political Co-operation under Strain* (London, 1988), ch. 5; C. Alden, *Apartheid's Last Stand: The Rise and Fall of the South African Security State* (Basingstoke, 1998), pp. 188–9; Howe, *Conflict of Loyalty*, pp. 476–500; McIntyre, *Significance of the Commonwealth*, pp. viii, 37–9, 115–23; *Hansard*, 6th series, 99 (1986), cols 492–3; Sharp, *Thatcher's Diplomacy*, pp. 226–34.

16. G. Segal, 'Asia and the Pacific', in Byrd, *British Foreign Policy under Thatcher*, pp. 118–21.

17. Segal, 'Asia and the Pacific', pp. 122–4; Sanders, *Losing an Empire*, pp. 126–7, 133; *Economist*, 23 Jan. 1988.

18. Segal, 'Asia and the Pacific', pp. 125–8.

19. Crockatt, *Fifty Years War*, pp. 279–86; Dumbrell, *American Foreign Policy*, pp. 23–5; 103–7; Paterson and Clifford, *America Ascendant*, pp. 204–5, 247; Spanier, *American Foreign Policy since World War Two*, pp. 202–4, 244–7; Ulam, *Dangerous Relations*, pp. 177–82; Steele, *World Power*, pp. 29–30, 35, 64–5, 169–71, 226–44; Nogee and Donaldson, *Soviet Foreign Policy since World War Two*, pp. 202–4, 288–92; Savigear, *Cold War or Détente*, pp. 47, 154, 162, 164; Legum, 'Communal Conflict and International Intervention in Africa', pp. 26, 33, 39–41, 43, 45–8, 50, 53–6, 59–62, 64. See also C. Legum and W. Lee, *Conflict in the Horn of Africa* (London, 1977), pp. 10–14; W.M. James, *A Political History of the Civil War in Angola, 1974–90* (New Brunswick, New Jersey, 1992), chs 6–7; C. Legum, 'Foreign Intervention in Angola', in C. Legum and A. Hodges, *After Angola* (London, 1976), pp. 9–41; and Shearman, *The Soviet Union and Cuba*, ch. 5 on Angola, 1975–76, and ch. 6 on the Horn of Africa, 1977–78.

20. Johnson, *Modern World*, pp. 539–40; R. Oliver and J.D. Fage, *A Short History of Africa* (London, 1977), pp. 246, 268, 272–4; and on the general context C. Legum, *Africa since Independence* (Bloomington, Indiana, 1999), ch. 2.

21. *The Times*, 26 Nov. 1974; *Observer*, 24 Nov. 1974; *Economist*, 30 Nov. 1974; *Washington Post*, 28 Nov. 1974; *Chicago Tribune*, 24, 28 Nov. 1974.

22. *The Times*, 9 June 1978; *Guardian*, 2 June 1978; *New York Times*, 1 June 1978; *Los Angeles Times*, 3 June 1978; Harrison, *Reluctant Ally*, pp. 191–2.

23. Morgan, *Callaghan*, pp. 749–50; McGrew, 'Security and Order', p. 109; Gromyko, *Memories*, pp. 263–4; R. Patman, 'Ideology, Soviet

Policy and Realignment in the Horn', and E. Moreton, 'The East Europeans and the Cubans: Surrogates or Allies?' both in *The Soviet Union in the Middle East: Policies and Perspectives*, ed. A. Dawisha and K. Dawisha (London, 1982), pp. 45–61, 62–84; Z. Cervenka and C. Legum, 'Cuba: The New Communist Power in Africa', in C. Legum and W. Lee, *The Horn of Africa in Continuing Crisis* (New York, 1979), pp. 137–52; Mayall, 'Africa in Anglo-American Relations', p. 328; *Hansard*, 5th series, 943 (1978), cols 1019–95.

24. Curtis, *Ambiguities of Power*, pp. 47–8.

25. S. Ellis and T. Sechaba, *Comrades Against Apartheid* (London, 1992), chs 1–2; S. Thomas, *The Diplomacy of Liberation: The Foreign Relations of the ANC since 1960* (London, 1996), chs 8–9; L. Thompson and A. Prior, *South African Politics* (New Haven, 1982), pp. 226–43; Kantowicz, *Coming Apart, Coming Together*, pp. 406–7, 411–12, 415; J. Barber and J. Barratt, *South Africa's Foreign Policy: The Search for Status and Security, 1945–88* (Cambridge, 1990), pp. 152–4; N. Worden, *The Making of Modern South Africa* (Oxford, 2000), pp. 152–7; Freund, *Contemporary Africa*, pp. 239–43; Dumbrell, *American Foreign Policy*, pp. 103–7, 172; Ambrose and Brinkley, *Rise to Globalism*, pp. 278–9, 343–4, 361–2; Paterson and Clifford, *America Ascendant*, pp. 246–7, 276–7, 303–5; Alden, *Apartheid's Last Stand*, pp. 23, 185–6, 190.

26. Morgan, *Callaghan*, pp. 456, 593; Barber, 'Southern Africa', pp. 109–14; *Hansard*, 5th series, 959 (1978), cols 1738–1833; R. Hyam and P. Henshaw, *The Lion and the Springbok: Britain and South Africa since the Boer War* (Cambridge, 2003), pp. 333–6; Curtis, *Ambiguities of Power*, pp. 124–6; Alden, *Apartheid's Last Stand*, pp. 186–8; Thomas, *Diplomacy of Liberation*, pp. 203–4; Thatcher, *Downing Street Years*, pp. 519–35.

27. *The Times*, 5 Sept. 1989; *Economist*, 9 Sept. 1989; *Observer*, 10 Sept. 1989; *Guardian*, 13, 15 Sept. 1989; *Washington Post*, 5 Sept. 1989; *Wall Street Journal*, 8 Sept. 1989.

28. *Hansard*, 6th series, 166 (1990), cols 871–2; Curtis, *Ambiguities of Power*, pp. 127–9; Mayall, 'Africa in Anglo-American Relations', p. 339; Hyam and Henshaw, *The Lion and the Springbok*, p. 337; Thomas, *Diplomacy of Liberation*, pp. 220–1, 228; Holland, *The European Community and South Africa*, ch. 5.

29. Ulam, *Dangerous Relations*, pp. 184–5; Savigear, *Cold War or Détente*, pp. 7, 172; Steele, *World Power*, p. 243; Nogee and Donaldson, *Soviet Foreign Policy since World War Two*, p. 204; Crockatt, *Fifty Years War*, p. 366; Barber and Barratt, *South Africa's Foreign Policy*, pp. 341–4; Gorbachev, *Memoirs*, p. 620; R.J. Payne, *The Non-Superpowers and South Africa: Implications for US Policy* (Bloomington, Indiana, 1990), pp. 249–53.

30. K.M. Campbell, *Soviet Policy towards South Africa* (Basingstoke, 1986), pp. 42–7, 164–8; Barber and Barratt, *South Africa's Foreign Policy*, pp. 341–4.

31. Murphy, *Brezhnev*, pp. 285–6; Steele, *World Power*, p. 206.

32. Hyman, *Afghanistan under Soviet Domination*, pp. 75–80, 100–1, 159–65; Kantowicz, *Coming Apart, Coming Together*, pp. 356–9; Ambrose and Brinkley, *Rise to Globalism*, pp. 287–9, 324, 360; Paterson and Clifford, *America Ascendant*, pp. 252, 258–9, 266–7, 328; Dumbrell, *American Foreign Policy*, pp. 44–5, 47–50, 52, 63, 100–1; Hammond, *Red Flag*, pp. 49–55, 61, 73–5, 79–82, 132–44; Ulam, *Dangerous Relations*, pp. 196–7, 209, 228, 232, 255–8; Steele, *World Power*, pp. 125–30; Crockatt, *Fifty Years War*, pp. 286–8, 362–3; Bell, *The Reagan Paradox*, pp. 56–7, 91, 119; Smith and Wertman, *US-West European Relations*, pp. 124, 131, 150–2, 165–6; H.S. Bradsher, *Afghan Communism and Soviet Intervention* (Oxford, 1999), pp. 48–52, 54, 75, 85; Nogee and Donaldson, *Soviet Foreign Policy since World War Two*, pp. 293, 295–6; Savigear, *Cold War or Détente*, p. 161.
33. Nogee and Donaldson, *Soviet Foreign Policy since World War Two*, pp. 293–5.
34. Steele, *World Power*, pp. 14, 117, 130.
35. Bradsher, *Afghan Communism and Soviet Intervention*, p. 86; Gromyko, *Memories*, pp. 239–40, 247; Gorbachev, *Memoirs*, p. 138; Nogee and Donaldson, *Soviet Foreign Policy since World War Two*, pp. 351–2; Pearson, *Rise and Fall of the Soviet Empire*, pp. 110–11, 123–4, 136.
36. Bradsher, *Afghan Communism and Soviet Intervention*, p. 87.
37. Nogee and Donaldson, *Soviet Foreign Policy since World War Two*, p. 296; Steele, *World Power*, pp. 65–6.
38. Thatcher, *Downing Street Years*, pp. 87–8, 477–8; Carrington, *Reflect on Things Past*, p. 384; Sharp, *Thatcher's Diplomacy*, pp. 43, 185.
39. *Hansard*, 5th series, 977 (1980), cols 655, 657, 727–9, 978 (1980), col. 276; *Economist*, 14 June 1980; *Guardian*, 23 June 1980; *The Times*, 19 June 1980.
40. Smith, 'Britain and the United States', p. 15; Clarke, 'Soviet Union and Eastern Europe', pp. 63–4; Allen, 'British Foreign Policy and West European Co-operation', p. 47, and idem, 'Britain and Western Europe', p. 189; Howe, *Conflict of Loyalty*, pp. 310–11; Thatcher, *Downing Street Years*, pp. 477–8; Curtis, *Ambiguities of Power*, p. 147; Sanders, *Losing an Empire*, pp. 231, 238, 241–2, 249, 254.
41. Hyman, *Afghanistan under Soviet Domination*, pp. 197–222; Carrington, *Reflect on Things Past*, p. 279.
42. Savigear, *Cold War or Détente*, pp. 27, 30–2.
43. Hammond, *Red Flag*, pp. 177–9.

9 Dealing with the Middle East

1. Kantowicz, *Coming Apart, Coming Together*, p. 371; Laqueur, *Confrontation*, pp. 11–75; Fraser, *Middle East*, pp. 130–1; Mansfield, *History of the Middle East*, pp. 291–4; Lea and Rowe, *Arab-Israeli Relations*,

pp. 8–9, 43–6; Edmonds, *Soviet Foreign Policy*, pp. 105–6, 120–1; Ulam, *Expansion and Coexistence*, pp. 757–9, and idem, *Dangerous Relations*, pp. 103–4; G. Golan, *Soviet Policies in the Middle East from World War Two to Gorbachev* (Cambridge, 1990), pp. 78–81; J.D. Glassman, *Arms for the Arabs: The Soviet Union and War in the Middle East* (Baltimore, 1975), pp. 116–17; Steele, *World Power*, pp. 167–8, 177, 194–6; Nogee and Donaldson, *Soviet Foreign Policy since World War Two*, pp. 177–8; J. Waterbury, *The Egypt of Nasser and Sadat: The Political Economy of Two Regimes* (Princeton, 1983), pp. 127, 393–4; Bundy, *Tangled Web*, pp. 428–9.

2. Kantowicz, *Coming Apart, Coming Together*, p. 374; Ulam, *Dangerous Relations*, pp. 103, 105, and idem, *Expansion and Coexistence*, pp. 756–7; W.B. Quandt, *Peace Process: American Diplomacy and the Arab-Israeli Conflict since 1967* (Washington DC, 2001), pp. 103–4; T.G. Fraser, *The USA and the Middle East since World War Two* (Basingstoke, 1989), p. 91; Steele, *World Power*, pp. 168, 194; Israelyan, *Inside the Kremlin*, pp. 16–19.

3. Laqueur, *Confrontation*, pp. 141–91; Fraser, *Middle East*, pp. 131–4, and idem, *The USA and the Middle East*, pp. 99–100, 103–10; Mansfield, *History of the Middle East*, pp. 295–8; Lea and Rowe, *Arab-Israeli Relations*, pp. 9–10, 46–51; Kantowicz, *Coming Apart, Coming Together*, pp. 373–5; Bundy, *Tangled Web*, pp. 434–52; Ambrose and Brinkley, *Rise to Globalism*, pp. 259–65; Quandt, *Peace Process*, pp. 105–24; Edmonds, *Soviet Foreign Policy*, pp. 145, 147–8; Israelyan, *Inside the Kremlin*, pp. 164–95; Steele, *World Power*, pp. 196–8; Nogee and Donaldson, *Soviet Foreign Policy since World War Two*, pp. 284–6; Waterbury, *Egypt of Nasser and Sadat*, p. 394; Ulam, *Expansion and Coexistence*, pp. 759–60, and idem, *Dangerous Relations*, pp. 105–10.

4. Glassman, *Arms for the Arabs*, pp. 171–2; Golan, *Soviet Policies in the Middle East*, pp. 93–4; Israelyan, *Inside the Kremlin*, p. 218; Fraser and Murray, *America and the World*, pp. 194–7; Kantowicz, *Coming Apart, Coming Together*, p. 376; Quandt, *Peace Process*, pp. 138–43, 197–204, 207–35; Fraser, *The USA and the Middle East*, pp. 119–22, 151–3, 156–7, idem, *Arab-Israeli Conflict*, pp. 116–27, and idem, *Middle East*, pp. 135–83; Paterson and Clifford, *America Ascendant*, pp. 243–5; Ambrose and Brinkley, *Rise to Globalism*, pp. 265–8, 291–3, 306; Dumbrell, *American Foreign Policy*, pp. 28–31; Mansfield, *History of the Middle East*, pp. 299–303; Lea and Rowe, *Arab-Israeli Relations*, pp. 10–13, 52–62; Smith, 'Arab-Israeli Conflict', pp. 229–30. For a copy of the Camp David Accords, see appendix C in *The Middle East: Ten Years after Camp David*, ed. W.B. Quandt (Washington DC, 1988), pp. 449–60, and pp. 357–409 for discussion of continuing superpower involvement in the region.

5. H. Beeley, 'The Middle East', in Louis and Bull, *Special Relationship*, pp. 291–2; Steele, *World Power*, p. 174; Waterbury, *Egypt of Nasser and Sadat*, pp. 394–5, 401–2.

6. R.D. McLaurin, *The Middle East in Soviet Policy* (Lexington, Massachusetts, 1975), p. 29; Golan, *Soviet Policies in the Middle East*, p. 94; Steele, *World Power*, p. 198; Nogee and Donaldson, *Soviet Foreign Policy since World War Two*, pp. 178, 286–7; Ulam, *Dangerous Relations*, pp. 115–16; Primakov, 'Soviet Policy', pp. 391–2.

7. S.L. Spiegel, 'The United States and the Arab-Israeli Dispute', in Oye, Rothchild and Lieber, *Eagle Entangled*, pp. 336–65; Steele, *World Power*, pp. 198–200; Waterbury, *Egypt of Nasser and Sadat*, p. 395; Golan, *Soviet Policies in the Middle East*, pp. 105–6.

8. Spanier, *American Foreign Policy since World War Two*, pp. 255–6; Garthoff, *Détente and Confrontation*, pp. 642–3; Nogee and Donaldson, *Soviet Foreign Policy since World War Two*, p. 290; M.I. Kamel, *The Camp David Accords: A Testimony* (London, 1986), pp. 14–15.

9. Kamel, *Camp David Accords*, pp. 358, 361, 363–4, 372.

10. W.B. Quandt, *Camp David: Peacemaking and Politics* (Washington DC, 1986), pp. 234–6.

11. Quandt, *Camp David*, pp. 236, 257–8; M. Dayan, *Breakthrough: A Personal Account of the Egypt-Israel Peace Negotiations* (London, 1981), p. 190; *Conversations with Carter*, ed. D. Richardson (Boulder, Colorado, 1998), pp. 159, 162, 164; Stueck, 'Carter's Foreign Policy', pp. 256–7; Morris, *Jimmy Carter*, p. 273; Gromyko, *Memories*, pp. 265, 272, 274–5; *Dangerous Relations*, pp. 202–4.

12. Spanier, *American Foreign Policy since World War Two*, pp. 256–8.

13. Primakov, 'Soviet Policy', pp. 396–7; Ulam, *Dangerous Relations*, pp. 202–4; Spanier, *American Foreign Policy since World War Two*, pp. 258–9.

14. Hill and Lord, 'Foreign Policy of the Heath Government', p. 301.

15. F.G. Gause, 'British and American Policies in the Persian Gulf, 1968–73', *Review of International Studies*, 11 (1985), pp. 247–73; Reynolds, 'A "Special Relationship"?' pp. 14–15.

16. McLaurin, *Middle East in Soviet Policy*, pp. 42, 57, 60.

17. N. Ashton, ' "A Special Relationship Sometimes in Spite of Ourselves": Britain and Jordan, 1957–73', *Journal of Imperial and Commonwealth History*, 33 (2005), pp. 221–44.

18. Reynolds, *Britannia Overruled*, pp. 229–30; Campbell, *Heath*, pp. 348–50; Heath, *Course of My Life*, pp. 500–1; Sanders, *Losing an Empire*, p. 177; Hill and Lord, 'Foreign Policy of the Heath Government', pp. 301–2, 311.

19. Home, *Way the Wind Blows*, pp. 258–60.

20. *Los Angeles Times*, 24 Oct. 1973; *Washington Post*, 27 Oct. 1973; *Economist*, 20 Oct. 1973; *Guardian*, 25 Oct. 1973; *The Times*, 23 Oct. 1973.

21. *Hansard*, 5th series, 863 (1973), cols 17–19, 34–6.

22. Heath, *Course of My Life*, pp. 500–1; Campbell, *Heath*, pp. 348–50, 558, 780.

23. *The Times*, 10, 21 Dec. 1973; *Guardian*, 13 Dec. 1973; *Observer*, 30 Dec. 1973.
24. *Hansard*, 5th series, 867 (1974), cols 1202–7.
25. Carrington, *Reflect on Things Past*, pp. 236–7, 334.
26. Morgan, *Callaghan*, pp. 401–2, 441, 454; Pimlott, *Harold Wilson*, p. 669; Callaghan, *Time and Chance*, pp. 289–91, 486.
27. Morgan, *Callaghan*, pp. 607–9; Sanders, *Losing an Empire*, p. 177; Callaghan, *Time and Chance*, pp. 292, 486–8, 490.
28. Kamel, *Camp David Accords*, pp. 26, 82, 96; Dayan, *Breakthrough*, ch. 11.
29. *Guardian*, 29 Sept. 1978; *Economist*, 30 Sept. 1978; *Hansard*, 5th series, 963 (1979), cols 1717–20.
30. *Daily Telegraph*, 15, 27 Mar. 1979; *Observer*, 18 Mar. 1979; *Economist*, 17 Mar. 1979.
31. Allen, 'Britain and Western Europe', p. 180.
32. A. Parsons, 'The Middle East', in Byrd, *British Foreign Policy under Thatcher*, pp. 81–2.
33. Parsons, 'The Middle East', pp. 82, 94–5.
34. Sanders, *Losing an Empire*, pp. 162–3.
35. Beeley, 'Middle East', pp. 292–3; Carrington, *Reflect on Things Past*, pp. 330, 336–44.
36. Sharp, *Thatcher's Diplomacy*, pp. 31, 45–6; Carrington, *Reflect on Things Past*, pp. 344–7, 367–8. The talks were cut short because of the Falklands crisis.
37. Sanders, *Losing an Empire*, p. 179; Thatcher, *Downing Street Years*, p. 162.
38. Sanders, *Losing an Empire*, pp. 164, 180–1.
39. S. Chubin, 'Soviet and American Rivalry in the Middle East: The Political Dimension', and J. Alford, 'Soviet-American Rivalry in the Middle East: The Military Dimension', both in Dawisha, *The Soviet Union in the Middle East*, pp. 124–33, 134–46.

10 The Falklands Crisis: Causes and Consequences

1. Sanders, *Losing an Empire*, pp. 125–7, 133; Reynolds, *Britannia Overruled*, p. 241.
2. Dockrill, *British Defence*, p. 116; L. Freedman, *Britain and the Falklands War* (Oxford, 1988), ch. 2; G.M. Dillon, *The Falklands, Politics and War* (Basingstoke, 1989), ch. 1; P. Eddy, M. Linklater and P. Gillman, *The Falklands War* (London, 1984), pp. 44–52; L. Freedman and V. Gamba-Stonehouse, *Signals of War: The Falklands Conflict of 1982* (London, 1990), pp. 3–22.
3. Reynolds, *Britannia Overruled*, p. 244; Carrington, *Reflect on Things Past*, pp. 348–9; Morgan, *Callaghan*, pp. 460–2, 594.

4. M. Hastings and S. Jenkins, *The Battle for the Falklands* (London, 1983), p. 15.

5. Hastings and Jenkins, *Battle for the Falklands*, pp. 22–3, 25–6, 28–30, 32–6.

6. *Hansard*, 5th series, 953 (1978), cols 626–8.

7. M. Clarke, 'The Policy-Making Process', in Smith, Smith and White, *British Foreign Policy*, p. 94; Sanders, *Losing an Empire*, pp. 124–5; Morgan, *Callaghan*, pp. 594, 725; *Hansard*, 6th series, 17 (1982), cols 856–7.

8. Callaghan, *Time and Chance*, pp. 370–8; Howe, *Conflict of Loyalty*, p. 245; Dockrill, *British Defence*, p. 117; Thatcher, *Downing Street Years*, pp. 175–6; Reynolds, *Britannia Overruled*, p. 243.

9. Carrington, *Reflect on Things Past*, pp. 362, 364, 369–70.

10. Sanders, *Losing an Empire*, p. 125; Hastings and Jenkins, *Battle for the Falklands*, pp. 313–14.

11. Dockrill, *British Defence*, pp. 118–19; Smith, *Reagan and Thatcher*, pp. 70–1; *The Times*, 3 Apr. 1982.

12. *Guardian*, 3 Apr. 1982; *Observer*, 4 Apr. 1982.

13. *Economist*, 10 Apr. 1982.

14. *Washington Post*, 4 Apr. 1982; *Los Angeles Times*, 6 Apr. 1982.

15. Dockrill, *British Defence*, pp. 119–21; Hill, 'The Historical Background', pp. 40, 46; Sharp, *Thatcher's Diplomacy*, pp. 57, 60.

16. Thatcher, *Downing Street Years*, p. 177; Carrington, *Reflect on Things Past*, pp. 368–9. For a copy of the Franks Report, see appendix C in Hastings and Jenkins, *Battle for the Falklands*, pp. 361–72.

17. Farrands, 'State, Society, Culture and British Foreign Policy', pp. 58–9, 61–2; Carrington, *Reflect on Things Past*, pp. 349–58; Hastings and Jenkins, *Battle for the Falklands*, pp. 37–42; Freedman, *Britain and the Falklands War*, pp. 26–8; Dillon, *Falklands, Politics and War*, ch. 2; Eddy, Linklater and Gillman, *Falklands War*, pp. 52–6.

18. Hastings and Jenkins, *Battle for the Falklands*, pp. 42–4.

19. Reynolds, *Britannia Overruled*, pp. 244, 248; Hastings and Jenkins, *Battle for the Falklands*, pp. 336–7.

20. Clarke, 'The Policy-Making Process', p. 88; Thatcher, *Downing Street Years*, pp. 185–6; Carrington, *Reflect on Things Past*, pp. 370–1; Reynolds, *Britannia Overruled*, p. 245; Eddy, Linklater and Gillman, *Falklands War*, p. 169.

21. Sharp, *Thatcher's Diplomacy*, p. 30; White, 'Britain and East-West Relations', pp. 152, 165; Ambrose and Brinkley, *Rise to Globalism*, pp. 314–16; Dumbrell, *American Foreign Policy*, p. 78; Sanders, *Losing an Empire*, p. 180.

22. Thatcher, *Downing Street Years*, pp. 176–7; Smith, *Reagan and Thatcher*, pp. 78–9; Rogers, 'The "Unspecial Relationship" in Latin America', pp. 342–4.

23. Hastings and Jenkins, *Battle for the Falklands*, p. 142; Bartlett, *The 'Special Relationship'*, pp. 154–7; Smith, *Reagan and Thatcher*, pp. 39, 79–81, 83–4; Dobson, *Anglo-American Relations*, pp. 153–5.

24. Hastings and Jenkins, *Battle for the Falklands*, pp. 107–13, 139–41; Smith, *Reagan and Thatcher*, pp. 89–91. On Haig's mediation see also Freedman and Gamba-Stonehouse, *Signals of War*, chs 13–15, and 'James Rentschler's Falklands Diary' at www.margaretthatcher.org/archive/arcdocs/Rentschler.

25. Savigear, *Cold War or Détente*, pp. 156–9.

26. Regelsberger, 'EPC in the 1980s', p. 23; Sanders, *Losing an Empire*, p. 164; G. Bonvicini, 'Mechanisms and Procedures of EPC: More than Traditional Diplomacy?' in Pijpers, Regelsberger and Wessels, *European Political Co-operation*, pp. 61, 64–5; Sanders, *Losing an Empire*, p. 165; Allen, 'Britain and Western Europe', p. 180.

27. G. Edwards, 'Europe and the Falkland Islands Crisis, 1982', *Journal of Common Market Studies*, 22 (1984), pp. 295–313.

28. Curtis, *Ambiguities of Power*, pp. 6, 118–19, 134.

29. Thatcher, *Downing Street Years*, pp. 214–16, 218, 222–3, 230–1; Smith, *Reagan and Thatcher*, pp. 94–6.

30. W. Little, 'Anglo-Argentine Relations and the Management of the Falklands Question', in Byrd, *Foreign Policy under Thatcher*, pp. 137–56; Hill, 'The Historical Background', p. 38.

31. McGrew, 'Security and Order', pp. 106–7; Allen, 'Britain and Western Europe', p. 175; Sanders, *Losing an Empire*, p. 252; Dillon, *Falklands, Politics and War*, pp. 237–42; Reynolds, *Britannia Overruled*, pp. 245, 261–2; Bowles, 'Defence Policy of the Conservative Government', pp. 186, 197–8.

32. *Hansard*, 6th series, 25 (1982), cols 729–32.

33. *Economist*, 26 June 1982; *Guardian*, 30 June, 1, 6, 7 July 1982; *Observer*, 11 July 1982; *The Times*, 30 June 1982.

34. *Chicago Tribune*, 24 June 1982; *New York Times*, 1, 2 July 1982.

35. Howe, *Conflict of Loyalty*, p. 247; Thatcher, *Downing Street Years*, p. 235; Reynolds, *Britannia Overruled*, pp. 241, 243; Sharp, *Thatcher's Diplomacy*, p. 95; Dillon, *Falklands, Politics and War*, pp. 234–5.

36. E. Shaw, *The Labour Party since 1945* (Oxford, 1999), pp. 162–8; D. Clark, *We Do Not Want the Earth: The History of South Shields Labour Party* (Whitley Bay, 1992), p. 123; A. Thorpe, *A History of the British Labour Party* (Basingstoke, 1997), pp. 209–10; D. Sanders, H. Ward and D. Marsh, 'Government Popularity and the Falklands War', H. Clark, W. Mishler and P. Whiteley, 'Recapturing the Falklands: Models of Conservative Popularity, 1979–83', and 'Reply' by Sanders, March and Ward, all in *British Journal of Political Science*, 17 (1987), pp. 281–313, 20 (1990), pp. 63–81, 83–90; Freedman, *Britain and the Falklands*

War, pp. 84–6, 100–4; T. Benn, *The Benn Diaries*, ed. R. Winstone (London, 1996), pp. 531–7.

37. Young, *Britain and the World*, pp. 203, 205–6, 210.
38. Hastings and Jenkins, *Battle for the Falklands*, pp. 315–16.

Conclusion

1. Heath, *Course of My Life*, p. 492; Smith, *Reagan and Thatcher*, pp. 72, 130.
2. I. Elliot, 'The Helsinki Process and Human Rights in the Soviet Union', in *Human Rights and Foreign Policy*, ed. D.M. Hill (Basingstoke, 1989), pp. 91–114.
3. Reynolds, 'A "Special Relationship"?' pp. 14–15.
4. Morgan, *Callaghan*, pp. 621–3.
5. White, 'Britain and East-West Relations', pp. 150–3, 165–7; Howe, *Conflict of Loyalty*, p. 312.
6. For a particularly forthright exposition, see M. Curtis, *The Great Deception: Anglo-American Power and World Order* (London, 1998), and idem, *Ambiguities of Power*, pp. 147, 180–1.
7. Garthoff, *Détente and Confrontation*, pp. 1087–9; White, *Britain, Détente and East-West Relations*, ch. 7; Clarke, 'A British View', p. 107.
8. Clarke, 'A British View', pp. 107–9.
9. Smith, *Reagan and Thatcher*, p. 92; Freedman and Gamba-Stonehouse, *Signals of War*, p. 417; Thatcher, *Path to Power*, pp. 508–9, and idem, *Downing Street Years*, pp. 173–4.
10. M. Clarke, *British External Policy Making in the 1990s* (London, 1992).
11. *British Defence Choices for the Twenty-First Century*, ed. M. Clarke and P. Sabin (London, 1993).

Select Bibliography

D. Baker and D. Seawright (eds), *Britain For and Against Europe* (Oxford, 1998).

D.S. Ball (ed.), *The Conservative Government, 1979–84: An Interim Report* (London, 1985).

S. Ball and A. Seldon (eds), *The Heath Government, 1970–74: A Reappraisal* (London, 1996).

C.J. Bartlett, *The 'Special Relationship': A Political History of Anglo-American Relations since 1945* (London, 1992).

J. Baylis, *Anglo-American Defence Relations, 1939–80: The Special Relationship* (London, 1981).

A. Bloed and P. van Dijk (eds), *Essays on Human Rights in the Helsinki Process* (Dordrecht, Netherlands, 1985).

K. Burk (ed.), *The British Isles since 1945* (Oxford, 2003).

P. Byrd (ed.), *British Foreign Policy under Thatcher* (Oxford, 1988).

M. Chalmers, *Paying for Defence: Military Spending and British Decline* (London, 1985).

M. Clarke, *British External Policy Making in the 1990s* (London, 1992).

M. Clarke and P. Sabin (eds), *British Defence Choices for the Twenty-First Century* (London, 1993).

C. Coker, *The Future of the Atlantic Alliance* (London, 1984).

R. Coopey and N. Woodward (eds), *Britain in the 1970s: The Troubled Economy* (London, 1996).

P. Cornish, *Partnership in Crisis: The United States, Europe and the Fall and Rise of NATO* (London, 1997).

N. Crafts and N. Woodward (eds), *The British Economy since 1945* (Oxford, 1991).

M. Curtis, *The Ambiguities of Power: British Foreign Policy since 1945* (London, 1995).

A. Daltrop, *Politics and the European Community* (London, 1986).

R. Davy (ed.), *European Détente: A Reappraisal* (London, 1992).

G.M. Dillon, *The Falklands, Politics and War* (Basingstoke, 1989).

D. Dinan, *Ever Closer Union: An Introduction to European Integration* (Basingstoke, 1994).

A.P. Dobson, *Anglo-American Relations in the Twentieth Century* (London, 1995).

M. Dockrill, *British Defence since 1945* (Oxford, 1988).

K. Dyson (ed.), *European Détente: Case Studies in the Politics of East-West Relations* (London, 1986).

R. Floud and P. Johnson (eds), *The Cambridge Economic History of Modern Britain* (3 vols, Cambridge, 2004).

B. Fowkes, *The Rise and Fall of Communism in Eastern Europe* (Basingstoke, 1995).

T.G. Fraser and D. Murray, *America and the World since 1945* (Basingstoke, 2002).

L. Freedman, *Britain and Nuclear Weapons* (London, 1980).

L. Freedman and V. Gamba-Stonehouse, *Signals of War: The Falklands Conflict of 1982* (London, 1990).

M. Fulbrook (ed.), *Europe since 1945* (Oxford, 2001).

C. Gati, *The Bloc That Failed: Soviet-East European Relations in Transition* (Bloomington, Indiana, 1990)

A.J.R. Groom, *British Thinking about Nuclear Weapons* (London, 1974).

A.J.R. Groom and P. Taylor (eds), *The Commonwealth in the 1980s: Challenges and Opportunities* (London, 1984).

A. Heraclides, *Security and Co-operation in Europe: The Human Dimension, 1972–92* (London, 1993).

B. Heuser, *NATO, Britain, France and the FRG: Nuclear Strategies and Forces for Europe, 1949–2000* (Basingstoke, 1997).

D.M. Hill (ed.), *Human Rights and Foreign Policy* (Basingstoke, 1989).

J. Hollowell (ed.), *Britain since 1945* (Oxford, 2003).

A. Hunter (ed.), *Rethinking the Cold War* (Philadelphia, 1998)

P. Johnson, *A History of the Modern World* (London, 1984).

D. Judd, *Empire: The British Imperial Experience from 1765 to the Present* (London, 1997).

D. Judd and P. Slinn, *The Evolution of the Modern Commonwealth, 1902–80* (London, 1982).

E.R. Kantowicz, *Coming Apart, Coming Together* (Grand Rapids, Michigan, 2000).

P. Kennedy, *The Realities Behind Diplomacy: Background Influences on British External Policy, 1865–1980* (London, 1981).

P. Kennedy, *The Rise and Fall of the Great Powers: Economic Change and Military Conflict from 1500 to 2000* (New York, 1987).

R.O. Keohane, J.S. Nye and S. Hoffman (eds), *After the Cold War* (Cambridge, Massachusetts, 1993).

K. Larres and E. Meehan (eds), *Uneasy Allies: British-German Relations and European Integration since 1945* (Oxford, 2000).

C. Legum, *Africa since Independence* (Bloomington, Indiana, 1999).

W.R. Louis and H. Bull (eds), *The 'Special Relationship': Anglo-American Relations since 1945* (Oxford, 1986).

P. Malone, *The British Nuclear Deterrent* (London, 1984).

N. Mansergh, *The Commonwealth Experience* (2 vols, London, 1982).

V. Mastny, *The Helsinki Process and the Reintegration of Europe, 1986–91: Analysis and Documentation* (London, 1992).

W.D. McIntyre, *The Significance of the Commonwealth, 1965–90* (Basingstoke, 1991).

R. Middleton, *The British Economy since 1945: Engaging with the Debate* (Basingstoke, 2000).

P. Nailor, *The Nassau Connection: The Organization and Management of the British Polaris Project* (London, 1988).

R. Ovendale, *British Defence Policy since 1945* (Manchester, 1994).

W. Park, *Defending the West: A History of NATO* (Brighton, 1986).

A. Pijpers, E. Regelsberger and W. Wessels (eds), *European Political Co-operation in the 1980s: A Common Foreign Policy for Western Europe?* (Dordrecht, Netherlands, 1988).

J.B. Poole, *Independence and Interdependence: A Reader on British Nuclear Weapons Policy* (London, 1990).

A. Pravda and P. Duncan (eds), *Soviet-British Relations since the 1970s* (Cambridge, 1990).

O. Ramsbotham (ed.), *Choices: Nuclear and Non-Nuclear Defence Options* (London, 1987).

R. Renwick, *Fighting with Allies: America and Britain in Peace and War* (Basingstoke, 1996).

D. Reynolds, *Britannia Overruled: British Policy and World Power in the Twentieth Century* (Harlow, 2000).

G. Richey, *Britain's Strategic Role in NATO* (Basingstoke, 1986).

K. Robbins, *The Eclipse of a Great Power: Modern Britain, 1870–1992* (London, 1997).

D. Sanders, *Losing an Empire, Finding a Role: British Foreign Policy since 1945* (Basingstoke, 1990).

D.N. Schwartz, *NATO's Nuclear Dilemmas* (Washington, DC, 1983).

P. Sharp, *Thatcher's Diplomacy: The Revival of British Foreign Policy* (Basingstoke, 1997).

J. Simpson, *The Independent Nuclear State: The United States, Britain and the Military Atom* (London, 1983).

A. Sked and C. Cook, *Post-War Britain: A Political History* (London, 1993).

G. Smith, *Reagan and Thatcher* (London, 1990).

M. Smith, S. Smith and B. White (eds), *British Foreign Policy: Tradition, Change and Transformation* (London, 1988).

J. Sperling and E. Kirchner, *Recasting the European Order* (Manchester, 1997).

G. Swain and N. Swain, *Eastern Europe since 1945* (Basingstoke, 1998).

H. Temperley, *Britain and America since Independence* (Basingstoke, 2002).

D.W. Urwin, *The Community of Europe: A History of European Integration since 1945* (London, 1991).

W. van Eekelen, *Debating European Security, 1948–98* (The Hague, 1998).

R. Vinen, *A History in Fragments: Europe in the Twentieth Century* (London, 2002).

R. Wakeman (ed.), *Themes in Modern European History since 1945* (London, 2003).

D.C. Watt, *Succeeding John Bull: America in Britain's Place, 1900–75* (Cambridge, 1984).

O.A. Westad (ed.), *Reviewing the Cold War: Approaches, Interpretations, Theory* (London, 2000).

B. White, *Britain, Détente and Changing East-West Relations* (London, 1992).

J.W. Young, *Britain and the World in the Twentieth Century* (London, 1997).

Z.A.B. Zeman, *The Making and Breaking of Communist Europe* (Oxford, 1991).

Index

Index